SCHELLING VERSUS HEGEL

Schelling versus Hegel
From German Idealism to Christian Metaphysics

JOHN LAUGHLAND

ASHGATE

© John Laughland 2007

All rights reserved. No part of this publication may be reproduced, stored in a retrieval system or transmitted in any form or by any means, electronic, mechanical, photocopying, recording or otherwise without the prior permission of the publisher.

John Laughland has asserted his moral right under the Copyright, Designs and Patents Act, 1988, to be identified as the author of this work.

Published by
Ashgate Publishing Limited
Gower House
Croft Road
Aldershot
Hampshire GU11 3HR
England

Ashgate Publishing Company
Suite 420
101 Cherry Street
Burlington, VT 05401-4405
USA

Ashgate website: http://www.ashgate.com

British Library Cataloguing in Publication Data
Laughland, John
  Schelling versus Hegel : from German idealism to Christian metaphysics
  1. Schelling, Friedrich Wilhelm Joseph von, 1775-1854
  I. Title
  193

Library of Congress Cataloging-in-Publication Data
Laughland, John.
  Schelling versus Hegel : from German idealism to Christian metaphysics / John Laughland.
    p. cm.
  Includes bibliographical references.
  ISBN 978-0-7546-6118-4 (hardcover) 1. Schelling, Friedrich Wilhelm Joseph von, 1775-1854. I. Title.

B2898.L37 2007
193--dc22

2006035444

ISBN: 978 0 7546 6118 4

Printed and bound in Great Britain by Antony Rowe Ltd, Chippenham, Wiltshire.

Contents

Chapter 1	The Creation, Liberty and Evil	1
Chapter 2	The Question of Being	11
Chapter 3	Schelling's Beginnings	37
Chapter 4	The Metaphysics of Evil	61
Chapter 5	Christian Cosmogony and the End of Idealism (Schelling's Development from Stuttgart to Munich, 1810–27)	93
Chapter 6	The Religious Flowering in Schelling's Late Philosophy	123

Bibliography   *151*

Index   *157*

Chapter 1

The Creation, Liberty and Evil

> If we read a book which contains incredible or impossible narratives, or is written in a very obscure style, and if we know nothing about its author, nor the time or occasion of its being written, we shall vainly endeavour to gain any certain knowledge of its true meaning.
>
> Spinoza, *Tractatus theologico-politicus*, Chapter VII[1]

Philosophy is not written in a void, nor should it be studied in one. Philosophers write in reply to their predecessors, and within an overall philosophical context which varies with time and place. The aims of a philosopher – certainly philosophical, perhaps political – can often be better discerned if this context is understood. This is not to attribute greater importance to the ancestry of ideas than to their truth or meaning: to take a text as anything other than something which aims at truth is to mistreat it. Rather, it is essential to understand the points of view against which a writer is arguing in order to understand the writer herself. The need to look at the philosophical context is especially acute when the debates of the time and the assumptions behind them are difficult or unfamiliar.[2]

This is certainly the case with the long philosophical career of Friedrich Wilhelm Joseph von Schelling (1775–1854). Throughout his life Schelling adopted different and sometimes conflicting philosophical views but much of his thinking revolved around the same set of questions. In particular, the Creation, liberty, evil and God were issues on which he wrote throughout his life: his very first work was his 1792 master's thesis on the origin of evil (*Antiquissimi de prima malorum humanorum origine philosophematis Genes. III. explicandi tentamen criticum et philosophicum*). As we shall see, his trajectory turns on his developing interpretations of these problems. It is therefore important to put them in context before examining Schelling himself.

Any such discussion must begin with the question of creation. Certain views about the origins of the world entail certain views about its metaphysical and ontological structure, as well as about God, human liberty and evil. In particular, the distinction is important between Judeo-Christian theories of the Creation and competing cosmogonies including Gnosticism, Manicheism, neo-Platonism and Orphism. This distinction is important precisely because the central claim of this book is that Schelling progressively disentangled himself from those competing cosmogonies,

---

1 Translated by R.M. Elwes (New York: Dover, 1951), p. 111.
2 Horst Fuhrmans makes this point in his introduction to Schelling's *Über das Wesen der menschlichen Freiheit* (Stuttgart: Reclam, 1964), p. 3. So does Arseni Gulyga, *Die klassische deutsche Philosophie, ein Abriß* (Leipzig: Reclam, 1990), p. 5.

which had themselves so heavily influenced the German idealist tradition into which he was born and which he initially espoused, and became progressively closer to the Judeo-Christian model, embracing along the way an increasingly overtly Christian metaphysics to go with it.

The Metaphysics of Christianity

The fundamental distinction between Judeo-Christian and these other cosmogonies is fairly easy to state. In the Judeo-Christian tradition, the creation is the result of a free and loving act of God: as a result, the created universe is basically good, orderly and intelligible. The opening words of the Gospel of St John (I:3) state, 'Through him all things were made; without him nothing was made that has been made', while the sentence, 'God saw that it was good' is repeated six times in the first chapter of Genesis.[3]

The universe is therefore not itself eternal or divine. Nor is the creation a necessary progression from an impersonal Absolute, as neo-Platonism was to affirm, or a degradation or a collapse, as numerous Oriental myths were to argue. Souls are not 'imprisoned' in their bodies following a 'catastrophe', and their existence did not precede the creation, any more than anything else did. Souls are not parcels of the divine substance, although they enjoy intelligence and freedom, and although man was created in God's image, man is ontologically separate from God. Man is called to return to God and to become unified with Him, but in this union, separateness is preserved: the Christian and Jewish theology of union is precisely the opposite of a cosmogony of unity, according to which everything, including man, is ontologically contiguous with the Absolute. Moreover, in the Judeo-Christian view, the created world is real: it is not an illusion, as Orientals maintained, hiding the fundamental oneness of reality.[4]

Because the creation is good, evil is not inherent in it. Evil comes instead from man, that is, from the liberty which God created. Man's separation from God is the result of moral rebellion, and only from this.[5] Far from being a fact intrinsic to the existence of creation, evil (in the Jewish and Christian view) is precisely that which attempts to destroy creation. Claude Tresmontant writes, 'Evil is a destruction of creation, it is an opposition to the creation, it is an inversion of it. It is properly

---

3   To be precise, the sixth formulation is: 'And God saw every thing that he had made, and, behold, it was very good'. Genesis I:31.

4   For this and the succeeding paragraphs on cosmogony, I am greatly indebted to the works of Claude Tresmontant: *La prescience de Dieu, la prédestination et la liberté humaine* (Paris: François-Xavier de Guibert, 1996); *Les idées maîtresses de la métaphysique chrétienne* (Paris: Seuil, 1962); *L'opposition métaphysique au monothéisme hébreu de Spinoza à Heidegger* (Paris: François-Xavier de Guibert, 1996); and, above all, Tresmontant's thesis, published as *La métaphysique du christianisme et la naissance de la philosophie chrétienne: problème de la création et de l'anthropologie des origines à Saint Augustin* (Paris: Seuil, 1961).

5   Leszek Kolakowski, *Religion, If There is No God: On God, the Devil, Sin and other Worries of the So-called Philosophy of Religion* (London: Fontana Press, 2nd edn, 1993), p. 40.

spiritual and not physical.'⁶ Evil is not matter, but will, or self-will. The separation between man and God is certainly in part ontological – because man is not divine – but mainly moral.

The goodness of creation is underlined by the specifically Christian doctrines of the Incarnation and the Resurrection of the Flesh. The Gospels tell us, 'God so loved *the world* that He gave His only Son so that whoever believed in Him should not perish, but have everlasting life.'⁷ In doing this, God sanctified the body and emphasised His love for the world He had created. Christians, and to a lesser extent Jews, 'believed in the goodness, albeit relative and derivative, of the physical world, of profane history, of secular life; this attitude was confirmed in the Christian dogma of Incarnation, of the resurrection of the body and the soul being the form of body.'⁸ There can surely be no stronger illustration of the view that the eternal can inhere in the finite than the Incarnation of Christ as man, and as we shall see, the later Schelling will lard his desire to create a 'real-idealism' with religious vocabulary.

Man's rebellion was made possible by his genuine liberty, which God also created. That liberty also made possible a genuine dialogue between God and man which permeates the whole of Holy Scripture:⁹ Abraham haggles with God over how many righteous there must be in Sodom to prevent the entire city being wiped out;¹⁰ the Virgin Mary replies freely to the angel Gabriel, 'Be it unto me according to thy word,'¹¹; Jesus himself teaches, 'Ask, and it shall be given you …'¹² The outcome of the dialogue and, *a fortiori*, salvation is no foregone conclusion, precisely because man is a free being. 'When the son of man cometh, shall he find faith on earth?'¹³ There is a genuine contingency in the history of the world which theories of eternal return and logical emanation cannot accommodate. Henri Bergson emphasised that the flow of time, and the succession of events in the real world, are genuinely unpredictable.¹⁴ Indeed, time is the medium in which these events occur. It is not a measure of degradation or of distance from the absolute One, but rather an indication of the fullness of the creation. Indeed, the very existence of time flows from the fact of creation: without a theory of creation, the existence of time cannot be accounted for. The universe, as Plato first argued in the *Timaeos*, is a living being, not the fixed reflection of some immutable Absolute.

Man is called upon to cooperate actively and intelligently with the ongoing development of the cosmos. In the Christian and Jewish view, human liberty is not an uncomfortable problem which needs to be subsumed into a larger rationalist system, it represents the very *raison d'être* of creation; man's vocation is to exercise his liberty in accordance with God's command. Although the creation is imperfect,

---

6 Tresmontant, *La prescience de Dieu*, p. 67.
7 John III:16, emphasis added.
8 Kolakowski, *Religion*, pp. 205–6.
9 See Tresmontant, *La prescience de Dieu*, pp. 91ff., for a long list.
10 Genesis XVIII:26ff.
11 Luke I:38.
12 Matthew VII:7–11.
13 Luke XVIII:8.
14 Henri Bergson, 'Le possible et le réel', in *La pensée et le mouvant* (Paris: Presses Universitaires de France, 5th edn, 1996), p. 99.

fragile and transient ('Heaven and earth shall pass away, but my words shall not pass away'[15]), this does not mean that creation is the source of evil.

As a consequence, God's liberty and man's liberty stand in a relation of mutual philosophical reciprocity: if the creation were not the result of God's free choice – if it had occurred as the result of a collapse, or a fall, or some other catastrophe within the Absolute – then evil would not be the result of man's liberty, but rather an ineradicable and necessary ontological fact inherent in the very fabric of creation itself. Theories which compromise God's own liberty to create the world therefore generally compromise man's liberty also. Human liberty, in other words, is intertwined with cosmogony at the deepest level. As Claude Bruaire writes, 'Not only does creation signify that there is not derivation or emanation ... it also demands the conversion of the concepts of identity, the absolute, difference and multiplicity in terms of personal liberty.'[16]

Other Cosmogonies

The early Church had to struggle vigorously to establish the philosophical coherence of this cosmogony against various competing ancient Greek and Oriental ones. The most important competing view was that the cosmos was itself eternal and therefore divine. Supporters of such cosmogonies tried to accommodate this view with the obvious fact that there are new developments in the world over time, and that things are born and die. To do this they adopted either theories of eternal return or theories which attributed the creation to a fall or a collapse in the Absolute. Both variants tended to adopt a cyclical and determinist view of cosmic development, according to which everything returns to its original condition. If the soul was a parcel of the Absolute which had fallen into matter, for instance, its vocation was to return, purified, to the One from which it had proceeded. Time, according to such schemes, was a lack: it was a sign of the deficiency of the material world and of its separation from the eternal absolute. It was the area of corruption and death. The world was an illusion.

These metaphysical doctrines had very direct ethical implications. Above all, the doctrine that existence is an illusion, and that only the undivided One is real – a doctrine which probably originated in the Upanishads but which, as we shall see, is implied by numerous modern philosophies including those of Spinoza (1632–77), Kant (1724–1804) and Hegel (1770–1831) – is incompatible with the traditional Christian view that man is free and that human life is sacred. If the whole of history is nothing but a cyclical eternal return then nothing, in reality, ever happens. There is little or no place for the genuine unpredictability of free human choice within such determinist fatalism, and therefore little room for the uncertainties of personal salvation. Similarly, if only the One truly exists, then individual human life is itself only illusory. If we will all die and return to the true One in the end, then it makes

---

15 Matthew XXIV:35.
16 Claude Bruaire, *Schelling ou la quête du secret de l'être* (Paris: Seghers, 1970), p. 37.

little difference if our death comes sooner or later. In the words of the Bhagavad-Gita,

> Who thinks this (self) can be a slayer, who thinks that it can be slain, both these have no (right) knowledge; it does not slay nor is it slain. Never is it born or dies; never did it come to be nor will it ever come to be again ... It is not slain when the body is slain ... If a man knows it as indestructible, eternal, unborn, never to pass away, how and whom can he cause to be slain or slay ? As a man casts off his worn-out clothes and takes on other new ones, so does the embodied (self) cast off his worn-out bodies and enter other news ones ... For sure is the death of all that is born, sure is the birth of all that dies: so in a matter that no one can prevent you have no cause to grieve.[17]

Such Oriental myths hold that only death liberates us from this illusory world and from the malediction of individuality. There is no such thing as crime against another man, and human love has no ontological value for it is in reality only love for oneself. Wherever individuality and personal existence are illusions, good and evil, love and liberty can only be illusions too.[18] Moreover, if the descent of the Absolute into multiplicity and materiality is a catastrophe, as such myths hold, then the world itself has a fall or a collapse as its first principle. It can only therefore be disorderly. As we shall see, the traditional Christian belief is that God's creation is fundamentally orderly and intelligible.

For instance, the school of Orphism, like the Oriental schools from which it flowed, believed that the soul had to liberate itself from the body in which it was imprisoned. This is the view expressed poetically by William Wordsworth in his 'Intimations of immortality from recollections of early childhood'. Only by contemplating the Absolute, and not by acting this way or that in the world – which is only illusory and futile anyway – can the soul be saved. The ethics of Orphism are thus profoundly ascetic: they demand total withdrawal of the self from the world and, as such, are un-civic. The only duty incumbent on the individual in the world is to free himself from it. Consequently, it is doubtful whether such injunctions can properly be called 'ethical'.

By the same token, Gnosis in its numerous forms holds the world to be bad in itself. Hans Jonas explains the Gnostic view: 'The universe ... is like a vast prison, whose innermost dungeon is the earth, the scene of man's life. The vastness and multiplicity of the cosmic system expresses the degree to which man is removed from God.'[19] The Gnostic believes that the world is ontologically out of joint with the Absolute as a result of its very existence, because it has arisen from a fall or a catastrophe. In the Gnostic tradition, it is as if the original sin were God's because He created the world. It is as if it were not the result of man's rebellion. The same applies to religions with strong Gnostic elements: Kolakowski writes, 'One is tempted to say

---

17 *Bhagavad-Gita*, Chapter 2, Verses 19, 20, 21, 22, 27; translated and with a commentary by R.C. Zaehner (Oxford: Clarendon Press, 1969), pp. 132ff.

18 See *Bhagavad-Gita*, Chapter 2, *passim*; also Tresmontant, *La métaphysique du christianisme*, p. 264.

19 Hans Jonas, *The Gnostic Religion* (Boston: Beacon, 2nd edn, 1963), p. 43.

that in a consistent Buddhist framework the act of creation itself, by producing more than One, amounts to producing evil.'[20]

This leaves little room for the human freedom. Gnosis differs from traditional Christianity in that it considers the soul is saved by knowledge – self-knowledge, of its own divine substance – and not by God's grace, which is itself a manifestation of divine liberty. It is through coming to know (or more precisely, to recall) its divine essence that the soul saves itself. For the Christian, the soul is not divine, although created by God. As Claude Tresmontant emphasises, 'The Christian theology of grace and charity is organically linked to a metaphysics of the creation. Gnosis, which ignores or dispenses with the effective creation of beings, also dispenses with the relationship of love between God and man which constitutes the essence of Christianity.'[21] In other words, God's liberty and man's are philosophically necessary for each other.

Plotinus

The thought of Plotinus (203–69 AD) is important in this regard, for he influenced numerous Christian mystics, both Catholic and Protestant, some of whom Schelling was to draw on, in particular Giordano Bruno, in whom Schelling displayed a great interest for a short time, and Meister Eckhart. The influence on Christian thinkers was strong in spite of the fact that Plotinus enrolled in the Persian army deliberately to learn about Oriental cosmogony, which duly influenced him. Plotinus' thought was dominated by the framework of the One and the many: he held that creation was a necessary progression from the perfect One, and that it was a degradation, a movement from the greater to the lesser. The closer reality approximated the One, the more perfect it was; the more multiple, the more imperfect and degraded.[22] The One is at the origin of everything: it is so abundant that it eternally overflows, cascading downwards, creating things which in turn create others below them on the ontological ladder: intelligence, soul, animate bodies, matter. Its creative activity is like that of a light which shines, or a hot body which necessarily imparts heat.[23] This movement of progression (or procession) is complemented by an equal and opposite movement, that of contemplation by inferior beings of superior ones.[24]

This, which one might label 'downward emanationism', is common to all currents of neo-Platonism, and it is the opposite of the Christian and Jewish doctrines of creation, according to which creation is an elevation of beings out of nothing. For the latter, the creation is an act of love, *agape*: it is not the result of a necessity, as Plotinus thought, and is not a fall or a catastrophe. Emanationism is also incompatible with

---

20 Kolakoswki, *Religion*, p. 40; see also Etienne Couvert, *La Gnose contre la Foi* (Chiré en Montreuil: Editions de Chiré, 1989), *passim*.

21 Tresmontant, *La métaphysique du christianisme*, p. 291.

22 Plotinus, *Enneads*, VI, 6, 1ff.; see also André Bord, *Plotin et Jean de la Croix* (Paris: Beauchesne, 1996), p. 22ff. and Émile Bréhier, *La philosophie de Plotin* (Paris: Vrin, 1998), Chapter IV.

23 Plotinus, *Enneads*, V, 1, 6.

24 Plotinus, *Enneads*, VI, 7, 17.

the Christian and Jewish doctrine of the creation *ex nihilo*. (In fact, emanation is not really creation at all.) Finally, the notion of a perfect and self-contained Absolute is not easily compatible with the personalisation of God as a loving Father.[25] Plotinus' doctrine that the higher does not look down on the lower is certainly incompatible with the love of the Christian God for man, which caused him to sacrifice His only Son. In contrast to the Christian universe, of which the fundamental ontological cause is love, Plotinus' universe is logical and ultimately impersonal. Schelling is to say much the same thing about Spinoza, as we shall see.

This makes the notion of human personality and freedom problematic too: Tresmontant explains, 'From the point of view of Platonism and neo-Platonism, there is no creative uncreated liberty because there is no creation. There is necessary and eternal procession from the One, without the One wanting it ... There is therefore no created liberty either.'[26] On the other hand, the Plotinian emphasis on lower beings contemplating the higher, and achieving their fulfilment through this (the soul is not soul unless it contemplates the intelligence which engendered it, for instance) was not in obvious conflict with Christianity, and the thought attracted many Christians, especially mystics.[27]

Moreover, perhaps by a process of osmosis, other Christian ideas do penetrate into Plotinus' system. At one point, he writes of God engendering a son,[28] and even attributes to the One the words 'I am, I am', which recall Yahweh's words to Moses in Exodus, 'I am that I am'.[29] This is why neo-Platonism was able to influence Christian mysticism so greatly: Meister Eckhart, for instance, was to write of the procession (*Usfluss*) of beings which multiply on the basis of primal unity, and of their reversion (*Widerfluss*) which reintegrates them into unity.

However, as with other kinds of Gnosis, it is difficult to see where ethics can have a place in the Plotinian system. To escape evil the soul must dispossess itself of that which is foreign to it, the body, in order to regain its original purity. As Tresmontant justly remarks, what Plotinus requires the soul to practise is not so much ethics as a sort of hygiene.[30] In the Christian and Jewish faiths, evil does not come from the soiling of the soul, but from an act of iniquity and crime which it commits freely and willingly. Such crimes wound other people and are an offence to God. In other words, in Christian and Jewish ethics, the problem of ethics is not that of the material world, but rather of the existential relationship between man, his fellow men and God. This consideration is to be of fundamental importance to our assessment of the relationship between Schelling and Christian metaphysics.

Plotinian ethics therefore bear strong resemblance to the shortcomings of Oriental ethics mentioned above. Plotinus seemed to reduce the importance of killing, for instance, when he adopted a simple fatalism towards death, whether violent or natural: 'If men take up arms against one another, let us remind ourselves

---

25 Kolakowski, *Religion*, pp. 139–40.
26 Tresmontant, *La préscience de Dieu*, p. 42.
27 Bord, *Plotin et Jean de la Croix*, pp. 37–8.
28 Plotinus, *Enneads*, V, 8, 12.
29 Plotinus, *Enneads*, V, 3, 10; cf. Bord, *Plotin et Jean de la Croix*, pp. 34–5.
30 Tresmontant, *La métaphysique du christianisme*, p. 360.

that they are mortal ... The great affairs of men are just games ... Death has nothing redoubtable; to die in war and combat is only to bring old age forward a little.'[31] Neo-Platonism, which does not allow other people to enter into a person's moral horizon, takes us a long way from Biblical ethics, which, holding birth to be a real event and death to be a serious reality, believes murder and any other harm committed against a neighbour to be a crime.[32]

Unlike the Upanishads, unlike Plotinus, the neo-Platonist tradition, and Gnosis, Manicheism emphasised the nature of evil. The Manichees believed that there were two principles in the world in the beginning, and that as a result of a struggle between them, the good principle had exiled itself in the evil realm of matter. Parcels of the good principle were thus prisoners in the material realm of evil, and this mixture constituted the world.[33] As with Orphism, however, Manicheism considered that salvation came from the separation between the body and the soul – the very opposite of the Christian dogma of the resurrection of the body. The Manichees believed that the body came from Satan and only the soul from God. In other words, the Manichees did not regard the world as simply evil, but rather as a great defensive machine constructed by the good principle in order to counteract the advances of the evil principle. Although matter itself was evil, the orderly manner of its construction in the world was good.[34] Despite its emphasis on evil, Manichean metaphysics led to an eradication of human freedom and responsibility. Evil was not the result of man's rebellion against God, but rather of the cosmic struggle between the two principles. Human responsibility was thus shoved off onto mythical entities. In other words, as the early Church fathers were eager to point out, in the Manichean universe, no true ethics was possible at all.[35]

St Augustine

It was precisely to escape Manicheism that St Augustine became a Christian. His philosophy thus represented one of the clearest statements of the traditional Christian understanding of the relationship between ethics and ontology, and it was one on which Schelling was to draw. Augustine's starting point was what has been called 'the ontology of Exodus'. We need, wrote Augustine, 'to understand clearly what God said by the mouth of his angel when sending Moses to the children of Israel: God said, "I am HE WHO IS" (Exodus III:14). For God is existence in a supreme degree – he supremely *is* ...'[36] According to this Father of the Church, God was the creator of all being: He was absolute, uncreated, eternal and ontologically self-sufficient.

---

31 Plotinus, *Enneads*, III, 2, 15, lines 33ff.
32 Tresmontant, *La métaphysique du christianisme*, p. 367.
33 *Ibid.*, p. 293.
34 *Ibid.*, p. 307.
35 *Ibid.*, pp. 318–19.
36 St Augustine, *City of God*, Book XII, Chapter 3, translated by John O'Meara (Harmondsworth: Penguin, 1984), p. 473.

The world was neither the shadow of the Absolute, nor its emanation, nor a modality of divine substance. On the contrary, it displayed a radical ontological difference from the Absolute. The world was created by God alone: that creation was His free choice (a theme which is to become a crucial element in Schelling's rejection of Spinoza). It was not the result of a necessity, nor did the Absolute need to create the world in order to fulfil itself or to become conscious of itself, as Hegel was to contend. The creation was the work of God's love, of His liberty, and He supported all things in their being; Christianity is a metaphysics of charity. As a result, the created world was unimpeachably good. Indeed, it was a heresy (the Manichean heresy, to be precise) to hold that there were two principles, good and evil, in the universe.

At the same time, the world in its fallen condition existed in a deficient but real continuity with its true and original order.[37] In the Fall, man's being did not remain in God. By aspiring to be self-sufficient, man fell away from Him who truly suffices him. The Fall represented the defection from that which supremely is, to that which has less being. Evil had no essence, for it was parasitic upon being. There was indeed no evil nature: instead, evil came from human liberty. It was not the flesh which corrupted the soul, but *vice versa*. Evil was expressed in defiance of divine law, and to consent to evil was precisely to will to offend against the law.[38] Augustine wrote, 'Not even the nature of the Devil himself is evil, in so far as it is a nature; it is perversion that makes it evil.'[39] Sin consisted in the overturning by man of the proper order of submission of the passions to the eternal law; and the cause of sin was freedom.[40] All this will be of great importance for Schelling's theory of liberty and evil.

Man chose not liberty, but bondage to sin by rebelling against God, a state which St Augustine described as one of moral sickliness.[41] Only divine grace could help man overcome his desire for vice. Fallen will, which habitually turned from being at the most fundamental level, inclined fallen man to turn away from the truth about being. Although knowledge was not enough for salvation, the mind should apprehend being – including beauty, justice, charity, kindness, goodness, and so on – through intellectual vision.

St Augustine argued that pervasive doubt was pervasive madness, for doubt itself is possible only on the assumption of some knowledge. He deduced from the certainty one has of one's own existence not only the fact of that existence, but also that one can have knowledge of one's existence and therefore of being.[42] This was to become a key argument for Schelling too. Augustine was convinced that human knowledge could converge upon real moral truth. At the same time, goodness and

---

37 See Graham Walker, *Moral Foundations of Constitutional Thought: Current Problems, Augustinian Prospects* (Princeton: Princeton University Press, 1990), p. 88.
38 Alasdair MacIntyre, *After Virtue: A Study in Moral Theory* (London: Duckworth, 1981), p. 175.
39 St Augustine, *City of God*, Book XIX, Chapter 13, p. 871.
40 St Augustine, *De Libero Arbitrio, Liber Primus, Pars Secunda*, I, VII, 16.
41 St Augustine, *City of God*, Book XV, Chapter 6.
42 *Ibid.*, Book XI, Chapter 26.

justice were properly objects not of neutral intellection, but of love, because man should love God's being. Indeed, Augustine maintained that it was wrong to think that our apprehension of reality should be dispassionate or 'rationalist'.

To this day, the Catholic Church maintains that what changed in the Fall was not human nature – which Luther and Calvin thought so distorted that freedom of choice was eradicated[43] – but the relationship between man and God.[44] Man's liberty is fallible because it is created from nothing, and has not been stabilised and confirmed in ultimate beatitude. Augustine conceives truth as reason irradiated by love, and morality as love irradiated by reason.[45] Both love and reason are inseparable parts of the human constitution. Indeed, the problem of moral epistemology – of knowing what is good – is not really a problem of knowledge but instead a problem of love, and of the orientation one adopts towards being. Fallen man spurns the good he knows. This is why Augustine considered that the fundamental obstacle to the knowledge of good was not obscurity but pride: 'And what is pride except a longing for a perverse kind of exaltation? For it is a perverse kind of exaltation to abandon the basis on which the mind should be firmly fixed and to become, as it were, based on oneself.'[46]

Pride fuels falsehood as the soul loves its own power, and this leads to ideology. Because of the fallen nature of man and his consequently disordered desires, disagreement about the good and the true is inevitable. It is a mistake to think that there is an inverse correlation between controversiality and truth: on the contrary, we might expect the most important truths to be hopelessly controversial, especially in society at large, precisely because of men's dissonant loves. The Manichees, in Augustine's view, did not turn away from the order of being because they thought it morally blank; rather, they proclaimed reality morally blank because they had already rebuffed it.[47] Like them, modern rationalists tend to believe that reason is not a matter of loving the truth, and they conclude from the fact that the good appears not to be deducible from calculative reason, that it does not exist.

In the next chapter, we shall look at how the question of being evolved in the modern period, and how Schelling progressively liberated himself from the 'Oriental' cosmogonies described above, to embrace a more traditionally Christian ontology.

---

43 Tresmontant, *Les idées maîtresses de la métaphysique chrétienne*, p. 74.
44 St Augustine, *City of God*, Book XII, Chapter 3.
45 St Augustine, *City of God*, Book XI, Chapter 28; *Confessions*, Chapter X.
46 St Augustine, *City of God*, Book XIV, Chapter 13, p. 571.
47 Walker, *Moral Foundations of Constitutional Thought*, pp. 117, 123 and 125.

Chapter 2

The Question of Being

> Pilate said to him, 'What is truth?'
> And when he had said this, he went out ...
>
> John XVIII:37–8

Plato and Aristotle

Different cosmogonies imply different ontologies. There is a long tradition among Christian philosophers that ontological realism is the cornerstone of Christian philosophy, although of course many centuries have been spent arguing over just what realism actually is.[1] The basic questions about ontology were formulated in Porphyry's commentary on Aristotle, the 'Introduction to the *Categories*', and in his *Isagoge*. What is the ontological status of genera and species? Are universals real things which exist on their own, or are they mere conceptions of the mind? Are universals things, concepts or names? If they are real things with their own independent existence, are they corporal or incorporal and do they exist separately from or only within particular things? In addition to these questions about the status of being (ontology), in other words about what is really true and what is not, there is the related issue of how we come to know the truth at all (epistemology). As we shall see, these twin questions of knowledge and being were at the centre of the preoccupations of the German idealists, especially Schelling.

Plato and Aristotle famously gave different answers to all these questions, which in any case had also preoccupied the pre-Socratic philosophers, but the answers of both giants fall within the category of realism. The original formulation of Platonic realism came in the *Meno*, where Plato moved from the fact of resemblance (between bees or virtues) to the suggestion that there must be a common essence which unites different manifestations of 'bee' or 'virtue'.[2] This is the basis for his idea that the Forms are the ontological 'causes' of things which bear their name.[3] Plato had taken Parmenides' side and argued that true being was changeless: as is well known, he came to argue that true reality consisted in a set of 'ideas' or universals which have their own independent existence famously illustrated by the parable of the cave in *The Republic*. Plato was an idealist–realist in the sense that he equated reality with definition, that is universality, and that the world of individual objects was but a shadow of the world of true being. Plato's belief in the world of really existing

---

1   Alain de Libera, *La querelle des universaux de Platon à la fin du Moyen Age* (Paris: Seuil, 1996).
2   Plato, *Meno*, 72a–b.
3   Libera, *La querelle des universaux*, p. 56.

independent abstract ideas (the Germans use the word '*Idee*' for this Platonic 'idea', as opposed to '*Vorstellung*' for ideas in the mind) made him a realist, but only in an intellectualist and essentialist (or even 'idealist') sense of the word. In many respects he was the father of German idealism, to the extent that he seemed to give priority to thought over existence: as we shall see, it was precisely in affirming the absolute priority and givenness of existence, as well as its inability to be subsumed into the concept, variable or otherwise, that the late Schelling, drawing heavily on Aristotle,[4] was to come to differ from this position. On the other hand, Plato was also the father of realism because he made concepts into real things. His theory of Forms concluded that there really existed a world of universal intelligible essences outside our thought, which was independent of the real world we know.

Aristotle retorted that what Plato called the real in fact had nothing to do with reality at all.[5] He was convinced it was wrong to say that only the Forms were real and that they inhabited a separate ontological realm; he insisted instead that a thing's essence was to be found in the thing itself.[6] Whereas Plato accorded a lesser ontological status to particular things, Aristotle argued that they were just as real as the knowable essences which they exemplified. He was convinced, indeed, that we come to know essences only by knowing real things, and that existence (not abstract contemplation) was itself a key to knowledge: 'It is impossible to know *what* a thing is if we do not know whether it exists ... To inquire what a thing is when we are not sure that it exists is no inquiry at all.'[7] He was, in this sense, an empiricist who believed that knowledge came from induction.[8] 'Experience, that is the universal when established as a whole in the Soul – the One that corresponds to the Many, the unity that is identically present in them all – provides the starting point for art and science.'[9] Order emerges from disorder rather as a new formation of soldiers emerges after a strategic retreat. 'General concepts are conveyed to us by sense-perception.'[10]

Aristotle's central theory, in other words, was that the form and the individual were inseparable: he made no radical distinction between the particular and the universal. Unlike Plato, Aristotle did not find the notion of change threatening to being, but instead regarded it as the very quality which defined the true being of that which exists: without being, there could be no teleology or development towards each thing's nature or towards the supreme principle of being.[11] Aristotle thus defined as *ousia* not things like colour or dimensions which can exist only in other things, nor

---

4   See, for example, Albert Franz, *Philosophische Religion, eine Auseinandersetzung mit den Grundlegungsproblemen der Spätphilosophie F.W.J. Schellings* (Amsterdam: Rodopi, 1992); Rüdiger Bubner, 'Dieu chez Aristote et Schelling', in Jean-François Courtine and Jean-Francois Marquet (eds), *Le dernier Schelling: raison et positivité* (Paris: Vrin, 1994).
5   Aristotle, *Metaphysics*, I, xi, 991b; VII (Z), xiii–xv, especially ch. xiv.
6   See especially Aristotle, *Metaphysics*, XIII, iv–x.
7   Aristotle, *Posterior Analytics*, II, viii, 93a.
8   See *Metaphysics*, I (A), i.
9   Aristotle, *Posterior Analytics*, II, xix, 100a.
10 *Ibid.*, II, xix, 100b.
11 Jean Brun, *Aristote et le Lycée* (Paris: Presses Universitaires de France, 1961), pp. 27–8.

indeed general notions like Man or Horse (because they are not things), but instead that which exists on its own and can have attributes.[12] Substance was thus the term used to describe the being of real things which are found in experience. The question of universals and of the intelligibility of being did not therefore impact only on the question of the ontological status of universals, but also on the epistemological question about the intellectual knowledge of particulars. Indeed one of Aristotle's clinching arguments against the Platonic theory of Ideas or Forms was to say that there was knowledge of the essence of things even when there was only one of them in the world (the sun, the moon).[13] More generally, he argued that our first knowledge of universals occurred precisely when we perceived particulars: when we see Callias, we see also the universal, 'man'.[14]

To be sure, Aristotle's work is replete with ambiguities and contradictions.[15] However, in his criticism of Plato, Aristotle anticipated many of the criticisms of Kant's transcendental idealism which itself drew on Platonism. Aristotle asked how the Forms could inhere in, or participate in, real things.[16] (For Kant and critics of Kant, the analogous question was 'How does the thing in itself relate to the phenomenal world?') Aristotle thought Plato had difficulty – a difficulty Kant also encountered – of explaining how it is we come to know true being (the Forms) if it is (they are) ontologically separate from the real world. Aristotle's replies to Plato are thus an interesting background to the reply of the post-Kantians, especially Schelling, to Kant.

Aristotle differed from his predecessors because he knew he could not explain being fully. He was conscious of the irredeemably given nature of actual being, but he did not try to expel it from his philosophy. In other words, the difference between Plato and Aristotle turns on the intelligibility of being: Plato began with pure intelligibility, and pushed real things off into the domain of illusion. Aristotle, by contrast, did not insist that that which is real must be entirely satisfying for thought, but instead started by accepting brute facts as they are, waiting until later to discuss their intelligibility.[17] As we shall see, this was close to the position which Schelling was to adopt in later life.

Aquinas

It is no exaggeration to say that the whole of medieval philosophy was preoccupied with the question of the relationship between the universal and the particular, and with how to reconcile Plato and Aristotle.[18] Aristotle's position was famously the inspiration for the Thomist view that universal essences can be discovered in real things. Aquinas

---

12   Aristotle, *Metaphysics*, VII, xiii, 1038b 10ff.; *Posterior Analytics*, II, *passim*.
13   Aristotle, *Metaphysics*, VII (Z), xv, 9 (1040a30–1040b).
14   Aristotle, *Posterior Analytics*, II, xix, 100b.
15   Libera, *La querelle des universaux*, pp. 72, 77 and 86–7.
16   Aristotle mocks Plato for this in *Metaphysics*, I, ix, 991a21–991b.
17   Etienne Gilson, *L'être et l'essence* (Paris: Vrin, 1994), pp. 54–5.
18   Libera, *La querelle des universaux*, p. 105; Etienne Gilson, *The Unity of Philosophical Experience* (London: Sheed & Ward, 1938), p. 3.

held that existence was prior to essence, and that humans could attain knowledge of independent reality through thought, perception and the use of reason. In *De ente et essentia*, Aquinas' main work on universals, he emphasised that a thing could be known only by knowing its essence and that this knowledge was achieved by a process of abstraction from individual things which today we would call 'induction'.[19] 'Essence is what is meant by the definition of a thing', wrote the Angelic Doctor.[20] Essence, for Aquinas, had a twofold existence, in the thing itself and in the human mind, but not its own being in an independent realm: Aquinas used Aristotle to wage his war against Plato, whose multiple errors, he insisted, all flowed from his one fundamental error, that he did not know the nature of being. In contrast, Aquinas wanted to examine being from the point of view of existence.[21] One of Aquinas' central beliefs was that metaphysics was the study of the intelligible, and that it was natural and possible for man to know and to ask about the ultimate cause of the things he observes. He was convinced that man could attain knowledge, albeit partial knowledge, of this ultimate cause of all being, God, via his knowledge of the real world. He therefore disagreed profoundly with Plato that intelligibility had to be placed in some other realm.

Aquinas' rejection of an essentialist ontology along Platonist or even Augustinian lines led him, as Etienne Gilson was at pains to show, to develop a double ontology by distinguishing existence from essence.[22] In fact, Gilson spent his life pleading with his readers to understand this Thomist priority of being and the dangers to philosophy of forgetting it. In *The Unity of Philosophical Experience*, Gilson urged that metaphysics needed to return to the concept of being and he documented the various attempts by modern philosophers (since Descartes) to replace the study of being with other disciplines (for example ethics or logic). Gilson never ceased to emphasise the key importance of the notion of *esse*, and we shall see at the end of this study that Schelling comes to adopt a similar view. Things have quiddity in virtue of their form, Gilson writes, but the act of their actual existing (*esse*) must be added for the thing actually to exist.[23] In other words, everything has essence and existence: in *id quod est* there is *id quod* and *est*. Every being demanded the co-presence of these two elements. All beings were acts of *esse* which were qualified to be this or that being by having an essence added to them: as Gilson writes, 'If *esse* were not something other than *id quod est*, then different individual things within one species, having the same quiddity, would not be distinguishable from one another.'[24] More generally, and especially in his great work, *The Unity of Philosophical Experience*, Gilson repeatedly urged that being was the key to all metaphysics, but that post-Cartesian philosophers had forgotten it. 'What is it which the mind is bound to conceive both as belonging to all things and as not belonging to any two things in the same way? The word is – Being. Our mind is so made that

---

19 Aquinas, *De Ente et essentia*, Caput I.
20 Aquinas, *De Ente et essentia*, Caput II.
21 Anton C. Pegis, *Introduction to Saint Thomas Aquinas* (New York: Randon House, 1948), p. xvi.
22 Etienne Gilson, *Le thomisme* (Paris: Vrin, 6th edn, 1989), p. 109.
23 Gilson, *L'être et l'essence*, p. 104.
24 *Ibid.*, p. 106.

it cannot formulate a single proposition without relating it to some being.'[25] We will see later how Schelling himself became increasingly convinced of the same thing.

Aquinas was indeed convinced of the specificity and importance of being (*esse*). His form of ontological realism – his conviction of the existence and intelligibility of being – was to form the bedrock of Catholic thinking. Aquinas differed from Aristotle in that he did not consider that the heart of the real lay either in substance or in form, but instead in *esse* – in that act of existence which cannot be conceptualised but which is indissociable from substance. Because the existence which belongs to each thing cannot be conceptualised, we have to content ourselves with apprehending it.[26] Although other philosophers have certainly distinguished existence from essence, Aquinas put existence at the very root of being rather than making it an accident of essence.[27]

We have already seen how St Augustine began with the 'ontology of Exodus' to attribute supreme being to God; St Thomas agreed and insisted on the primacy of existence too. He also sought to show the specificity of the existence of God, namely that it was contained within his essence. 'God is in all things as the *esse* which causes their *esse*, or imparts it to them. He is their sustaining ground. For all other things, a distinction must be drawn between *quo est* and *quod est*, between that something is and what it is.'[28] In Aquinas, it is clear that each individual thing is supported in existence by the *esse* which God imparts to it as a loving gift: the multiplicity of existing things is therefore not the sign of degradation, but instead of God's love. We will see later that God's liberty in imparting *esse* to all existing things is the key prerequisite for the existence of human liberty as well.

Nonetheless, Aquinas used this priority of existence, and especially his belief that existence was ascertained rather than deduced, to reject the ontological argument of St Anselm, by saying that the argument could work only if God, in fact, existed. The idea of something existing was in no way equivalent to something existing.[29] This was to be exactly Schelling's reaction to Descartes' use of the argument centuries later. Thomists like F.M. Genuyt argue precisely, as Schelling was to do, that experience of bodily reality was a key element of self-knowledge, and that any interpretation of being which made corporal human existence incomprehensible had to be dismissed:[30] this basic experience of being is that which leads us to an affirmation of the existence of God and the world. As we will see later, there are many other similarities between Aquinas in particular, Thomism in general and Schelling, especially in the later Schelling's emphasis on the facticity of, and in his discussion of, creation *ex nihilo*.[31] It is precisely the primacy of existence over essence, or of being over thought, which

---

25   Gilson, *The Unity of Philosophical Experience*, pp. 318–19.
26   Gilson, *L'être et l'essence*, pp. 113–22; *Le thomisme*, pp. 174ff.
27   Gilson, *Le thomisme*, p. 180.
28   Aquinas, *De ente et essentia*, Caput V.
29   Aquinas, *Scriptum super sententiis*, I, d.3, q.1, a.2, arg. 4 and resp.; Gilson, *Le thomisme*, p. 61.
30   F.M. Genuyt, *Vérité de l'Etre et Affirmation de Dieu, Essai sur la philosophie de Saint Thomas* (Paris: Vrin, 1974), p. 43.
31   Cf. Harald Holz, *Spekulation und Faktizität, Zum Freiheitsbegriff des mittleren und späten Schelling* (Bonn: Bouvier, 1970), p. 252, note 18.

will be the crucial point separating Schelling from the fundamentally essentialist ontology of Hegel.

This Thomist position was, of course, undermined by the rise of modern rationalism. Following the counterintuitive discoveries of Copernicus and Galileo, men had less and less confidence in their senses as instruments for discovering the truth. They turned inwards, to reason, as a seemingly better source of certainty. The rise of secularism coincided with this growing faith in autonomous human reason, which was autonomous both from God and also from the outside world. The laws of nature themselves were increasingly thought not to be of divine authorship, still less evidence of divine revelation, but instead an autonomous logical-mathematical body which man could easily and clearly comprehend with his mind alone. This intellectual movement was linked to the Reformation project of enabling the individual to establish truth for himself, without being aided or taught by the Church. These processes culminated in the philosophy of Descartes (1596–1650). However, the attempt to escape the pit of Cartesian doubt often seemed only to emphasise the extent to which modern man seemed trapped inside his private sense-impressions, like Descartes in his stove.

Rationalism and Descartes

> And new Philosophy calls all in doubt,
> The Element of Fire is quite put out;
> The Sun is lost, and th'earth, and no mans wit
> Can well direct him, where to looke for it ...
> 'Tis all in pieces, all cohaerence gone;
> All just supply, and all Relation:
> Prince, Subject, Father, Sonne, are things forgot ...
>
> John Donne, *The First Anniversary, An Anatomy of the World*[32]

Descartes' attempt was precisely to solve the problems caused by this sudden loss of self-confidence in the truth-revealing (but common-sense disturbing) capacity of the senses. However, it is not clear that he succeeded: he is the author *par excellence* of the modern world's doubt of the objectivity of the outside world. Schelling's disagreements with Descartes from 1804 onwards are one of the main causes of his gradual move away from idealism and from Hegel.

The novelty of the kind of secular philosophy introduced by Descartes (no doubt against his intentions) lies precisely in the paradox that the pretensions of the modern mind grow in proportion to the suspicion that truth and objective reality are unknowable. Because of the idealist and post-idealist tendency to rely only on subjective states as the best or only source of certainty, philosophy since Descartes and Kant has tended to value sincerity as the necessary and sufficient condition for truth. The modern mind wants to be the absolute master of its own thought, and to be emancipated from traditional sources of authority. This risks just what Augustine

---

32   John Donne, *The First Anniversary: An Anatomy of the World*, lines 205ff.

feared: that those who do not believe in reality, let alone love it, will try to replace the perceived void with a hubristic philosophical bricolage of their own. As we shall see, Schelling – who made God the 'master of Being', and who was convinced throughout his life that 'nature' could tell us a lot about the structure of being – implicitly and later explicitly refused such attempts to put man in God's place.

Thomists and Catholic thinkers have traditionally accused the idealist tradition of undermining the ability of man to know any truth at all, let alone the most important truths.[33] They have said it leads to atheism, pantheism, materialism or rationalism (anathemised by both Pius IX's *Syllabus of Errors* and the First Vatican Council in 1870) or to the kind of moral cynicism epitomised by Pilate's remark above.[34] Thinkers who might broadly be described as traditionally religious have expressed the fear that modern ontology undermines the possibility of there being an objective reality which the human mind can come to know. They have instead championed objectivity and the ability of all men endowed with right reason to know it and to know God, for 'Subjectivism implied excessive freedom, relativism, the absence of obedience to God's word and the Church's voice.'[35]

Idealism is a broad term, and, as we shall see below, there are many different variants of it. But the word always implies a move towards subjectivity. Idealism is based on the primacy of the idea, and thus of the thinking subject, and idealist philosophy is often characterised by a study of the structures of thought. Descartes is the author of the quintessential belief of idealism, which is that thought is prior to being. It is a belief which, as we shall see, Schelling came to refute. Realists in the Thomist tradition see in the project to make human thought completely autonomous of reality an 'angelism', a monstrous pride which refuses to accept any truth not discovered by oneself. Indeed, the religious implications of Cartesian philosophy are considerable. Even though it must be stressed that, in theology as much as in epistemology, Descartes was trying to save what he could – it was certainly not his intention to undermine faith – God in fact became for Descartes an Archimedian point by which to lever the basically isolated individual into the real world. But as Leszek Kolakowski has shown, 'The theory which made logical, mathematical, and moral laws dependent entirely on God's free and arbitrary decree was, historically speaking, an important step in getting rid of God altogether ... Descartes barred the road from Nature to God by breaking the link between God's essence and His actual legislation; he was thereby, in spite of his intentions, to become a forerunner of deists.'[36] This point is to be especially important in the light of Schelling's lifelong interest in the natural world, where he believed variously (in his early life) that idealist philosophy itself could be observed at work and (later on) that the natural world was the oldest 'testament' of God's revelation. Schelling, in other words,

---

33 Jean Daujat, *Y a-t-il une vérité?* (Paris: Téqui, 1974), *passim*.

34 For example Jean Ousset, *Pour qu'il règne* (Grez-en-Bouère: Dominique Martin Morin, 1986), p. 25.

35 Thomas O'Meara, O.J., *Romantic Idealism and Roman Catholicism: Schelling and the Theologians* (Notre Dame and London: University of Notre Dame Press, 1982), p. 13.

36 Leszek Kolakowski, *Religion, If There is No God: On God, the Devil, Sin and other Worries of the So-called Philosophy of Religion* (London: Fontana Press, 2nd edn, 1993), p. 21.

repeatedly sought to re-open the road from nature to God, over which Descartes had lowered a barrier which his successors then bolstered with philosophical sandbags. Idealism was to demote existence to the level of conjecture, in the name of a higher certainty, and this why it took on a certain Gnostic and dualistic allure.

Spinoza

Spinoza was a crucial reference point for German idealism in general and for Schelling in particular, who was fascinated by him throughout his life. Spinozism was the direct cause of the *'Pantheismusstreit'* (the argument about pantheism) which Friedrich Heinrich Jacobi (1743–1819) launched when he attacked Spinoza as pantheist, rationalist and atheist in 1785. Spinoza's system encapsulates many of the themes on cosmogony discussed in Chapter 1: he was a clearly 'emanationist' thinker who, like Plotinus, did not believe that God freely created the world, but instead that it emanated necessarily from Him. It is significant that, from early on, Schelling was to wrestle with the problems associated with this view, especially with the difficulties it creates for human freedom.

Spinoza was a radical anti-creationist. He made it clear, against Aquinas and the whole theory of Judeo-Christian creationism, that 'No substance can be produced or created by anything else',[37] and that it was absurd to suggest that substance in general was created.[38] Instead, substance was eternal and infinite.[39] Nature was a timeless and changeless single individual 'whose parts – that is, the constituent bodies – vary in infinite ways without any change in the individual as a whole.'[40] Nature was an emanation of the Absolute, and the creation never really happened as such: the world did not come about as the result of God's free choice – 'not from God's free will or absolute pleasure'[41] – but rather by the necessity of His essence. There was therefore no 'end' or purpose to nature.[42]

Spinoza severely downgraded the veracity of Revelation and considered that 'the Bible leaves reason absolutely free, that it has nothing in common with philosophy.'[43] Knowledge and faith were entirely separate domains, and neither was the handmaid of the other:[44] indeed, it was precisely the purpose of the *Tractatus theologico-politicus* to separate faith from reason.[45] This is precisely the view which the later Schelling was to

---

37 Spinoza, *Ethics*, I, 15, Scholium, translated by Samuel Shirley (Indianapolis: Hackett, 1982); see also I, 6.
38 *Ibid.*, I, 8, Scholium 2.
39 *Ibid.*, I, 10, Scholium.
40 *Ibid.*, II, 13, Lemma 7, Scholium.
41 *Ibid.*, Appendix to I.
42 *Ibid.*; also IV, Preface.
43 Spinoza, *Tractatus theologico-politicus*, trans. R.M. Elwes (New York: Dover, 1951), Preface, p. 9.
44 *Ibid.*, p. 10.
45 *Ibid.*, Chapter 14, p. 189.

attack. Indeed, Spinoza came as close to saying that religion is the opium of the people as was possible at the time, even in Holland.[46]

Quite apart from making theological objections, some have argued that Spinoza's ontological monism had unwelcome political implications too, because of the apparent reduction of the human individual to utter passivity, even if Spinoza was himself politically moderate. Bertrand de Jouvenel, for instance, claims to find sources of despotism in the *Tractatus theologico-politicus*.[47] As Roger Scruton says, 'Something is missing from Spinoza's philosophy of mind: ... the self, or subject.'[48] Even in the early period, Schelling too saw that Spinoza's was a fundamentally anti-individualist doctrine which demanded of the individual that he destroy himself as an autonomous subject. Schelling saw that Spinoza's freedom was mere causality, and that that causality was in turn merely a derived version of the causality of the Absolute.[49]

Spinoza has rightly been called the prophet of modern science, for his pantheist system anticipates the modern materialism which has no room for self-consciousness or the human soul. As the full title of the *Ethics* reveals – 'Ethics demonstrated in geometrical order' – the rationalist has a mathematical or geometrical model in his mind when he starts to give an account of reality. For rationalists like him, mathematics is the perfect illustration of the possibility that one may gain *a priori* knowledge of something which is not oneself.

Spinoza also makes human consciousness the criterion for freedom: it is through absolute *knowledge* that man becomes free. This is the definitive Gnostic idea, as we saw in Chapter 1. Emotions are ranged on a scale, depending on the 'adequacy' of the idea involved in them: 'An emotion which is a passion ceases to be a passion as soon as we form a clear and distinct idea of it ... The more an emotion becomes clear to us, the more it is within our power, and the less the mind is passive to it.'[50] In Spinoza, it is by obeying and understanding necessity that we are free: any other idea of freedom is an illusion which creates bondage. Spinoza intentionally removed contingency from the picture. Freedom was not freedom from necessity but instead the consciousness of necessity.[51] 'Self-complacency is the highest object for which we may hope.'[52]

Spinoza made the Absolute as impersonal as he made humans. In his early life, Schelling was to defend Spinoza against this attack of impersonalism because by that stage the religious elements of Schelling's philosophy were relatively undeveloped. Later, however, Schelling came to agree with Spinoza's Christian critics who condemned both the impersonality of the Spinozist God as well as the necessity

---

46 See also Tresmontant, *L'opposition métaphysique au monothéisme hébreu de Spinoza à Heidegger* (Paris: François-Xavier de Guibert, 1996), pp. 13–61.

47 See Bertrand de Jouvenel, *Du Pouvoir: Histoire naturelle de sa croissance* (Geneva: Cheval Ailé, 1947), p. 49.

48 Roger Scruton, *Spinoza* (Oxford: Oxford University Press, 1986), p. 72.

49 Andrew Bowie, *Schelling and Modern European Philosophy* (London: Routledge, 1993), p. 27.

50 Spinoza, *Ethics*, V, 3 ... V, 3, Corollary.

51 *Ibid.*, V, 6.

52 *Ibid.*, IV, 58.

of His creation.[53] Traditional Christian theology may itself be vitiated by trying to hold the twin yet perhaps incompatible beliefs that God is both Absolute and Father, but nonetheless Christians have traditionally stuck to the view that God is both recognizably a person, and also that His creation was a free act of love.[54] Neither of these qualities can be found in Spinoza's God, as Schelling was later to see.

German Idealism

The relationship between German idealism and the broader movement we have called 'modern rationalism' is close and yet full of tension. Schelling initially joined in with the Romantic attack on rationalism until he realised that German idealism, especially Hegel's philosophy, was itself a child of it. As such, Schelling came to turn his fire on the rationalist elements within German idealism itself.

Charles Taylor offers a masterly sketch of the causes and motives of the German idealist movement in his *Hegel*.[55] Attributing the change between modern and premodern philosophy to a change in the concept of the self (a correct interpretation, which will help us to understand why Schelling's approach to human liberty is so different from that of his contemporaries) Taylor writes, 'The essential difference can perhaps be put in this way: the modern subject is self-defining, where on previous views the subject is defined in relation to a cosmic order.'[56] The brilliant but dangerous[57] French reader of Hegel, Alexandre Kojève, made a similar point but went one step further when he emphasised that this eminently modern goal of self-definition reached its summit in Hegel's philosophy itself: 'Der seiner selbst gewisse Geist – the spirit which has the certitude of itself – is in the final analysis Hegel himself, that is to say his system of philosophy (the *Phenomenology* plus the *Enclyclopedia*) which is no longer the search for wisdom but wisdom (= absolute knowledge) itself.'[58]

For the ancients, the idea that the self could be demonstrated without any reference to a cosmic order was simply inconceivable, since the exercise of reason was precisely the grasping of that order. Teleology, in other words, the science of ends, was a crucial element in theories of the self, and it is a concept which was to interest Schelling. By contrast, the modern Cartesian and post-Cartesian self precisely draws back in on itself, defining itself and the world from within, cut off from everything else. These remarks help us to understand the background to the Kantian revolution, which was the philosophical context in which Schelling wrote.

---

53 *Zur Geschichte der neueren Philosophie (Münchener Vorlesungen)* (1833), I/10, 40; *Über die Natur der Philosophie als Wissenschaft (Erlanger Vorträge)* (1821–25), I/9, 218.
54 Kolakoswki, *Religion*, p. 140.
55 Charles Taylor, *Hegel* (Cambridge: Cambridge University Press, 1975), Chapter 1.
56 *Ibid.*, p. 6.
57 On the political implications of Kojève see Shadia Drury's magnificent *Alexandre Kojève and the Roots of Postmodern Politics* (New York: St Martin's Press, 1994).
58 Alexandre Kojève, *Introduction à la lecture de Hegel* (Paris: Gallimard, 1947), 'C. Der seiner selbst gewisse Geist. Die Moralität', p. 145.

If there is one outstanding preoccupation of German Idealist philosophy, as of rationalism generally, it is the search for an all-encompassing system, describing the whole of being, and constructed on the alleged certainties of the self or of the concept. Heidegger drew attention to six defining characteristics of this desire to construct systems, which various seventeenth- and eighteenth-century philosophies have in common despite their other differences.[59] The first was the pre-eminence of the mathematical approach. (Heidegger is perhaps wrong not to draw a distinction between pre- and post-Kantian idealism, for Hegel's system sometimes seems to draw more inspiration from biology than mathematics: post Hegelian philosophers like Engels were convinced that their theories of the dialectic had been 'proved' by the latest discoveries in biology, especially those of Charles Darwin.[60]) The mathematical approach is a particular concept of the essence of knowledge itself, whose roots lie at least as far back as Descartes. It conceives of knowledge as consisting in a unity of demonstrable conclusions based upon a demonstrable and absolute premise. The system is self-enclosed and self-supporting.

As a consequence, the traditional religious experience of being is re-forged according to rules of thought which describe all being in the form of mathematical coherence. In this concept of 'system', which starts with Spinoza, the notions of the mathematical, the mind giving itself its own law, the emancipation of man into freedom within the whole of being, are all interlocked. As Rüdiger Bubner remarks, 'The effects of idealism, which can still be felt, proceed from the idea of thought working its way out *(sich herausarbeiten)* towards independence; thought which earns the strength to know its own limitations, and thus to extend its horizons step by step.'[61] At the deepest level, this view leads to the typically idealist belief that being can be subsumed in thought. As Spinoza wrote, and as Hegel was also to argue, 'The order and connection of ideas is the same as the order and connection of things.'[62]

The second characteristic of the desire to create systems to which Heidegger drew attention is the demand for self-grounding knowledge. Critics attack this as betraying a priority of certainty over truth and of method over content. The 'method' is obviously principally a Cartesian invention. Systems of knowledge of this kind are believed to be properly grounded when they are sure of themselves. This certainty and this self-assuredness become the ground of all knowledge, and thus the ground of the truth of the knowable. Such an approach reinforces the modern preference for sincerity over truth, an idea with ultimately Oriental roots which becomes important in Kantian ethics.

Third, the foundation of certainty is the self-certainty of the thinking self. In other words, the self-certainty of thought decides what is. It takes its own certainty

---

59 Martin Heidegger, *Schellings Abhandlung über das Wesen der menschlichen Freiheit (1809)* (Tübingen: Max Niemeyer, 1971), pp. 36ff; p. 41.

60 Friedrich Engels, 'Anti-Dühring, Einleitung, I. Allgemeines', in Karl Marx, Friedrich Engels, *Werke*, Vol. 20 (Berlin: Dietz, 1990), p. 22; see also 'Dialektik der Natur, Alte Vorrede zum "Anti- Dühring", Über die Dialektik', in *Werke*, Vol. 20, pp. 335–6, also p. 319.

61 Rüdiger Bubner, 'Einleitung', in *Geschichte der Philosophie in Text und Darstellung*, Vol. 6, *Deutscher Idealismus* (Stuttgart: Reclam, 1978), p. 18.

62 Spinoza, *Ethics*, II, 7, p. 66.

as its foundation, and thus pronounces on the fundamental nature of being. Thought and its certainty become the measure of truth and of being.

Fourth, 'The self-certainty of thought becomes the court which decides what can be and what cannot be: indeed, further, it decides what being is.'[63] In addition to the requirement that a system be based on a mathematical model – that is, that the totality of the system be transparent to the light of human reason – the essential understanding was also added that such knowledge had to be absolute knowledge akin to the knowledge one has of a mathematical truth. This is a concept foreign to Aquinas.[64]

Fifth, the desire for systems is fundamentally secular and modern. Heidegger pointed out that Aquinas' thought began with God and descended into practical and moral human life; the modern system, by contrast, made man's thought its base and attempted thence to encompass the whole universe. This is why the search for this self-grounded certainty was the exact opposite (and indeed enemy) of the religious disposition. Faith was henceforth measured according to its conformity with the self-certainty of pure thought. To be sure, Pascal, Descartes and others were not consciously trying to undermine religion but instead to ground it more surely according to the new criterion of pure thought. However, as Schelling was to argue, their attempts were doomed to failure.

Sixth, the rise of the autonomy and self-assurance of human thought can be seen as leading to political, and not just philosophical, emancipation. What man is in himself, what his being consists in, was now decided by men themselves. Art and human genius became the law of human being, as of being in general. This is why Charles Taylor writes, 'The modern shift to a self-defining subject was bound up with a sense of control over the world – at first intellectual and then technological. The modern certainty that the world was not to be read as a text or an embodiment of meaning ... grew with the mapping of the regularities in things, by transparent mathematical reasoning, and with the consequent increase of manipulative control.'[65]

All this was conducive to a new notion of freedom, one in which the self-defining subject enjoyed power with respect to, and over, the world. This new concept of freedom needed rising secularism as its pre-requisite, for the Church obviously assumed that man was dependent on God. It encouraged an appropriately deferential attitude to God and to His creation. The divorce between the mind and the outside world, inherent in the idealist project, had its obvious counterpart (and no doubt source) in the theology of the sixteenth century: while Luther struggled to explain the real presence of Christ in Holy Communion, radicals like Zwingli gave up the attempt completely, preferring instead to understand the Mass as a mere act of remembrance. Whereas Catholics drew on Aquinas and Aristotle to explain the Incarnation and the Mass as the inhering of the universal in the particular, the various strands of Protestantism made the notion of the presence of the divine in real things increasingly problematic. Emptied of the divine, the world became meaningless. There can be no doubt (it is not just 'probable' as Taylor says) that the Protestant

---

63 Heidegger, *Schellings Abhandlung*, p. 37.
64 For example Aquinas, *Summa Contra Gentiles*, Book III, Chapters 53 and 81.
65 Taylor, *Hegel*, p. 7.

war waged for a devotion to God unmitigated by any 'idolatry' 'helped to destroy the sense that the creation was a locus of meanings in relation to which man had to define himself'.[66] This point will be crucial in assessing Schelling's relationship to Catholicism and traditional Christian metaphysics.

The use of mathematical or rationalistic models for interpreting the structure of being also led to important problems where the question of freedom and the problem of evil were concerned. These two problems were at the very heart of Schelling's preoccupations. As we shall see, Schelling started off his 1809 *Freedom* essay by admitting that a 'system of freedom' sounded like a contradiction in terms. We shall also see that Schelling's specific concept of evil played an absolutely key role in the development of his ontology. The main problem, as Henri Bergson said, is,

> Most philosophers ... are unable to conceive of radical novelty and unpredictability. I am not just speaking of those philosophers who believe that phenomena and events are so rigorously linked to one another that effects can be deduced from causes: these people imagine that the future is given in the present, that it is theoretically visible there, and that, consequently, it brings nothing new. But even those very few who believed in free choice have reduced it to a simple 'choice' between two or several options, as though these options were 'possibles' destined in advance and as if the will were restricted to 'realizing' one of them. In other words, they still hold – even if they are unaware of it – that everything is given. Of an action which might be entirely new ... and which would not pre-exist in any fashion, not even in the form of a pure possible to be realised, they seem to have no idea.[67]

Very few philosophers have been prepared to pay the real price of true contingency for freedom, especially not if evil comes with the purchase. This is why philosophers have often tried to spirit away the problem of evil as well. Evil presents similar problems for the systematic mind to those posed by radical contingency. This is why systematists often explained evil away as an optical illusion (the fault is with our limited intellect), on the assumption that only the whole is actually real, as Hegel maintained. Duns Scotus also recognised the problem, writing that evil, like freedom, belonged to those 'things about which the most learned and ingenious men can know almost nothing'.[68] For the religious mind, by contrast, evil is a conscious act of rebellion against God: it is an act of will. When Augustine or Aquinas wrote of evil as a privation, they did not wish to attenuate its effects or its magnitude. Not only did the optimistic rationalists of the seventeenth and eighteenth centuries try to dissolve the problem of evil away in the elixir of man's progressive reason, but they also (especially Hobbes, Rousseau and Kant) made the human will – the very source of evil itself – the cornerstone of their system.

---

66   *Ibid.*, p. 9.
67   Bergson, *La pensée et le mouvant* (Paris: Presses Universitaires de France, 5th edn, 1996), p. 10.
68   Duns Scotus, *Philosophical Writings: A Selection*, trans. Allan Wolter (Indianapolis and New York: Library of Liberal Arts, 1962), p. 171.

Kant and Transcendental Idealism

It was in German idealism that freedom and the self-constitution of reason became the highest values. The twin desire to know being as it is and to construct a system came together in this current of philosophy. Kant, in particular, attempted to ground the validity of knowledge by undertaking a critique of reason and explaining its limits. In fact, as Schelling was to argue, his attempt led him to shut reason off from access to the very linchpins of his whole system, freedom and the thing in itself.

Kant's system was an attempt to ground a system of philosophy based on the free and autonomous use of reason. At the heart of his ethics are the notions of self-determination and autonomy: freedom consists in giving oneself one's own law out of one's own essence. The famous first sentence of the essay *What is Enlightenment?* ('*Aufklärung ist der Ausgang des Menschen aus seiner selbstverschuldeten Unmündigkeit*' [Enlightenment is when man leaves the state of tutelage for which he is himself responsible]) reads like a political manifesto. Certainly, his own proclamation that his metaphysics was revolutionary (in the preface to the second edition of the *Critique of Pure Reason*[69]) made it clear that his project had political as well as philosophical implications.

Kant's transcendental idealism differed crucially from previous idealisms such as Berkeley's. Unlike Berkeley, Kant repeatedly insisted that the independent existence of a real world was not in the least problematic for him. He strenuously rejected the charge of 'absolute idealism', claiming that his transcendental idealism was based on the crucial empirical affirmation that reality in itself exists. Kant even argued against Descartes, who did not conclude that the outside world did not exist, but who doubted it at the beginning.

On the other hand, Kant's critical or transcendental idealism ended up contesting the idea that we can know the noumenal world – reality as it really *really* is. The division between the phenomenal and noumenal worlds meant that, for the phenomenal world, our minds decide what is and what is not while the thing-in-itself remains unknowable. As Alan White says, 'While Kant uses transcendental knowledge to develop arguments proving that our mathematical and empirical knowledge is reliable, he leaves transcendental knowledge itself ungrounded.'[70] In other words, Kant's determination to establish a mathematical or scientific model – a method by which reason would establish a single all-encompassing system – led him away from the realist element in transcendental idealism. For Kant, system was 'the unity of multifarious cognitive acts under one idea';[71] it was 'the systematic in cognition, that is, the connectedness of it out of a principle' (*das Systematische der Erkenntnis ..., d.i. der Zusammenhang derselben aus einem Prinzip*).[72] He wrote,

---

69   Thirteenth paragraph, beginning, 'In jenem Versuche ...'.
70   Alan White, *Schelling: An Introduction to the System of Freedom* (New Haven: Yale University Press, 1983), p. 9.
71   Kant, *Kritik der reinen Vernunft, II. Transzendentale Methodenlehre*, 3. Hauptstück, *Die Architechtonik der reinen Vernunft*, A 832; B 860 (for example on p. 696 of Immanuel Kant, *Werke*, Vol. 2, ed. Wilhelm Weischedel [Wiesbaden: Insel, 1956]).
72   Kant, *Kritik der reinen Vernunft, I. Transzendentale Elementarlehre, Anhang zur transzendentalen Dialektik*, A 645; B 673; p. 566 in Vol. 2 of Kant, *Werke*.

This unity of reason presupposes an idea of the form of the totality of cognition, which precedes particular cognitions of individual parts, and contains the conditions for determining *a priori* the position and relationship of each part to the others. This idea thus presupposes the full unity of the understanding through cognition, through which the latter is not simply an aggregate, but a system which hangs together through necessary laws.[73]

It was thus reason, and not an inherent order in the world, which made the acts of our understanding 'systematic'. Reason made cognition possible. Without it, it would be impossible to find any intelligibility in the world. Reason constructed the greatest degree of unity out of the greatest degree of plurality: it was simultaneously the demand for, and the creation of, a system. This is why Kantian reason can be called 'creative': his view was the direct opposite of the Thomist or Aristotelian view, which held that intelligibility obtained *in things themselves* and in the world itself. Intelligibility was given and found, not created or constructed. In a dramatically revealing passage, Kant wrote,

> Reason should go to nature with, in one hand, its principles, according to which alone concordant appearances can count as laws, and, in the other hand, the experiment that it has thought of according to them. To be sure, it will be instructed by nature, but not in the quality of a schoolboy who lets the teacher tell him whatever he likes, but rather like a judge appointed to a case (*eines bestallten Richters*) who compels witnesses to answer the questions which he puts to them.[74]

'Objects', he went on, 'must orient themselves according to our knowledge.'[75] Consequently, despite his own assurances, Kant ended up with a system in which, for things as we know them at least, there is nothing other than that which is perceived. The existence of the noumenal realm, which Kant said he wanted to ensure, was incapable of being apprehended by human reason: it therefore became radically problematic and ultimately unknowable after all. Kant himself admitted that, in his system, there was an 'unavoidable chasm' between the (knowable) phenomenal world and the (unknowable) noumenal one '… so that from the former [the domain of nature as the sensory] to the latter [the domain of freedom as the super-sensory] (through the theoretical use of reason) there can be no transition, just as if they were different worlds, with the first having no influence on the second …'[76] To this extent, Kant's transcendental idealism really was idealism *tout court*: unlike Berkeley, Kant did admit a reality other than appearance, but, like Berkeley, he thought that *esse est percipi* for things in the real world. As Robert Pippin shows, 'Kant's position is idealistic because it asserts that what we experience is always subject to (the requirement of *our* apprehension).'[77]

---

73   *Ibid.*
74   Kant, *Kritik der reinen Vernunft, Vorrede zur zweiten Auflage*, 8th paragraph (beginning 'Als Galilei seine Kugeln …').
75   *Ibid.*, 11th paragraph (beginning 'Ich sollte meinen …').
76   Kant, 'Einleitung II', in *Kritik der Urteilskraft* (Stuttgart: Reclam) p. 28.
77   Robert Pippin, *Hegel's Idealism: The Satisfactions of Self-Consciousness* (Cambridge: Cambridge University Press, 1989), p. 34.

This radical unknowability of the world is bad enough for ordinary day-to-day pieces of knowledge about this or that. It becomes even more problematic when it applies to the very building-blocks of the Kantian system itself. Yet it is very striking that in the *Grundlegung der Metaphysik der Sitten*, where Kant elaborated on the significance of the good will; where he defined the categorical imperative and its relationship to rationality, autonomy and freedom; where he distinguished two different sorts of law to which man was subject (natural and moral); and where he explained how this dovetailed with the idea of a kingdom of ends – all of these with great clarity and conviction – he remained nonetheless resolutely unable to say *how* freedom was possible, and how free acts determined by the moral law could be in harmony with the law of nature. In other words, the so-called *Grundlegung* did not lay the ground of anything at all. As he himself wrote, when discussing the essential question of how free action was compatible with causality in the phenomenal world,

> Reason would overstep all its limits if it undertook *how* pure reason can be practical, which would be exactly the same as the task of explaining *how freedom is possible* ... Freedom is a mere idea, whose objective reality cannot be represented in any way according to the laws of nature nor in any possible form of experience ... It can therefore never be conceived or even seen. It is valid merely as a necessary presupposition of reason in a being which believes ... it is conscious of its own will.[78]

In other words, freedom – for Kant, the key to the dignity of man, as well as the crown of his whole philosophical system – is a mere unprovable postulate. Indeed, precisely because it was for Kant a mere postulate of reason, freedom, and the morality which goes with it, was resolutely abstract from all fact or contingency: the Kantian imperative can enjoin no particular practice and no particular action. The 'essence' out of which the free man supposedly determines himself in Kant is the most universal and abstract thing possible, reason: what is autonomous in Kant is not man, and certainly not particular men, but instead the rational, abstract, universal moral law. Despite Kant's clear affirmation of a 'positive' sense of freedom as self-determination, his model can never accommodate the individuality of a chooser or an agent. Individual human character is dissipated away into the thin cold air of Prussian formalism, and into the anonymity of a soldier who receives a command. Kant's is the philosophy of that worst of German qualities, *Kadavergehorsam* – the obedience of the corpse. No doubt this is why *Zum ewigen Frieden*, his enormously influential tract on world peace through federalism, takes it title – albeit wryly – from an inn sign depicting a cemetery.

This abstractness (or deadness) of the Kantian self is the inevitable counterpart to the equally abstract 'thing in itself'. The mutual emptiness of man and the thing in itself in Kant's system is the exact opposite of that symmetry between God's full, loving and personal liberty and the man he created in His own image. Although Kantian morality is one of duty, the duty is entirely to oneself, not to one's Creator. Any sense of intrinsic debt, the foundation-stone of all religiosity, is completely absent from Kant, who held that a man was free when he 'stands for himself', when

---

78 Kant, *Grundlegung der Metaphysik der Sitten*, p. 121 in Reclam edition (pp. 458–9).

he is *selbstständig*. Kant's conception of freedom defined his concept of man as that which determines its nature out of its own ground. As Taylor remarks, 'Kant's principal interest was that man should draw his moral precepts out of his own will and not from any external source, including God.'[79] The highest Kantian values are self-clarity, self-possession and self-determination. For Kant, it is not God, but the self-given command of Reason, which inspires awe.[80] The reference point for judgement on good and evil is not being as it is (for this is unknowable), but one entirely internal to the agent, good will. The reason for this abstractness – which seemed to threaten the very things it was trying to establish, namely the knowability of the world and human freedom – lay precisely in Kant's determination to establish a system in which human reason would be sovereign. It lay, in other words, in his desire for a self-contained system.

From a traditional theological perspective, of course, things are supposed to be the other way around. Man is supposed to have his ground in God, not in himself. Schelling, as we shall see, will adopt the idea that God, not man, has His ground within Himself as the linchpin of the metaphysical structure of the 1809 *Freedom* essay. We shall thus see that Schelling provided an ontological setting which allows Kantianism to be overcome, while Hegel, despite his criticism of Kant, does not.

It is hardly surprising if Kant's successors dispensed with the *Ding an sich*, having very quickly identified the problems associated with it. For, in Gilson's words, 'Critical idealism is one of the most instructive attempts to avoid the obstacle which existence presents to understanding, for it represents the most consistent effort which any philosopher has ever undertaken to neutralise existence as completely as possible without actually denying it ... There may be existence in the Kantian system, but luckily for the understanding, everything can carry on as if there were none.'[81] Gilson says Kant's attitude was one of 'rebellion against the given as it is, and the deliberate refusal to submit to it'.[82] It was this rebellion which Schelling sought to redress.

German idealism therefore devoted its principal efforts to reconciling Kant's notorious dualism of nature and freedom. This was not least for moral reasons, since Kantian dualism seemed to subject man to the determinism of the laws of nature after all.[83] The fact that German idealism grew out of the Kantian system explains why it was asserted earlier that the relationship between it and rationalism was close but full of tension: although German idealism was consciously reacting against specifically French rationalism, embodied in the French Revolution – a reaction which was given added impetus by the victories of Napoleon, and the final *coup de grâce* the Emperor delivered in 1806 to the Holy Roman Empire – it also drew much energy from sources which were in fact closer to home.

In particular, it drew on the religious currents of mysticism which had inspired Luther. The theories of Böhme, for whom wrath was one of God's fundamental

---

79   Taylor, *Hegel*, p. 31.
80   *Ibid.*, p. 32.
81   Gilson, *L'être et l'essence*, pp. 204 and 206.
82   *Ibid.*, p. 200.
83   Pippin, *Hegel's Idealism*, pp. 12 and 44.

attributes, and the neo-Platonist Meister Eckhart, were important, as was the individualist Protestant creed, pietism (itself an important influence on Kant). Pietism was also mystic enough to allow some later post-Kantian German Romantics to collapse into the warm embrace of irrationalism. Mysticism was the perfect weapon of the German heart against the philosophy of the over-intellectual French. Like Luther, some neo-Kantians seemed simultaneously to hold the contradictory beliefs that the human mind had an inherent ability to come to know the Absolute unaided, and also that human reason was so corrupt and limited that in fact it could never be relied on. Mysticism traditionally spurned the world as a source of knowledge of God: St John of the Cross, for instance, fought against contemplating the world, regarding it as a distraction from eternal truths. He emphasised that there was nothing in common between the divine Absolute and the world of nature, and that nature was in fact an obstacle to accession to God: this is why he rejected the Thomist attempt to accede to the infinite by using man's faculties for natural knowledge.[84] The opposition between mysticism and the world-doubting Enlightenment was therefore less sharp than its protagonists, the German idealists, supposed. Rationalism soon led to irrationalism, as Hegel noted in his criticism of the Terror.

It was precisely this deep congruence between mysticism and Enlightenment rationalism (both of which questioned the powers of human reason to know being as it really is) which Schelling was to perceive. He was to devote his later life to navigating a painful path between the two. Part of what Marc Maesschalk calls Schelling's 'successive ruptures with transcendental philosophy'[85] was driven by his belief that 'both the rationalism of transcendental thought, as well as the pietism of spiritualist metaphysics, are to be put in question.'[86] This is why his later positions are so close to those of traditional Christian philosophy.

Fichte

In other words, we stand here in a whirlpool of opposing and complicated currents, flows of ideas, eddies and counter-reactions in which it is easy to lose one's bearings. Fichte, for instance, professed in politics (in *Reden an die deutsche Nation*) a metaphysical superiority of the German people which stood in utter contradiction to the universal principles of Kantianism which he also claimed to endorse.[87] Like Luther, he seemed to be trying to compensate for Germany's political weakness by

---

84 Leszek Kolakowski, *Chrétiens sans église: la conscience religieuse et le lien confessionel au 17ème siècle* (Paris: Gallimard, 1969) (first published in Polish in Warsaw, 1965) pp. 368–70.

85 M. Maesschalk, *L'anthropologie politique et religieuse de Schelling*, Editions de l'Institut supérieur de Philosophie, Louvain-la-Neuve (Paris: Vrin and Leuven: Peeters, 1991), p. xii.

86 *Ibid.*, p. xi.

87 Pierre Béhar, *Du 1er au IVe Reich, Permanence d'une Nation, Renaissance d'un état* (Paris: Desjonquères, 1990), p. 118. See also pp. 31–60 on the Reformation.

cooking up a potent brew of spiritual pre-eminence for her (a position caricatured by Heinrich Heine in *Deutschland – Ein Wintermärchen*[88]).

In philosophy, the cross-currents were as clear as in politics. Fichte was trying, among other things, to overcome Kantian dualism. He did this by arguing that the two realms, phenomenal and noumenal, had a common source, the 'I'. He simply replaced the partly obscure Kantian notion of the 'transcendental unity of apperception' with the self. Moreover, while for Kant the representing 'I', upon which the system rested, was an assumption which depended on the contingent existence of such an 'I', Fichte wanted to found an absolute system which excluded all such mere facts, because he felt that Kantian criticism would collapse into simple empiricism or scepticism if it could not ground itself necessarily and absolutely.

Fichte made the affirmation of the self the source of all being. I = I was an act or a demand, which, its form being identical to its content, was supposed to represent the logical and ontological foundation of all being. The principle of identity – the source of all intelligibility and all being – reposed for Fichte on this fundamental 'act' of the self-positing I. Fichte, indeed, presented the *cogito* as the absolute substance. 'I am' had the ontological privilege of being the most fundamental proposition imaginable: 'der erste, schlechthhin unbedingter Grundsatz.'[89] The being of the I was thus entirely founded on itself, in virtue of this positing activity which is its very essence. 'The positing of the I by itself is its pure activity.'[90] It would be difficult to think of a more radical de-throning of God than this, Fichte's transposition of the majestic ontology of Exodus onto the allegedly self-grounding powers of the human individual.

Moreover, the real world (the 'not-I') was nothing but an instrument for the self-realisation of the 'I', the subject which underlies everything. Fichte admitted no ultimate reality outside the thinking 'I', which engendered its own thought through its creative dynamism. Fichte therefore took Kant a step further, precisely because he believed that the noumenal realm, which for Kant was radically transcendent and unknowable, was intimately accessible to man because it was his innermost self. He seemed to believe, again against Kant, that the transcendent could be incarnated clearly on earth, and that it was incarnated in man. The world might not be in a grain of sand but the individual certainly had the Absolute within himself. Whereas, therefore, there is at least the possibility of interpreting Kant as a modest philosopher who was aware of the limitations of the human mind, and who perhaps erred by pushing ultimate reality away into an unknowable realm, this is impossible for the megalomaniac Fichte, who held that the law of self-determination (freedom) was not some unknowable state at which man could only aim, but instead a principle which could inspire him in full clarity.

This is a metaphysical position with notoriously unwelcome ethical implications. The demand of the self-affirming self is that it achieve absolute autonomy against all

---

[88]   '*Franzosen und Russen gehört das Land, / das Meer gehört den Briten, / wir aber besitzen im Luftreich des Traums / die Herrschaft unbestritten.*'

[89]   Fichte, *Grundlage der gesammten Wissenschaftslehre, Erster Theil*, para. 1, in *Werke*, ed. R. Lauth, H. Jacob and H. Gliwitzky (Stuttgart-Bad Canstatt: Friedrich Fromann, 1964), I, 2, p. 255.

[90]   *Ibid.*, p. 259.

that which is not itself ('not-I'). Indeed, that which is not-I is considered irrational. This is even coherent with one aspect of Kant: the demand that the moral law be realised implies that everything which is opposed to it (in Kant's case, my natural passions; in Fichte's case, the whole world) must be suppressed. Fichte's is literally an egotistical philosophy. As Taylor says, rational awareness, the classical view of man, was abandoned in favour of rational self-awareness: 'What man defines himself in relation to is not an ideal order beyond, but rather something which unfolds from himself, is his own realisation, and is first made determinate in that realisation.'[91] As a consequence of his exaggerated faith in the human self, will and reason, Fichte wanted to institute a new society by means of the forced indoctrination of youth in the principles of reason. In the famous *Reden an die deutsche Nation*, Fichte advocated taking advantage of the collapse of the German states in order to create a new social order from scratch. His thought therefore followed the well-known revolutionary pattern of *solve et coagula* which was to reach its apogee in the Hegelian and, later, Marxist, dialectic. In an anticipation of the harshest practices of communism, Fichte wanted children to be separated from their parents at birth in order for them to be educated in the absolute novelty of reason; he also wanted to close the economy to all outside influences (*Der geschlossene Handelsstaat* was his tract on political economy). Fichte's ideal state was thus a sort of parody of Plato's: rationality would control everything, conflicts would be erased, and decisions would be taken by philosopher–kings. As Alan White says, 'The practical doctrine that truly flows from Fichte's principles is that each subject should demand subordination of all to himself, each should strive to become a tyrant.'[92]

Fichte thus typified how important was the Spinozist doctrine of *conatus* or endeavour for the German Romantics. Just as Spinoza depicted the world as the unfolding of the Absolute's self-determination, so Fichte depicted it as the unfolding of the (absolute) I. Charles Taylor rightly says that such 'expressionism' was the key concept uniting various German Romantics whom we associate with the cult of genius: 'It was Herder and the expressivist anthropology developed from him which added the epoch-making demand that my realisation of the human essence be my own, and hence launched the idea that each individual … has its own way of being human, which it cannot exchange with that of any other except at the cost of distortion and self-mutilation.'[93] Fichte depicted more forcefully even than his immediate predecessors the human form as 'an inner force imposing itself on external reality, perhaps against external obstacles'.[94] Freedom as self-determination obviously was the central Kantian theme too, but it was taken to even higher levels by his successors. Schelling initially bought into this Enlightenment and Romantic schema but it was precisely against its subjectivism that he was to rebel so radically as his philosophy developed.

Finally, it is absolutely crucial to understand that Fichte's idealism renders any theory of the creation impossible. Indeed, Fichte explicitly and emphatically rejected

---

91   *Ibid.*, pp. 17–18.
92   White, *Schelling*, p. 97.
93   Taylor, *Hegel*, p. 15.
94   *Ibid.*

the very notion of it. In his lecture series, *Die Anweisung zum seligen Leben, oder auch die Religionslehre* (Initiation to the Holy Life, or the Doctrine of Religion), given in Berlin in 1806, Fichte discussed the Gospel of St John and wrote,

> The assumption of a creation ... is the absolutely fundamental error of all metaphysics and all doctrine of religion, and especially the basic principle of Judaism and heathens. Required to recognise the absolute unity and unchangeability of the divine being (*des göttlichen Wesens*), and not wishing to give up the autonomous and true existence of finite things, they allow these latter to come about out of (*hervorgehen*) an act of absolute arbitrariness (*Willkür*).[95]

Fichte spoke disparagingly of such an idea – 'a creation cannot even be properly conceived of' (*eine Schöpfung läßt sich gar nicht ordentlich denken*) – and said that the positing of a creation was the first sign of falsehood in a philosophical theory. He claimed to show that the Gospel of St John proved this, because 'the Word' was in the beginning and because therefore there had always been something. Genesis, meanwhile, wrongly posited a creation. It is no coincidence that Fichte insisted on the lack of God's freedom to create the world, given that he was not interested in any freedom for man on earth either.

Hegel

All this brings us to Hegel, the key figure against whose philosophy Schelling struggled for nearly half a century. Like Fichte and Kant, Hegel thought that freedom was the highest value and that human reason ought to ground itself. To this extent, he was a child of the Enlightenment against which he came to rebel. Although he attacked the French Revolution (he thought the abstractness of its concept of freedom led directly to the Terror) he liked the idea that the Revolution should erase the past and start anew – *du passé faisons table rase!* – and wanted philosophy to do the same thing (as Kant had too). Hegel believed, like Descartes and so many others, that, 'Any philosophical system must begin without any presuppositions and develop everything out of that presuppositionless beginning.'[96]

With Hegel, indeed, the originally Cartesian project of establishing a self-grounded system of thought was pursued with the most extreme thoroughness. As Robert Pippin argues, Hegel talks about the self-legislation by reason in far more expansive and dramatic language than even Kant: he realised more deeply and thoroughly than his contemporaries that Kant had not gone far enough in developing a theory of 'thought's *self*-determination'.[97] Indeed, the very purpose of the *Logic* was to show that reason could not presuppose anything, not even its own rules. It had to be totally free to make them up itself. Hegel was animated by a desire to free thought from all constraints, in order to turn criticism even on thought itself. In his

---

95 Fichte, *Die Anweisung zum seligen Leben*, 6. *Vorlesung*, 8th paragraph, beginning 'Aus Unkunde ...'.
96 Terry Pinkard, *Hegel's 'Phenomenology': The Sociality of Reason* (Cambridge: Cambridge University Press, 1994), p. 20.
97 Pippin, *Hegel's Idealism*, pp. 8 and 38.

determination to pursue the Cartesian project to the bitter end, Hegel insisted that knowledge be preceded by universal doubt: the only thing which philosophy should take for granted was the imperative that it take nothing for granted.[98]

Like many post-Kantian idealists, Hegel was preoccupied with the problems posed by the fact that what we think is true changes over time. It is for this reason that he came to embrace a 'historical' understanding of being, according to which being is the result of a dynamic interaction between real and ideal.[99] For him, self-determining thought set the standards of what was to count as true rationality.[100] He described a process by which everything flowed into its opposite, making the principle of contradiction, the dialectic, the driving force of the development of *Geist* and the fundamental principle of being. This is obviously the very antithesis of Aristotle's identity-based logic. Hegel took up the Spinozist thesis, *omnis determinatio est negatio*, to argue that all determinate being involved negation, and that the development of being was thus the result of permanent negation and contradiction. Contradiction made things move and change, yet the Absolute went on living through both the affirmation and the denial of finite things. Thus the Absolute was essentially life and movement and change.[101] It was precisely this neo-Heraclitean flux in Hegel which attracted Engels and Marx to him.[102] In a phrase which anticipates and probably inspired the greatest relativist of them all, Nietzsche, the man who reduced truth itself to power, Hegel calls truth '*der bacchantische Taumel*' (the Bacchanalian frenzy).[103]

> Indeed, mind is not conceived as being at rest, but in constantly progressing movement ... So knowledge, the crown of the world of mind, is never perfected in its beginnings ... The reality of this simple whole consists in the fact that those formations which have become moments develop again into new formations in their new element and in a developed sense.[104]

Hegel rejected, in other words, the view that philosophy could lay claim to a fundamental ground, which he thought instead could only ever be an unending dialectic.

> Only this identity which reestablishes itself is true ... not an *original* or *immediate* unity as such. It is the becoming of itself, the circle, which presupposes its end as its purpose and also has it as its beginning, and which is real only through its enactment (*Ausführung*) and its end ...

---

98   Stephen Houlgate, *Freedom, Truth and History: An Introduction to Hegel's Philosophy* (London and New York: Routledge, 1991), pp. 45–50.
99   Pinkard, *Hegel's Phenomenology*, pp. 14–15.
100 Houlgate, *Freedom, Truth and History*, p. 67.
101 Taylor, *Hegel*, p. 107.
102 Engels, 'Dialektik der Natur, Einleitung', in Marx and Engels, *Werke*, p. 320.
103 Hegel, *Phänomenologie des Geistes, Vorrede* (Stuttgart: Reclam, 1987), p. 42.
104 *Ibid.*, pp. 16–17.

> The true is the whole. But the whole is only that essence which perfects itself through its development. It is to be said of the Absolute that it is essentially *Result*, that it is only at the end that which it truly is ...[105]

This, the constant movement of the Hegelian dialectic, is that of the successive embodiment of concept which reveals itself and then passes on to another manifestation. The whole is infinite and imperishable, but it manifests itself in the eternally perishing finite – a finite or sensible world which does not exist in itself, and which therefore can never be the final ground of knowledge. '*Das reine Seyn ist das Nichts. Being and nothing are the same; only becoming is true.*'[106] It is not difficult to see parallels between this Hegelian ontology of eternal flux and some of the Oriental cosmogonies discussed earlier. His is, after all, 'the drama of an Absolute Being which, not satisfied with its empty self-identity, alienates itself and, through the struggles and tragedies of human history, matures to perfect self-consciousness, re-assimilates its products and eventually abolishes the distinction of subject and object ...'[107] Hegel wrote, 'The being of finite things as such is that they have the kernel of their disappearance (*Vergehen*) in their being-in-themselves (*Insichseyn*), the hour of their birth is the hour of their death.'[108] Such a schema recalls the myths of cycles of death and re-birth found in Persia and India. Indeed, Hegel himself compared his system with that of Eastern religions: in the *Wissenschaft der Logik* (Science of Logic), Hegel says, 'The popular, especially Oriental, sayings that everything which is has the seed of its end in its beginning, and that death is the entrance to new life, basically express this very union of being and nothing.'[109]

> Thus *intelligibility* is a becoming, and as this becoming it is *reasonableness* ... As the concept is the own self of the object, which represents itself as *its becoming*, it is not a resting subject, which carries accidents unmoved, but the concept which moves itself and which brings its determinations back into itself ... the firm ground, which reasoning has in the subject, begins to shake, and only this movement itself becomes the object.[110]

The reason why Hegel adopts this model of ontological development lies in his very aims: to develop a presuppositionless philosophy, and to explain how determinacy develops out of the Absolute. As Stephen Houlgate writes, 'The notion of pure, indeterminate being thus slides into the thought of *nothing* because of its

---

105 *Ibid.*, pp. 21–2.
106 Hegel, *Enzyklopädie der philosophischen Wissenschaften*, I, para 88.
107 Kolakowski, *Religion*, p. 138.
108 Hegel, *Wissenschaft der Logik, Zweites Kapitel, Das Daseyn, B. Die Endlichkeit, c. Die Endlichkeit.*
109 Hegel, *Wissenschaft der Logik, Erstes Buch, Die Lehre vom Seyn, Erster Abschnitt, Bestimmtheit (Qualität), Erstes Kapitel, C. Werden, Einheit des Seyns und Nichts, Anmerkung I.*
110 'So ist die *Verständigkeit* ein Werden, und als dies Werden ist sie die *Vernünftigkeit* ... Indem der Begriff das eigene Selbst des Gegenstandes ist, das sich als *sein Werden* darstellt, ist es nicht ein ruhendes Subjekt, das unbewegt Akzidenzen trägt, sondern der sich bewegende und seine Bestimmungen in sich zurücknehmende Begriff ... der feste Boden, den das Räsonieren an dem ruhenden Subjekte hat, schwankt also, und nur diese Bewegung selbst wird der Gegenstand' (Hegel, *Phänomenologie des Geistes, Vorrede*, pp. 50 and 53).

sheer indeterminacy ... Just as the thought of sheer, indeterminate being slides into the thought of nothing, so the thought of nothing slides into the thought of being.'[111] As Etienne Gilson spent his life trying to show, Hegel's attitude is typical of the Platonist tradition, which always tries to explain being by non-being: to say what a thing is is to say what it is not. We are back in the essentialist ontology, where being and non-being, far from being sheer opposites, mutually support and interpenetrate each other. It is thus that Hegel claims to have shown the how reflection comes out of negation:[112] negation, not identity, is the fundamental principle of being and truth.

Hegel was convinced that 'the spiritual is alone the real, it is the essence, or that which is in itself' (*das Geistige ist allein das Wirkliche, es ist das Wesen oder das An-sich-seiende*)[113]. He wrote approvingly that Kant had demonstrated 'the absolute identity of thought and being'[114] for this was indeed his own view. It is for this very reason that Gilson attacks Hegel: 'Thus reduced to a simple game of concepts which are formally abstract, taken out of sensory experience and governed only by the principle of contradiction, [Hegel's] ontology is nothing other than a logic.'[115] Indeed, as Manfred Frank pointedly remarks, 'If anything else were intended' (that is, if Hegel has intended anything other than to make the concept everything, and to allow nothing outside it) 'then Hegel's system would have few reasons for the certainty that he had started something thoroughly new *vis-à-vis* his predecessors with a logical foundation of being.'[116] Hegel reduces existence to a pure notion, shying away from any 'givenness' which might precede thought. As we shall see, it is precisely the accusation that Hegel's system remains too conceptual, and that it is a stranger to that true being which does indeed precede thought, which is to form the cornerstone of Schelling's attack on him.

Hegel on Freedom

On the questions of freedom and ethics, Hegel's reaction against Kant centred mainly on what he considered to be the excessive abstractness of the Kantian system. Hegel held that the moral will was not expressed in abstract thoughts or in maxims, but in deeds. He also argued that freedom was not simply the ability to get what one wants but also the ability to value it, thereby attaining a sense of the meaning of one's life. As Schelling was to do, he attacked 'negative freedom, or the freedom of the understanding' as being 'the freedom of the void – like the pure contemplation of the Indians'.[117] Sounding like Edmund Burke – the metaphysical assumptions of whose writings have been brilliantly laid out by Joseph Pappin[118] – Hegel argued

---

111 Houlgate, *Freedom, Truth and History*, p. 51
112 Manfred Frank, *Der unendliche Mangel an Sein* (Frankfurt: Suhrkamp, 1975), p. 54.
113 Hegel, *Phänomenologie des Geistes, Vorrede*, p. 25.
114 Hegel, *Glauben und Wissen, Teil A: Kantische Philosophie*.
115 Gilson, *L'être et l'essence*, p. 211.
116 Frank, *Der unendliche Mangel an Sein*, p. 33.
117 Hegel, *Grundlinien der Philosophie des Rechts*, para. 5 (Stuttgart: Reclam, 1970), p. 78.
118 Joseph L. Pappin III, *The Metaphysics of Edmund Burke* (New York: Fordham University Press, 1993); see also my own article, 'The Prodigies of Sacrilege: Edmund Burke

that Kantian abstractness led to fanaticism. 'It is only by destroying something that this negative will has a sense of its own existence. An abstract imagination (*Vorstellung*) and the realisation of it can only be the freedom of destruction.'[119] Like the very Thomist Burke, Hegel attacked the French Revolution for destroying all institutions, even its own 'because all institutions are repellent to the abstract self-consciousness'.[120] Indeed, his insistence that freedom and value can exist only in a social context are, of course, analogous to his view that truth and being itself develop in reality, and that *Geist* always embodies itself.

Hegel thus attacked freedom without personality. He believed that mere freedom of choice without a context of value was null and void: its content was not determined by the nature of a person's will but just through chance.[121] He argued that the choice made by pure reason alone said nothing about the individual person but was instead actually destructive of individuality since in reality people were not motivated by general or universal purposes but instead by individual impulses. Was Hegel thinking of the famous passage on love in II Corinthians 13 when he wrote, 'The thought of pure consciousness as such remains the formless clang of a bell, or a humid fog, a musical thought, which never comes to a concept...'[122]?

It is for these reasons that Roger Scruton argues that Hegel had a far more concrete notion of the self than Kant did.[123] Hegel insisted that the individual was part of his historical and social context, and that that culture informed his very self. Hegel's claim that 'the past runs through the individual ... the past existence is the earned property of the general spirit'[124] recalls what Burke called 'the partnership between those who are living, those who are dead, and those who are to be born'.[125] Moreover, according to Hegel, 'The individual cannot know what *he is* before having brought himself to reality through action.'[126] Hegel's ethics therefore had a strong realist flavour: he warmly recalled 'the wisest men of antiquity [who] had the following saying: that wisdom and virtue consist in living according to the morals of one's people.'[127]

In spite of all these efforts to distance himself from Kant, however, Hegel retained crucial elements of the Kantian system. Above all he agreed with the Kantian identification of morality with reason, and of freedom with self-conscious will and self-determination: he simply had a different understanding of those terms. For all his reaction against the Enlightenment and the French Revolution, therefore, Charles Taylor is right to identify Hegel himself with 'the modern Enlightenment [which]

---

on Money', *The Salisbury Review* (autumn 1999) and *The University Bookman* (spring 2000).
    119   Hegel, *Grundlinien der Philosophie des Rechts*, para. 5, p. 78.
    120   Hegel, *Phänomenologie, I. Die sinnliche Gewißheit*, p. 79.
    121   Hegel, *Grundlinien der Philosophie des Rechts*, para. 15, p. 92.
    122   Hegel, *Phänomenologie des Geistes*, IV, B, p. 162.
    123   Roger Scruton, 'Hegel as a Conservative Thinker', in *The Philosopher on Dover Beach* (Manchester: Carcanet, 1990).
    124   Hegel, *Phänomenologie des Geistes, Vorrede*, p. 29.
    125   Edmund Burke, *Reflections on the Revolution in France*, ed. Conor Cruise O'Brien (Harmondsworth: Penguin, 1968), p. 195.
    126   Hegel, *Phänomenologie des Geistes*, V.C., p. 284.
    127   Hegel, *Phänomenologie des Geistes*, V.B., p. 255.

does not just define man as thought, it is sure that the whole of reality conforms to thought too'.[128]

In the master–slave passage in the *Phenomenology*, for example, the struggle for recognition is understood as constitutive of political freedom. The escape from slavery leads to self-consciousness via the struggle for freedom. The harder the slavery, the bolder are the attempts to break loose from it. There are echoes of Fichte here. In other words, freedom is ultimately a matter of private mental states: the slave is unfree because he does not think of himself in the right way.

> Self-consciousness which purifies and raises its object, content and purpose to this generality, does this as thinking which *accomplishes itself* in will. Here is the *point at which it illuminates* that it is only as *thinking* intelligence that the will is free will. The slave does not know his essence, his infinity, the freedom, he does not know himself as essence; and he does not know himself thus, that is, he does not know himself as essence; and that he does not know himself thus means he does not *think* himself.[129]

Hegel seems to have shown that being, thought and freedom are the same. It is on this key issue that Schelling will split with him.

---

128 Taylor, *Hegel*, p. 400.

129 'Das Selbstbewußtsein, das seinen Gegenstand, Inhalt und Zweck bis zu dieser Allgemeinheit reinigt und erhebt, tut dies als das im Willen sich *durchsetzende Denken*. Hier ist der *Punkt, auf welchem es erhellt*, daß der Wille nur als *denkende* Intelligenz wahrhafter, freier Wille ist. Der Sklave weiß nicht sein Wesen, seine Unendlichkeit, die Freiheit, er weiß sich nicht als Wesen; – und er weiß sich so nicht, das ist, er weiß sich nicht als Wesen; und er weiß sich so nicht, das ist, er *denkt* sich nicht' (Hegel, *Grundlinien der Philosophie des Rechts*, para. 21, p. 96).

Chapter 3
Schelling's Beginnings

> Soon after ..., I was invited to a supper party at Schelling's. The evening was a jovial one, and showed that philosophers can unbend as well as other folk; and as it was only in a convivial way I could expect to be listened to by a great metaphysician, I ventured to spar with the Professor. Some strange and unintelligible remarks had been made on the mythology as well of the Orientalists as the Greeks, and the important part played by the serpent. A gentleman present exhibited a ring, received from England, in the form of a serpent. 'Is the serpent the symbol of English philosophy?' said Schelling to me. 'Oh, no!' I answered, 'the English take it to appertain to German philosophy, because it changes its coat every year.' 'A proof,' he replied, 'that the English do not look deeper than the coat.'
>
> Henry Crabb Robinson, *Diary*, 1802[1]

From his earliest days, Schelling was driven by an emotional urge to give an account of the real world, and to show how it could exist without the self.[2] This urge stayed with him until the day he died. In his youth he tried to achieve his goal by working within the structures of German idealism. Like Kant, like Fichte, and like Hegel and Hölderlin with whom he studied at Tübingen, he was obsessed with freedom, which he initially, like them, held to be of supreme value. Later, however, it was precisely his endless search for a true account of human liberty, and especially for an account of its relationship to being, which led him to smash his way out of the mould of German idealism and to return to an almost pre-Cartesian and neo-Thomist account of man, God and liberty. To put it bluntly, in his old age Schelling got God.

This explains an interesting phenomenon of contemporary Schelling studies. Many of today's Schelling scholars are either men of the cloth or philosophers with a strong interest in theology or the philosophy of religion. Of the clerics, the best known is doubtless the French Jesuit priest and professor at the Gregorian University in Rome, Xavier Tilliette, who has emphasised the links between Schelling and Catholic thought, and who has himself pointed out that among the best modern scholars of Schelling, one finds Catholic theologians like Walter Kasper (now a Cardinal and President of the Council for promoting Christian Unity), Claude Bruaire (1932–86)[3]

---

1 Henry Crabb Robinson, *Diary, Reminiscences and correspondence* (London: Macmillan, 1869), I, p. 129.

2 Thomas Buchheim, 'Das "objektive Denken" in Schellings Naturphilosophie', *Kant-Studien*, 81 (1990): 321–38.

3 See Claude Bruaire, *Schelling ou la quête du secret de l'être* (Paris: Seghers, 1970). On Bruaire, see Antonio Lopez FSCB, *Spirit's Gift: The Metaphysical Insight of Claude Bruaire* (Washington, DC: Catholic University of America Press, 2006).

and Thomas O'Meara (another Jesuit).[4] O'Meara himself, who calls Schelling the 'mentor' of numerous nineteenth-century German Catholic intellectuals, makes a similar point, adding the names of Guido Vergauwen and Klaus Hemmerle to the list, and arguing that their studies 'show Schelling's attractiveness for the Catholic mind'.[5] Indeed, one could add the following names of commentators on Schelling who have a strong interest in religion and theology: Alain Pernet, translator into French of Schelling's later works; the German Thomist theologian, Bernhard Welte; Christian Danz; Horst Fuhrmans; Marc Maesschalk, professor at the Catholic University of Louvain, and the Jesuit priests Emerich Coreth and Emilio Brito.[6]

Even during his lifetime, Catholic thinkers (especially Franz Baader) had a strong influence on Schelling, while he in turn influenced a school of Romantic Catholics in the nineteenth century, headed by Michael Sailer. Schelling's influence on Protestants like Sören Kierkegaard and ecumenical figures like Karl Barth and Paul Tillich has also been noted,[7] as has his influence on the Russian Orthodox religious philosopher, Nicolas Berdyaev.[8] Hans Urs von Balthasar, who was to become one of Pope John Paul II's favourite theologians, admired Schelling and called the 1809 *Freedom* essay, 'the most titanic work of German idealism'.[9] Schelling devoted his later life to trying to show the congruence between philosophy and revelation. The paradox is that, whereas Hegel and Kant said they wanted to ground their systems on freedom but ended up with freedom submerged by the (impersonal) Absolute, it was precisely what Xavier Tilliette call Schelling's determination to develop 'free philosophy' rather than 'absolute philosophy'[10] which drove him back into the arms of God. In other words, Schelling's drift away from idealism, and his move to Christian philosophy, were driven by a desire to develop a philosophy based on liberty – both man's and God's. This progressively undermined the idealist project of developing a self-enclosed philosophical system in which everything is deduced logically from the Absolute.

On the other hand, Schelling's relationship with Christianity was far from straightforward. He did not steer a direct course towards a union of religion and philosophy. Rather, he navigated somewhat uneasily between conflicting and treacherous doctrines, some of which threatened to wreck the whole enterprise. In particular, he took a long time to cast off the considerable neo-Platonist and Gnostic

---

4   Xavier Tilliette, *L'absolu et la Philosophie: essais sur Schelling* (Paris: Presses Universitaires de France, 1987), p. 8.

5   Thomas O'Meara, O.P., *Romantic Idealism and Roman Catholicism: Schelling and the Theologians* (Notre Dame and London: University of Notre Dame Press, 1982), p. 196.

6   See Bibliography.

7   Tilliette, *L'absolu et la Philosophie*, p. 242; O'Meara, *Romantic Idealism and Roman Catholicism, passim*; Emilio Brito, *Philosophie et théologie dans l'oeuvre de Schelling* (Paris: Cerf, 2000), p. 7.

8   Robert F. Brown, 'Resources in Schelling for New Directions in Theology', *Idealistic Studies*, XX/1 (January 1990): 15, note 1.

9   Hans Urs von Balthasar, *Prometheus, Studien zur Geschichte des deutschen Idealismus* (Heidelberg: Kerle, 1947), p. 240.

10 Tilliette, *L'absolu et la Philosophie*, p. 25.

ballast with which he began his voyage (even though, paradoxically, some elements of it are precisely what helped him along the way).

It may be for this reason that Schelling has also been adopted by some modern atheist and left-wing thinkers like Adorno, Bloch and Habermas. (Jürgen Habermas approvingly called Ernst Bloch 'a Marxist Schelling'.[11]) The reason for this is not difficult to discern. Schelling, as will be shown, was trying to inject realism into the prevailing idealism of his time. This led him to elaborate a philosophy at the end of his life, according to which existence was deemed prior to essence. Habermas, Adorno and others were certainly influenced by the Schellingian insistence that metaphysical thinking had become 'a narcissistic illusion'.[12] The discussion here will concentrate on the religiously orthodox nature of Schelling's claim – it is one embraced by Aristotle and above all Aquinas – but it is fairly easy to see that views about the primacy of existence will appeal to atheist thinkers if the references to God are ignored and overlooked. Without God the meaning of 'existence' changes radically. Under such circumstances, Schelling's philosophy might be construed (albeit falsely) as anticipating existentialism. Schelling's notion of man's absolute liberty is that it is a reflection of God's absolute liberty, and that the two belong intrinsically together: to take one of the two away (that is, God's) is to distort Schelling's message completely. As one commentator says, Ernst Bloch used Schellingian ideas and terminology 'with little regard for their meaning in Schelling's theological system'.[13] The founding fathers of Marxism did not make the same mistake as their twentieth-century epigones: Ludwig Feuerbach attacked Schelling's 'Philosophy of Revelation' as 'a theosophical farce' in *The Essence of Christianity* and Marx wrote to Feuerbach to congratulate him for the jibe.[14] Engels, meanwhile, attended Schelling's lectures in 1841 and wrote essays lampooning the philosopher, calling the positive philosophy the 'latest attempt of reaction against the free philosophy'.[15]

In the words of Alan White, Schelling had two choices:

> He could either focus exclusively on human beings as radically free agents confronted ... with the necessity of making decisions ..., or he could attempt to go beyond the human level, he could strive to uncover the supersensible source that gives rise both to humans and to the good and evil between which they must choose. A step along the former path would have been a step into the twentieth century, the beginning of the existentialist attempt to explain the world in human terms; *Schelling did not take that step*. Instead he stepped back ... reviving for the last time the classical attempt to understand all that exists

---

11   *Über Ernst Bloch, mit Beiträgen von Martin Walser, et al.* (Frankfurt am Main: Suhrkamp, 1968), p. 61.

12   Andrew Bowie, *Schelling and Modern European Philosophy* (London: Routledge, 1993), p. 10.

13   Wayne Hudson, *The Marxist Philosophy of Ernst Bloch* (London: Macmillan, 1982), p. 72.

14   Karl Marx letter to Ludwig Feuerbach, 30 October 1843.

15   Friedrich Engels, *Schelling und die Offenbarung, Kritik des neuesten Reaktionsversuchs gegen die freie Philosophie*, published anonymously in Leipzig (1842). See <www.marxists.org> for an English translation.

in terms of the transcendent absolute in which it is grounded. In choosing the latter path, Schelling remained true to the metaphysical tradition.'[16]

In other words, Schelling's lifelong interest in religious matters cannot be brushed aside – an omission for which Marc Maesschalk attacks both Habermas and Heidegger. 'To understand Schelling,' he writes, 'one must dare to draw the consequences of his religious anthropology of the divine Word.'[17] This book is guided by the sentiment expressed in that remark.

Nature Philosophy, Identity Philosophy and Schelling's Development within Idealism

As is well known, Schelling studied at the Lutheran seminary in Tübingen together with Hegel and Hölderlin and thus spent his formative years in the very crucible of German Romanticism and in the hothouse atmosphere generated across Europe by the excitement of the French Revolution. As a student, he seems to have been a goody-goody. (A handwritten report by the Dean, dating from 1795 and in Latin, describes the young Schelling as being of not very robust health, of medium stature, distinct in speech, with decent manners, an excellent intelligence, keen judgement, easy and tenacious memory, inelegant handwriting, honest morals, hard working and enjoying sufficient means, that is, wealth.[18]) Although Schelling was to swim against the modern current by overthrowing the long-held conception that freedom could be described in terms of the self-referentiality of the agent, and by describing it instead as the capacity to choose whether or not to live in accordance with God's law, his early work was thoroughly congruent with the very view he was later to reject.

In his initial period, Schelling was under the influence of the idealist and proto-idealist systems of Fichte and Spinoza, both of whom were suspected of being atheists (for good reason, since their systems made the concept of a free and loving God impossible to accommodate). On the other hand, Schelling very quickly started to disentangle himself from the Fichtean system. In other words, although Schelling's thought is certainly '*une philosophie en devenir*', the general direction and underlying continuity becomes clear early on.

In his early philosophy, Schelling was mainly interested in the freedom of the Absolute, which he identified, in a Fichtean way, principally with the I's power to act. Like Fichte, he was at first preoccupied with how reason came to constitute itself, and he believed that the thinking self could furnish the required foundation stone. Fichte's I and not-I meant that he equated the principle of identity with self-

---

16   Alan White, *Schelling: An Introduction to the System of Freedom* (New Haven: Yale University Press, 1983), pp. 1–2, emphasis added.

17   M. Maesschalk, *L'anthropologie politique et religieuse de Schelling*, Editions de l'Institut supérieur de Philosophie, Louvain-la-Neuve (Paris: Vrin and Leuven: Peeters, 1991), p. xxx. The attack on Habermas is on p. 114 and on pp. 100–101, note 24, where he also attacks Heidegger.

18   Facsimile reproduced in Bruaire, *Schelling ou la quête du secret de l'être*, p. 32.

consciousness, and urged that self-consciousness was the basis of being. From this equivalence, he reduced being to that which is for itself, and thus to selfhood.

This idea initially attracted Schelling. 'For me the highest principle of all philosophy is the pure, absolute I,' he wrote a little naively to his chum Hegel, 'that is, the I, insofar as it is mere I, not yet conditioned by objects, but posited through freedom. The alpha and omega of all philosophy is freedom.'[19] Elsewhere: 'I am! My I contains a being which precedes all thinking and representing.'[20] The Absolute circumscribes the infinite sphere comprising all reality: 'If substance is the unconditional, then the I is the only substance.'[21] In the Philosophical Letters of 1795, Schelling said that the vocation of critical philosophy was 'Strive towards immutable selfhood, unconditional freedom, unlimited activity. Be! is the highest command of criticism.'[22]

In this period, therefore, Schelling thought of the I as freedom, and thus of the Absolute as nothing but unlimited subjectivity. The 'I' was the 'principle of philosophy' and the 'unconditional in human knowledge'. Consequently, he subscribed initially to the exaggerated Fichtean admiration for power: 'The highest idea, which expresses the causality of absolute substance, is the idea of absolute power (*Macht*).'[23] As Xavier Tilliette comments, 'Liberty is to be understood as an infinite expansion, a rupture of all obstacles and of all chains, a destruction of all limits. Thus liberty, which escapes from the finite whose restrictions it destroys, reaches the suprasensible world to which Kant had forbidden access. It even transcends the personal being of God in order to immerse itself in the abyss of the one and the all.'[24]

In short, Schelling is up to his neck in the full-on, anti-individualist Gnosticism described in Chapter 1. Schelling himself wrote, 'The ultimate goal of all striving can also be understood as extension of personality to infinity, that is, as the destruction of it'[25] (because there is no consciousness in the infinite). Schelling's earliest philosophy is thus a perfect example of the kind of systematic thought described in Chapter 2: it tried to complete philosophy, understood as a systematic knowledge of all being, from the starting point of one supreme principle (*Grundsatz*) of internal unity and organisation, rather than starting from any given reality.

Yet Schelling's first personal innovation was, particularly with the benefit of hindsight, extremely significant. He soon saw that the notion of 'absolute I' had to be abandoned in favour of just 'the Absolute'. After all, how could the Absolute be assimilated to the self when the latter was finite? And how could it be absolute if it was constantly meeting limitations in the not-I? It was precisely on this question of the relationship between the Absolute and the particular that Schelling moved

---

19   Letter to Hegel, 4 February 1795.
20   *Vom Ich als Prinzip der Philosophie oder über das Unbedingte im menschlichen Wissen* (1795), I/1, 167.
21   *Ibid.*, I/1, 192.
22   *Philosophische Briefe über Dogmatismus und Kriticismus* (1795), I/1, 335.
23   *Vom Ich* (1795), I/1, 195.
24   Tilliette, *L'absolu et la Philosophie*, pp. 14 and 67.
25   *Vom Ich* (1795), I/1, 200.

away from Fichte. Whereas Fichte swooned at the apparent power of the self and its will, Schelling swooned at the forces of nature which seemed too immense. He came to believe that philosophers could say nothing about the Absolute, given the obvious differences between it and the human self. Being, in its simplicity prior to all positing (prior to all opposition or synthesis) could not be deduced or founded by the reflexivity of the self itself. (As Manfred Frank and Gerhard Kurz have shown, Schelling was helped towards this view by Hölderlin.[26])

Even by the time of the otherwise very Fichtean *Philosophical Letters on Dogmatism and Criticism* of 1795, according to Alan White, Schelling realised that as long as he focused solely on the problem of the subject, then his criticism would only remain complementary to Spinoza's dogmatism.[27] Soon enough, therefore, Schelling saw that this fixed point for all knowledge, which he sometimes also termed 'eternal liberty', could not in fact be assimilated or even compared to the thinking self at all. He soon came to argue, against Fichte, that the I's existence was secondary and dependent on reality, not constitutive of it. He and Hegel found it absurd and contradictory that man should be posited in the finite, when the system started by giving him immediate access to the infinite. Self-consciousness therefore required a pre-reflexive ground of undivided identity which bore all limitations and differences within it, that is, one which was neither I nor not-I but both in undivided identity.

Schelling also used the *Letters* to attack the Spinozist notion that all finite existing things, especially including human beings, were nothing but modifications of infinity.[28] He took Spinoza to task for failing to deduce any real content from the Absolute. He declared that the spirit of Spinozism was vulnerable to attack by the principle expressed in the old saw, *ex nihilo nihil fit*.[29] He realised the implications of this for human freedom:

> By demanding that the subject lose itself in the Absolute, he (Spinoza) also demanded the identity of subjective causality with absolute causality. He decided practically that the finite world was nothing but a modification of the infinite, and that finite causality was nothing but a modification of infinite causality. Thus, it is not through the subject's own causality, but through a foreign causality within him, that the demand is to be fulfilled. In other words, the demand is none other than: destroy yourself through absolute causality, or: behave with utter passivity towards absolute causality.[30]

In contrast to such fatalist monism, Schelling recognised that the very act of asking about one's ideas and representations put one above them. In virtue of asking how one comes to know things, one is a being which has its being within itself, independent from others, a free being: one's freedom cannot therefore be in doubt. 'I

---

26   Friedrich Hölderlin, 'Urtheil und Seyn', in Manfred Frank and Gerhard Kurz (eds), *Materialien zu Schellings philosophischen Anfängen* (Frankfurt am Main: Suhrkamp, 1975), p. 108.
27   White, *Schelling*, p. 37.
28   *Philosophische Briefe über Dogmatismus und Kriticismus* (1795), I/1, 315.
29   Ibid., I/1, 313.
30   Ibid., I/1, 316.

am free in that I raise myself above the connection between things and ask how this connection itself has become possible.'[31] If one were a mere link in a causal chain, as Spinoza suggests, then one could never step out of it and question. If one's self were just a thought in the mind of the infinite, or if one were just a focal point for a succession of images, then one could never achieve self-consciousness. That one can question one's ideas and impressions is proof of one's independence (freedom) from the world.[32]

In other words, here we see Schelling taking his distance from Fichte's subjectivist idealism in an equal but opposite way to that in which he distances himself from Spinoza's impersonal monism. For if the relationship between I and not-I is merely reflexive, that is, if the world of objects merely reflects myself back to me, as Fichte suggests, then it becomes impossible to understand how it is that I know myself. 'How would I know it was *my* reflection, unless I already knew in another way', that is, unless I already had an independent yardstick for measuring identity?[33] According to Fichte's conception, I am a mere thought, with no real external world beyond me. His decisive point is that the I is superior to all that is given in being: it is autarchic and absolute, and does not need the world for its own existence.

That Schelling should abandon this view for ontological and logical reasons meant that he moved away from the theory that it is the power of the self which supports all being, and from the theory that the source of all self-consciousness is will. Aware of Jacobi, and taking his distance from Spinoza, Schelling realised that Fichte's system contained that fatal narcissism which he was later to repudiate fully; and he was to do so on the basis that being and identity preexist the self.

> Whosoever feels and knows nothing real in himself and outside himself – whosoever lives only on concepts and plays with concepts – for whomsoever his own existence is nothing but a dull thought – how can he speak about reality?[34]

In this single early anti-Fichtean thought, therefore – in which Schelling clearly tries to replace the alleged certainty we have of ourselves with the certainty that we have knowledge of the outside world – is contained the germ of Schelling's rejection of one of the central tenets of German idealism, which, according to Walter Schulz, 'can be defined in very general terms as the method of absolute reflection, in which thinking cognition dissolves (*aufheben*) the whole of being into a concept and thus, having coming to itself and achieved certainty of itself, conceives itself as the form and content of being. This absolute positing of the concept was to find its bitterest opponent in the late Schelling.'[35]

---

31 *Ideen zu einer Philosophie der Natur als Einleitung in das Studium dieser Wissenschaft* (1797), I/2, 15.
32 *Ibid.*, I/2, 18.
33 Bowie, *Schelling and Modern European Philosophy*, p. 24.
34 *Abhandlungen zur Erläuterung des Idealismus der Wissenschaftslehre* (1796–97), I/1, 353.
35 Walter Schulz, *Die Vollendung des deutschen Idealismus in der Spätphilosophie Schellings* (Stuttgart and Köln: Kohlhammer, 1955), p. 11.

However, it is early days. Despite this apparent move away from Fichte's radical idealism, Schelling retained a strikingly Gnostic doctrine, that of intellectual contemplation (or intuition) (*intellektuelle Anschauung*). Intellectual contemplation was the self-knowledge of the absolute I: I know myself to be an I by intellectual contemplation, and that contemplation affords access to the Absolute itself, the absolute I. However, because it is knowledge of the Absolute, it is inexpressible. It is clear that what is being contemplated here is original, absolute and immutable being.[36] Schelling uses the notion of intellectual contemplation to attack Spinoza for having put the Absolute outside of the subject, but otherwise he maintained the bulk of the Spinozist system by simply subjectivizing it. So close, indeed, is the notion of intellectual contemplation to Oriental mysticism that Schelling himself even writes of it as 'a condition of death', saying that those for whom it would become a permanent state would 'go out of time into eternity'.[37] To see God is to die, yet intellectual contemplation is a vision of the Absolute – in which nothing is seen. It puts the Absolute out of the realm of philosophical discussion. Alan White writes, 'Since the Absolute is beyond all determination, intuition of it leaves nothing on which reason can reflect, and thus there is nothing to explain.'[38]

One of the main manifestations of Schelling's realist urge was his interest in Nature Philosophy. On the one hand, such an interest was fairly typical for the German Romantic that the young Schelling was. Romantics in Germany and England from Schlegel and Goethe to Keats and Wordsworth were notorious for communing with nature and having intimations of the sublime in the process. They admired in nature that sense of organic unity which, they felt, Enlightenment mechanism had stifled: they preferred apparently untamed English gardens to geometrical French ones – or, better still, a forest. Thomas Mann captured something of the eccentric atmosphere of the German Romantics' interest in natural science in his novel, Dr Faustus, whose hero, Leverkühn, obsessively conducts bizarre experiments: Schelling's Nature Philosophy is certainly replete with strange speculations about the metaphysical meaning of phenomena like electricity. For this reason, the Nature Philosophy is today largely dismissed as cranky and ridiculous. However, Schelling's interest in natural science was genuine and serious: when in 1802 he was awarded an honorary doctorate at Landshut, it was in medicine, a subject he had himself wanted to study.[39] In any case, the point is that Schelling believed that natural science revealed evidence of the Absolute at work. This thought was to develop in a religious direction in later life.

The Romantic notion of union with nature was also a way of overcoming Enlightenment dualism. The Spinozist system, which many equated with pantheism, was an obvious source of inspiration for this: as we have seen, Spinoza blurs the distinction between the human individual and the rest of the world. His system seemed to provide a template for the Romantic idea that universal life flows through nature. For his part, Schelling was trying to rehabilitate Kantian and Fichtean

---

36 *Vom Ich* (1795), I/1, 216.
37 *Philosophische Briefe über Dogmatismus und Kriticismus* (1795), I/1, 325.
38 White, *Schelling*, pp. 31–2.
39 O'Meara, *Romantic Idealism and Roman Catholicism*, pp. 38 and 67.

idealism, while overcoming their dualism, by conceiving nature out of the essence of mind. This is why, in his earliest philosophy, he described the essence of mind and the essence of nature as coming from one and the same source: he wanted his Nature Philosophy to be the description of the 'real' side of being, along the same lines as the description of the 'ideal' side offered by German idealist philosophy.

His idea, then, was to introduce a higher realism into the philosophy of idealism, trying to give back to the natural world that self-sufficiency which he felt Fichte had taken away from it. (For Schelling, as for many of his contemporaries, this project also dovetailed, in political philosophy, with a holistic, communitarian view of the state, for which Winkelmann's theories about ancient Greece were largely responsible, and which were later also taken up by such arch-Romantic figures as Richard Wagner, as well as by Hegel himself.)

Schelling's basic idea in the Nature Philosophy was that all nature should be thought of in terms of 'productivity'. This productivity is not a separate inaccessible thing in itself, because it is also at work in the subject. Schelling was concerned to understand how life emerges, without relying on the dualism of matter and life which creates the gulf between them which Kant could not cross.[40] Schelling wrote passionately of his frustration with that gulf:

> Whoever in scientific research is seized by the sheer pleasure at the richness of nature does not ask whether nature and experience are possible. It is sufficient for such a person that it is there for him ... Man is not born to waste his mental energy in struggling against the hallucination of an imagined world, but to wield all his forces on a world which has influence upon him, which allows him to feel its power, and against which he can react ... Mere reflection is a form of mental illness ... It makes the division between man and the world permanent, by making the latter into a thing in itself, unreachable by perception, imagination, understanding or reason.[41]

Arguing that 'one and the same principle connects inorganic and organic nature',[42] and that it was the 'world soul' which animated the natural world, Schelling claimed that both the organic and the inorganic were dynamic. His purpose was obviously to overcome mechanism and dualism. He argued that both 'reality' and 'ideality' had to be included in a true unity which left each of them separate, while conceiving them as arising from a common, higher ground. This unity was the principle of identity ($A = A$), something which was not just an object of knowledge, as in Kant, but the ground which bore the whole of being. Schelling was later to refer to these arguments as his attempts to achieve 'the mutual fusion of realism and idealism'.[43]

Fichte had conceived history as simply the history of human activity: Schelling was to come to view mind and nature not as totally separate static realms, but as two stages or epochs of a single development of the world acting one upon the other. He eventually came to hold that the world was in essence history: history of nature

---

40   Bowie, *Schelling and Modern European Philosophy*, p. 38.
41   *Ideen zu einer Philosophie der Natur* (1797), I/2, 12–14.
42   *Von der Weltseele* (1798), I/2, 350.
43   *Philosophische Untersuchungen über das Wesen der menschlichen Freiheit* (1809), I/7, 350.

and history of mind.[44] Hegel's *Phenomenology* subscribed to the latter idea: it is interesting that Schelling himself overcame it in response to the use Hegel made of it.

The Beginnings of Schelling's Change

This interest in science was to prove crucial. O'Meara argues that it was Schelling's interest in science, and especially medicine, which brought him into contact with Catholic circles, through Catholic doctors, and thereby into a dialogue between Romantic Idealism and the Catholic Church of which he was one of the main protagonists.[45] Catholic doctors in Landshut showed great interest in the Nature Philosophy, and this caused Schelling to frequent Catholic circles. 'The scientists set in motion a course of events that will establish Schelling as the philosophical mentor for Roman Catholic thinkers over the following 30 years.'[46] That dialogue led Schelling to 'become dissatisfied with the enterprise of pure transcendental philosophy and its abstract ideology of the Absolute'.[47] Like his *Frühromantik* colleagues, Schelling wanted to celebrate a 'monadology' of the universe, 'a biology of the divine presence'.[48]

However, it was more than a matter of contacts. Schelling's keen interest in nature, and in reality generally, was to become the Archimedean point by which he was to heave himself out of the Fichtean/Spinozist mould. His view that the workings of the Absolute could be observed in natural science (and that they were essentially the same workings as those of the human self) separated him from dualism and therefore, to some extent, from idealism. Just as Gnosis generally insisted that the created world was dark, that the created world was inherently evil, and that only God was light, so some mystics argued that no good would come from contemplating the real world. There are similarities between this view and Kant's view that the thing in itself in unknowable.

Schelling, by contrast, was convinced that if nature displayed an intelligible order, then this could not be only as a result of the organisational capacities of the I. There had to be order in nature itself:

> Because there is in our mind an endless striving to organise oneself, so in the outside world a general tendency to organisation must reveal itself. Indeed, this is what really happens. The world system is a kind of organisation, which has formed itself out of a common centre.[49]

Schelling specifically argued that nature had intelligibility and even *telos* in itself.

---

44   Walter Schulz, 'Freiheit und Geschichte in Schellings Philosophie', in *Schellings Philosophie der Freiheit, Festschrift der Stadt Leonberg* (Stuttgart: Kohlhammer, 1975), p. 30.
45   O'Meara, *Romantic Idealism and Roman Catholicism*, pp. 27 and 32–5.
46   *Ibid.*, p. 27.
47   *Ibid.*, p. 32.
48   Maesschalk, *L'anthropologie politique et religieuse de Schelling*, p. 245.
49   *Abhandlungen zur Erläuterung des Idealismus der Wissenschaftslehre* (1796–97), I/1, 386.

Schelling's Beginnings 47

> All concepts of purposefulness (*Zweckmäßigkeit*) can arise only in the understanding, and it is only with respect to such understanding that a thing can be called purposeful.
>
> You are similarly obliged to admit that the purposefulness of natural products dwells within them themselves, that it is objective and real, and that it does not belong to your arbitrary representations (*Vorstellungen*) but rather to necessary ones.[50]

Without such purposefulness (I have translated *Zweckmäßigkeit* as 'purposefulness' but 'finality' might do too) and organisation, indeed, any judgement about the world would be impossible.[51] The existence of such purposefulness was itself definitive of the intelligibility of the world. Schelling saw that there was a natural order in the universe, that natural occurrences were not chaotic or contingent, that order was not the result of an arbitrary projection by the mind onto indeterminate and unknowable nature, and that order and reason could not be attributed exclusively to the I. This teleological view is not incompatible with an Aristotelian one – the source, as it happens, of traditional views about justice and law.[52]

Schelling even adopted the view that order was not arbitrarily imposed by God, but that it inhered in the very natures of created things themselves. When human intelligence detects the finality of things, that finality is equivalent to their being, their essence, their reality.[53] According to this view, it was precisely the fault of nominalism and idealism (including Kantian transcendental idealism) to believe that order is that which is imposed, rather than that which inheres naturally in things, as a result of their essence. Schelling declared,

> But you destroy all idea of nature from the bottom up as soon as you allow purposefulness to be transferred from outside, through a transition from the understanding of any other being. If you ... extend the idea of the creator to infinity, then all concepts of purposefulness and understanding are lost, and one is left only with the idea of absolute power ... To explain purposefulness by saying that divine understanding is its author is not to philosophise, but to make pious observations.[54]

This is very similar to the Catholic philosopher, Jean Daujat, who says,

> One must not introduce into the affirmation of finality the idea of an external intention which is foreign to the natural movement of beings such as it results from their natures ... the principle of finality in no way affirms the intentions of Providence."[55]

Self-organisation, Schelling said, must be the primary process not only of mind but also of nature: the organised character of mind and of nature cannot be absolutely separate. Nature is visible mind and mind is invisible nature,[56] and the world is the

---

50   *Ideen zu einer Philosophie der Natur* (1797), I/2, 42–3.
51   *Ibid.*, I/2, 42.
52   See Michel Villey, *Le droit et les droits de l'homme* (Paris: Presses Universitaires de France, 1983), *passim*, esp. p. 42.
53   *Ideen zu einer Philosophie der Natur* (1797), I/2, 45f.
54   *Ibid.*, I/2, 45 and I/2, 55.
55   Jean Daujat, *Y a-t-il une vérité?* (Paris: Téqui, 1974), pp. 87 and 88.
56   *Ideen zu einer Philosophie der Natur* (1797), I/2, 56.

product of the Absolute working through nature and through mind. The difference between this and the Kantian view, according to which the laws of nature are foreign to nature itself, is clear enough.

This is doubtless why Xavier Tilliette has described the Nature Philosophy as 'cutting the transcendental umbilical cord'.[57] Because Schelling regarded the natural world as a manifestation of the Absolute, the Absolute was not pushed off into an unknowable realm. Reason and observation could provide a path towards knowledge of it. Schelling was henceforth inclined to move towards a slightly more realist ontological position: he 'accorded his system a vast ontological base of which (universal) nature furnished the elements'.[58]

Because the conscious I was itself part of the natural order (secondary, like nature, to primordial unity, not constitutive of it), Schelling saw that the philosophy which placed an absolute I in the centre of all being was a mistake. Thus he often sounded empiricist when discussing the kind of knowledge which scientific experimentation can give us.

> We do not know only this or that, we know absolutely nothing except through and thanks to experience, and thus all our knowledge consists in statements about experience. These statements only become *a priori* when we realise that they are necessary.[59]

Or in other words, *nihil est in intellectu quod non prius fuerit in sensu*. Because of his basic empiricism, Schelling's assessment of man's cognitive faculties was modest. He stressed that human knowledge, while progressive, was always only partial, 'because every experiment throws us back into a new state of ignorance, and because when it unties one knot another one ties itself, so it is understandable that the total discovery of all the links in nature – and thus natural science itself – is an endless task'.[60] He distanced himself from the hubristic pretence inherent in the Cartesian and idealist project, that the human mind can know everything.

Schelling never renounced the Nature Philosophy. This suggests either that he had a high opinion of himself, or that his philosophical development was always consistent and rectilinear. The latter is doubtful. However, it is true that his thought continued to gravitate around the same set of preoccupations. In the 1809 *Freedom* essay, for instance, he referred back to the mechanistic and dualistic views which the Nature Philosophy was trying to overcome:

> The firm belief in a purely human reason, the conviction that all thought and knowledge is completely subjective, and that nature is totally without reason and thought, together with the omnipresent domination of the mechanistic way of seeing things, in which even the dynamism which Kant reawakened merely turned into a higher form of mechanism,

---

57   Tilliette, *L'absolu et la Philosophie*, p. 54.
58   *Ibid.*, p. 55.
59   *Einleitung zu dem Entwurf eines Systems der Naturphilosophie, oder über den Begriff der spekulativen Physik und die innere Organisation eines Systems dieser Wissenschaft* (1799), I/3, 278.
60   *Ibid.*, I/3, 279.

and was never recognised in its identity with the spiritual, adequately justify the path of these reflections.[61]

In other words, in these few sentences, Schelling sketches what he sees as the inadequacies of modern philosophy from Descartes to German Idealism. During this period, freedom was generally equated with the faculties of the mind, and it had been given no place in the overall scheme of being. For the dualists, mind was just 'I', 'I think', and freedom was therefore experienced only as self-consciousness. Even in Kant, the question of freedom was posed in terms of nature on the one hand, and mind on the other. This conception of freedom was the definitive cause of the opposition between mind and matter, and the latter was forced into a purely mechanical mould. This is what Schelling was determined to destroy in his Nature Philosophy, and later.

It is important to emphasise that what we see here are mere germs which are to flourish later. Despite these similarities with some traditional Christian views – for instance about the inevitably limited and partial nature of human knowledge – Schelling initially adopted a kind of monism to solve his problems. One of the reasons why he admired Spinoza was precisely that he had argued that real and ideal were united in human nature and thought.[62] It is only later that this ontological mould would break up in favour of something more original – original for Schelling's period, at least.

This monism was expressed in the Identity Philosophy, which succeeded the Nature Philosophy. Schelling was in search of the Absolute, the fundamental principle underlying all knowledge and being.[63] He was convinced that, without a ground of identity which preceded all differences, there could be no identification or differentiation between subjects and objects, and therefore no knowledge or judgements. Schelling thus argued in the 1800 *System of Transcendental Idealism*, that absolute identity was prior to pure subjectivity. He based this system on the intuition of self-consciousness, which he described as a state of pure subjectivity, but it is clear that, for him, absolute identity was that which is there before that process of limitation occurs which produces the finite world and consciousness. Schelling wrote, 'The pre-established harmony between the objective (the lawful) and the determining (the free) is thinkable only through something higher, which is above both of them, which is neither intelligence [*sic*] nor free, but which is the common source of both the intelligent and the free.'[64] That higher thing was the basis of identity between the subjective and the objective, the unpredictable Absolute which is the ultimate source of the world. This identity was accessible only to intellectual intuition, in other words nothing can be known about it because it is prior to the self-reflexive act of knowledge.

---

61   *Philosophische Untersuchungen über das Wesen der menschlichen Freiheit* (1809), I/7, 333.
62   *Ideen zu einer Philosophie der Natur* (1797), I/2, 35–6.
63   *System der gesammten Philosophie und der Naturphilosophie insbesondere* (1804), I/6, 138.
64   *System des transcendentalen Idealismus* (1800), I/3, 600.

As Andrew Bowie shows, this is a sudden reversal of Kant. Whereas Kant had considered that positive knowledge was only of the empirical world, Schelling was now implying that positive knowledge was knowledge of the Absolute, while empirical knowledge was relative.[65] To this extent, the 1800 *System* and the Identity Philosophy generally remain firmly in the dualist and Gnostic groove, despite Schelling's differences with Fichte and Kant. The world is produced by subjectivity, and as such it is in fact only representation.[66]

To attribute to the real world an illusory quality, as here, is in fact hardly to liberate oneself from the Spinozist or Fichtean constructs, even if Schelling was now moving away from the subjectivist ontology of the latter. On the other hand, Schelling's repeated insistence during this period that the knowledge that things exist outside of the self does not derive from the fundamental prejudice that I exist, but instead from the act of knowledge itself – and that therefore being is both unquestionable and prior to thought – is to provide the basis for his later return to ontological realism (the belief in the reality of the outside world as an intelligible pre-existing entity).

Schelling's Move to Catholic Bavaria

These philosophical developments coincided with important evolutions in Schelling's relationship with religion. By 1803 Schelling had moved to Bavaria, where he took up a professorship at Würzburg. Schelling's language and philosophical endeavour took on a strongly religious tone which it was never to lose. Bavaria itself was at that stage undergoing a significant cultural revival, most of it inspired by the Enlightenment-minded Graf Montgelas[67] (although of course there was also much opposition to Enlightenment rationalism). The Catholic theologian Michael Sailer (1751–1832) was one of the most prominent Bavarian intellectuals of the period, and, being a friend of Schelling's, was greatly interested in and influenced by him. Two other Catholic theologians, Patriz Zimmer and J. Weber, belonged to the circle: the former tried to produce a reinvigorated Catholic theology with the help of Schelling's philosophy.[68] Horst Fuhrmans resumes the religious politics of Bavaria at the time very well:

> If believing theological circles had become used to seeing something deeply dangerous in the philosophy of Kantian and post-Kantian idealism (of Fichte, but also thereby of Schelling), which in the last resort even seemed to contain anti-Christian tendencies, for these people [Röschlaub the medic, Weber and Zimmer the theologians] Schelling was,

---

65   Bowie, *Schelling and Modern European Philosophy*, p. 67.

66   *System des transcendentalen Idealismus* (1800), I/3, 378.

67   On the influence of Enlightenment ideas on the Catholic parts of Germany in the late eighteenth and nineteenth century, see W. Trapp, *Vorgeschichte und Ursprung der liturgischen Bewegung, vorwiegend in Hinsicht auf das deutsche Sprachgebiet* (Regensburg, 1940 and Münster, 1979) and Aidan Nichols, *Looking at the Liturgy* (San Fransisco: Ignatius, 1996), Chapter 1, which draws heavily on Trapp.

68   See O'Meara, *Romantic Idealism and Roman Catholicism, passim*, and Horst Fuhrmans, *F.W.J. Schelling, Briefe und Dokumente*, Vol. 1 (Berlin: Bouvier, 1962), p. 295, note 10.

by contrast, a leader back into the religious, an area in which a rebirth of the religious took place ... In Landshut circles had formed around the great figure of the theologian Michael Sailer, whose deepest aim was to overcome the Enlightenment ... Into this front, Schelling had moved, not least with his Nature Philosophy. After the brittle (*spröd*) all too brittle, spirit of the Enlightenment, which put on airs and only permitted the 'moral' to count for anything, in order take a distance from religion, and in order to abjure everything living and flowing, everything which came from the area of feeling – including living religion – in Schelling, everything seemed to come back to life again.[69]

Catholics in Bavaria thus saw in Schelling's philosophy the chance to achieve a renewal of religion and to arrive at a new religious philosophy. It was precisely for this reason that the circles which opened themselves to Schelling's philosophy were not anti-religious or even pantheist ones, but religious and believing ones. By the same token, his enemies were not principally Christians, but rather men of the Enlightenment: even the ones who were nominally theologians were in fact rationalist Kantians whose main slogans were 'reason' and 'morality'. It was against such men that Schelling's appointment in Würzburg was understood as representing an important political victory.[70]

At this time, indeed, Schelling began to take his distance from pietism and mysticism. Individualist and partly mystic pietism had always been the bedrock of the Protestant environment in which Kant had been brought up: its influence is especially detectable in his ethics. Schelling began to feel at this period that it tended to render collective political and religious experience impossible, and he began to believe that the Church should strengthen its role in the modern state for that very reason. In his early philosophy, Schelling had supported an invisible Church of free spirits – 'Christians without a Church', to use the title of Kolakowski's book – but after moving to Bavaria he evolved away from pietism (and especially from the implicit support pietists' individualism paradoxically gave to the power of the modern state) and towards a greater appreciation of the ecclesiastical institution.[71]

This development was reflected in the 1803 *Vorlesungen über die Methode des akademischen Studiums* (Lectures on the method of academic study). Many of the lectures dealt specifically with Christianity. Schelling argued that the doctrines of Christianity were being destroyed through a merely empirical interpretation of them: he said he wanted to leave behind the rationalist philosophy of Kant[72] and return to the true spirit of Christianity instead. He argued that the Christian religion had a specifically historical nature ('in Christianity, the universe is observed as history, as

---

69   Fuhrmans, *F.W.J. Schelling, Briefe und Dokumente*, Vol. 1, p. 296. The following paragraph also draws on Fuhrmans.

70   Ibid., pp. 296–7.

71   Maesschalk, *L'anthropologie politique et religieuse de Schelling*, pp. 164–5. On the role of Protestantism in strengthening the state, see Murray N. Rothbard, *Economic Thought before Adam Smith* (*An Austrian Perspective on the History of Economic Thought*, Vol. I) (Aldershot: Edward Elgar, 1995), Chapter 5, 'Protestants and Catholics'.

72   *Vorlesungen über die Methode des akademischen Studiums* (1803), Neunte Vorlesung, 'Über das Studium der Theologie', I/5, 299.

a moral empire'[73]), and in a strikingly anti-Protestant vein, attacked the *Aufklärerei* which sought to undermine the system which the Church had built up over the ages, by supposedly going back to *Ur*-Christianity instead.[74] He criticised the Protestants' political attacks on the Catholic Church for allegedly preventing the study of early texts, saying that the Church's purpose was not to keep people in ignorance, but instead to maintain the Christian religion as a living organism in the present, rather than as an object of purely scholarly study.

Indeed, argued Schelling, Protestantism was wrong to think that only the early Church had legitimacy; the Catholics' purpose was to make Christianity 'a living religion, not only as something in the past', to make it 'continue as an eternal present'.[75] He accused Protestantism of creating 'a much worse slavery' than the one it had attacked, because it replaced the living authority of the present Church with the distant authority of something dead. It was thus inevitable, he said, that Protestantism should have subsequently declined into sects, for its appeal was by definition not universal.[76] He particularly attacked German scholars for removing all the symbolic and miraculous elements from Christianity, and for trying to prove the existence of God with empirical and historical arguments. Protestant bookishness had made theology decline into a profane science.[77]

In keeping with the realist (as opposed to mystic or pietist) drift in his thought, Schelling emphasised that art, morality, politics and religion were all realms where the real became the ideal: art and religion mirrored God. By contrast, he blamed the Enlightenment because it held religion to be a science of objects, and merely displaced religious dogma with moral imperatives. By the end of March 1805, as a result of a series of attacks upon him by representatives of the Catholic Enlightenment (that is, progressives), he published a rancorous open letter against his enemies, whom he called the 'darkening Enlightenmentalists' (*verfinsternde Aufklärlinge*).[78] Despite the evidence presented here, Schelling's lectures did not elicit the admiration of the Bishop of Würzburg, who forbade Catholic attendance at them after the inaugural one because he was shocked by what he thought was Schelling's neo-Platonism and mysticism.[79]

Identity Philosophy

As a matter of fact, the bishop had good grounds for his ruling. At this stage in his development, Schelling's work remained very neo-Platonist. However, it was also a hybrid position which was soon to move away from neo-Spinozist emanationism. Initially, the Gnostic elements were clear: Schelling insisted that the thinking subject

---

73   *Ibid.*, I/5, 287.
74   *Ibid.*, I/5, 300.
75   *Ibid.*, I/5, 301.
76   *Ibid.*
77   *Ibid.*, I/5, 302.
78   'Schellings Erklärung "An das Publikum", vom Ende März 1805', published in Fuhrmans, *F.W.J. Schelling, Briefe und Dokumente*, p. 325.
79   O'Meara, *Romantic Idealism and Roman Catholicism*, p. 69.

was identical with the nature it came to objectify in cognitive judgements. It was neither real nor ideal, but a combination of the two.[80] This explains why it was the starting point of the Identity Philosophy (as expressed in the 1804 *System of the Whole of Philosophy and of Nature Philosophy in Particular*) that, 'The first principle of all knowledge is that it is one and the same thing which knows and is known.'[81] The highest knowledge was therefore that in which the identity of subject and object is recognised: reason, indeed, was the self-recognition of this eternal identity.[82] For reason was either not knowledge at all, or knowledge of that which is eternal.

This Gnosticism was hybrid because, although it came from the same source as Cartesianism and other idealist currents, it also contained elements which caused Schelling to react against Cartesianism, in particular against its alleged 'mechanism':

> Most people think they can grasp the fact that a soul has concepts, representation and so on; but the idea that there can be living concepts in nature, concepts which are nothing further than these concepts themselves, which are not had by any one but which exist for themselves and by themselves without reflection – this does not only belong to the class of inconceivable propositions, but also to the utterly incomprehensible. In this respect, the same old moaning (*Jammer*) of the Cartesian period continues in our own philosophical age, which denied all dark, that is, not reflected, not subjective but objective concepts. It thereby demoted the whole of nature – not just so-called inorganic nature, but organic as well – into the realm of pure mechanism.[83]

This is why Schelling called the philosophy of identity 'real-idealism'. Similarly, although Schelling was being overtly neo-Platonist when he entitled his next work *Bruno* in honour of the heretic, Giordano Bruno, and when he declared in that work that everything flowed from an original unity – 'Everything which is, has a unity from which it has drawn its origin and from which it is separated by the relative opposition in it of the finite and the infinite; while this unity itself issues from a superior unity which contains the indifference of all things which are comprehended in it'[84] – nonetheless, this position allowed him to emphasise that the truth of being was incontrovertible. It is fundamental identity which makes subjects and objects possible;[85] the identity between subject and object in knowledge is derivative of this fundamental identity; and if there were no being, if there were no incontrovertible 'is', then knowledge as such would not be possible. This thought is to provide an important basis for the later philosophy: the (idealist) thought that there might be nothing in the world outside our subjective ideas is banished precisely by the knowledge that being necessarily affirms itself in knowledge and in reason.

---

80   Bowie, *Schelling and Modern European Philosophy*, p. 82.

81   *System der gesammten Philosophie und der Naturphilosophie insbesondere* (1804), I/6, 137.

82   *Ibid.*, I/6, 141.

83   *Aphorismen über die Naturphilosophie* (1806), I/7, 215.

84   *Bruno, oder über das göttliche und natürliche Prinzip der Dinge, Ein Gespräch* (1802), I/4, 268.

85   *System der gesammten Philosophie* (1804), I/6, 147, para. 3.

Non-being is eternally impossible and can never be known or grasped, and that last question of the understanding which stands dizzily at the abyss – the question, 'Why is there not nothing? Why is there anything at all?' – this question is driven out by the recognition that being is necessary, that is, through the absolute affirmation of being in knowledge. This absolute positing of the idea of God is in fact nothing other than the absolute negation of the nothing (*das Nichts*) and as certainly as reason eternally denies the nothing (*das Nichts*), and the nothing is nothing, just as certainly does it affirm the universe, and thus God is eternally.[86]

Or again, the strikingly Gnostic sentiments, 'It is not I who recognises the identity, but the identity which recognises itself, and I am the mere organ of it'[87] and, 'It is only in the supreme science that the mortal eye closes, there where man no longer sees, but where the eternal seeing has become seeing in him',[88] also allowed Schelling to attack Cartesian dualism: 'Since Descartes, the I think, I am has been the basic error of all knowledge: thinking is not my thinking, and being is not my being, for everything is only of God or of the universe (*des Alls*).'[89] Schelling undermined the central role played by the Cartesian subject by declaring, 'It is not I that knows, but rather only the universe (*das All*) knows in me.'[90] This is the as yet undeveloped germ of the rejection, prominent in the later philosophy, of any doubt that we can know reality, or that reality exists prior to our knowledge of it. Philosophy's primary certainty is that there is being: all reasoning is impossible without accepting that everything is what it is. Schelling writes,

> If there were not within our mind a knowledge, totally independent of all subjectivity, and no longer a knowledge of the subject as subject, but a knowledge of that which just is, and just can be known, the simple One, then we would in fact have to abandon philosophy altogether, we would be eternally locked inside the sphere of subjectivity with our thinking and our knowing, and we would have to regard the results of Kantian and Fichtean philosophy as the only possible ones and make them our own.[91]

Schelling was certainly neo-Platonist when he declared that philosophy was knowledge of 'that which is in itself, that which is eternal and unchangeable,' and, as such, he was still very much in the broad idealist mould. However, as he recognised here, this Gnosticism itself led him away from both Kant and Fichte who forbade knowledge of that which is in itself. If Fichte had been right, said Schelling, 'then the circle would indeed be closed (*unauflöslich*) in which Fichte thought he had captured the human mind'.[92]

---

86 *Ibid.*, I/6, 155.
87 *Ibid.*, I/6, 143.
88 'Kritische Fragmente' in *Aus den Jahrbüchern der Medicin als Wissenschaft* (1806), I/7, 248.
89 *Aphorismen zur Einleitung in die Naturphilosophie* (1806), 44, I/7, 148.
90 *System der gesammten Philosophie* (1804), I/6, 140. Bowie also quotes these passages in *Schelling and Modern European Philosophy*, pp. 61–2.
91 *System der gesammten Philosophie* (1804), I/6, 143.
92 *Ibid.*, I/6, 144.

Pantheism, Morality and the Problem of Evil

It was because of its pantheist and neo-Platonist elements that the 1804 *System* failed to elaborate an accurate account of evil and human freedom. Typically, pantheist systems – whether of the Spinozist or more overtly religious kind – do not leave much room for human freedom or evil. As Alan White puts it, 'According to the strictly scientific 1804 "System", human freedom is an illusion and is therefore not worthy of serious philosophical treatment.'[93] This was the concern which drove Schelling towards the 1809 *Freedom* essay. In the 1804 *System*, a rather flippant passage on crime and punishment emphasises how little space there is for human freedom, choice and personality.

> For him who acts wrongly, it is precisely the lesser degree of reality which is expressed in him, which is the punishment. Absolutely considered, he is also necessary as a member (*Glied*) of the world, and to this extent not punishable and not even excusable. But the stone is also excusable for not being a man, although it is nonetheless condemned to be a stone and to suffer what a stone suffers.[94]

At this stage, therefore, Schelling sidestepped the problem of evil, saying that the difference between good and evil was merely one of degree.[95] He thus reduced the reality and importance of evil, something he was to correct in the *Freedom* essay. On the other hand, in a passage which prefigures almost word for word a similar passage in the *Freedom* essay (I/7, 392), Schelling attacked Kant for arguing that a moral man must consciously consider the options if his otherwise good action is to qualify as really moral:

> Religion is higher than devotion or feeling. The primary meaning of this frequently misused word is conscientiousness: it expresses the highest unity of knowledge and action, which makes it impossible to contradict one's knowledge in action. A man for whom this is impossible – not in a human or physical or psychological way, but in a divine way – is called religious, conscientious in the highest meaning of the word. A man is not conscientious if he must first hold the command of duty in front of himself, and if it is only through respect for the law that he determines to do right. The conscientious man does not need this: it is impossible for him to act other than is right. Religiosity originally means that action is bound: it never means a choice between opposites, as one assumes for the freedom of the will. It does not mean an *aequilibrium arbitrii*, as it is called, but rather the highest decisiveness for that which is right, without choice.[96]

Schelling accused Kant of allowing ideas (*Ideen*) no reality: because his philosophy was only reflective, he made them into mere inventions of thought.[97] Schelling called it typical of the 'vain urge of selfhood'[98] to think that moral ideas exist only as

---

93   White, *Schelling*, p. 106
94   *System der gesammten Philosophie* (1804), I/6, 547.
95   Ibid., I/6, 546.
96   Ibid., I/6, 558.
97   Ibid., I/6, 186, middle.
98   Ibid., I/6, 187.

inventions of the mind, and do not describe any reality: Schelling's urge towards traditional realism – towards the views that ideas inhere in the very structure of reality – was already becoming visible.

Philosophy and Religion

It was to be precisely the problems of freedom and evil which caused the first cracks in Schelling's neo-Platonist mould to appear in the *Freedom* essay. For the time being, however, the problems presented for freedom and evil by Schelling's early ontology remained acute, as the short essay *Philosophy and Religion* showed. That essay represented the beginning of Schelling's attempt to elaborate what has been called 'a programme of speculative theology'.[99] As such, *Philosophy and Religion* can be seen as the beginning of the change in Schelling's philosophy which becomes explicit in 1809.

The key novel element in *Philosophy and Religion* was the notion of 'fall'. Although this notion was present in the 1804 *System* as well – concrete, real being was said to have a relatively lower ontological status as 'relative non-being'[100] – the notion of a sudden fall, rupture or collapse was the centrepiece of *Philosophy and Religion*, and it was eventually to destroy Schelling's earlier seamless ontological structure.

Schelling's purpose in the essay was to overcome the modern tendency to separate certain knowledge (philosophy) from religion.[101] He wanted to put the truths of religious dogma on a firm scientific footing,[102] and to develop an ontology that would allow 'the whole of ethics' to be grounded.[103] Moreover, that ontological basis had to be 'the living idea of the Absolute'[104] and not some dead conceptual construction.

What Schelling said about the creation is incompatible with traditional Christian teaching and shows that he remains firmly in a Gnostic-dualist mould:

> From the Absolute to the real there is no steady transition. The origin of the sensory world can only be thought of as a total breaking away from the Absolute, as a leap ... The Absolute is the only real, finite things on the contrary are not real; their ground can therefore not lie in a communication of reality to them or to their substrate from the Absolute, it can only lie in a distancing, in a fall from the Absolute.[105]

This is exactly the kind of Orphism discussed in Chapter 1. It is the opposite of the Christian tradition. However, what is intriguing is that this stark emphasis on the fall began to corrode Schelling's former harmonizing conception of his own philosophy,

---

99   Emilio Brito, 'La Création ex "nihilo"' selon Schelling', *Ephemerides Theologicae Lovanienses*, 60 (1984): 298.
100   *System der gesammten Philosophie* (1804), I/6, 189, para. 36.
101   *Philosophie und Religion* (1804), I/6, 16.
102   *Ibid.*, I/6, 20, para. 2.
103   *Ibid.*, I/6, 17.
104   *Ibid.*, I/6, 27.
105   *Ibid.*, I/6, 38.

according to which the Nature Philosophy and the transcendental philosophy were the 'real' and 'ideal' sides of the same coin, without any transition or rupture between them. His new conviction that the transition from the infinite to the finite was inexplicable[106] would separate him radically from Hegel, who by contrast tried to portray the development of determination out of the Absolute as a seamless, comprehensible and necessary logical dialectic. It also separated Schelling from his own early attachment to Spinozism: like Hegel's, Spinoza's is a fundamentally monist and seamless system. Although some emanationist systems, such as Plotinus', also contain the notion of a fall, the transition from the Absolute to the real is not one of sudden rupture. Here, by contrast, Schelling insisted not only that the creation was a fall but also that it was 'a total breaking away' from the Absolute.

The notion of the absolute fall is also not easily compatible with the view, propagated in the Nature Philosophy, that nature is the straightforward manifestation of the Absolute. It is therefore not clear what internal coherence there was in Schelling's new position. He seemed to want to retain the idea that God creates free human beings and thus reveals Himself in creation.[107] He thus placed freedom centre-stage.

> The exclusive mark of the Absolute is that it lends to its image not only the essence of itself but also autonomy (*Selbstständigkeit*). This being-in-itself, this actual and true reality of that which was first seen, is freedom, and from that first autonomy of the image there flows out that which in the phenomenal world appears as freedom, which is the last trace and at the same time the seal of divinity which has looked into the fallen world.[108]

Schelling's confusion, in other words, was between the fall which comes *after* human freedom has rebelled, that is, in the Garden of Eden, and the Oriental idea that the world is itself somehow guilty for its own existence or itself the consequence of a fall.

> The ground of the fall ... does not lie in the Absolute, it lies only in the real itself, in that which is observed, which is to be regarded as quite free and self-standing. The ground of the possibility of the fall lies in freedom, and insofar as this is posited by the informing (*Einbildung*) of the Absolute-ideal into the real, it lies in the form and thus in the Absolute; but the ground of *reality* lies only in the fallen itself, which producing the nothingness of sensory things only through and for itself.[109]

'The nothingness of sensory things' is a classic Oriental notion, of the kind which was to fascinate Schopenhauer. Schelling was at this stage convinced that the origin of no finite thing could be traced immediately to the infinite:[110] the finite was thus an eternal and absolute breaking-off from the infinite. Schelling also added that this fall was inexplicable, for it was itself absolute and came from the Absolute.[111] The

---

106   *Ibid.*, I/6, 42.
107   *Ibid.*, I/6, 39.
108   *Ibid.*, I/6, 39.
109   *Ibid.*, I/6, 40.
110   *Ibid.*, I/6, 41.
111   *Ibid.*, I/6, 42.

key point is that this essay represented an abandonment of Schelling's earlier view that a philosophical system could be elaborated in which all differences would be harmonised and reconciled. *Philosophy and Religion* therefore continued the first green shoots of the positive philosophy, for it implied that negative philosophy, as he begins to call it here, which moved only in a world of concepts, was mistaken in thinking that the source of the existence of the world could be explained logically.[112]

In keeping with his Orientalism at this stage, however, Schelling adopted a cyclical view of history and redemption which is incompatible with that genuine unpredictability which comes from true human freedom.

> Only the old, holy doctrine can put an end to all those knotty doubts with which reason has tired herself for millennia: the souls step down from the world of ideas into the world of senses, where as a punishment for their selfhood and for a guilt which precedes this life (according to the idea, not according to time), they are chained to a body as to a cell, and they bring with them the memory of the music and harmony of the true universe, but they apprehend in the noise of the world before them only in a disturbed manner, through disharmony and clashing tones, just as they can recognise truth not in that which is or which seems to be, but only in that which was for them, and to which they must strive back, the intelligible life.[113]

This is pure Orphism, especially the notion that the soul is imprisoned in the body. As we have seen, the idea that creation is a punishment and not a gift is utterly incompatible with Christianity. It is also difficult to reconcile with a true status for human freedom, for the cyclical nature of the soul's journey implies that salvation is ensured.

Philosophy and Religion thus sat on the cusp between various apparently contradictory convictions: that we have direct knowledge of the Absolute through our experience of being; that the world we know has fallen away from the Absolute; that human freedom is the cause of the world; and that the outcome of the world-historical process is inevitable.

Schelling was convinced until 1804 that philosophy itself was nearing completion. This was a typical conceit for his time. He thought he could complete the discipline by piecing together different parts of the Spinozist, Leibnizian, Kantian and Fichtean systems.[114] However, *Philosophy and Religion* put a spoke in the wheels of this happy plan: whatever new problems Schelling was preparing for himself by introducing the notion of a fall into his account of the creation, it is clear that if the world had come into being as the result of an inexplicable fall, then philosophy would have a hard time explaining the universe, particularly if it was to use logic. This inexplicability was to be the key to the later positive philosophy, for to describe the creation of the world as the result of a sudden catastrophe renders the comprehension of it within a single logical and systematic framework impossible.

---

112 *Ibid.*, I/6, 43.
113 *Ibid.*, I/6, 47.
114 White, *Schelling*, p. 28, note 11.

The Transition to the Philosophy of Freedom

In 1807 Schelling's close friend and former fellow student, Hegel, published the *Phenomenology of Spirit*. The foreword contained a barbed attack on the concept of the Absolute as 'the night in which all cows are black'. Schelling had publicly broken with Fichte the previous year and he perceived these words in the *Phenomenology* to be an attack on him and on his Identity Philosophy. He wrote to Hegel to express his annoyance.

> I have now read the Preface. Inasmuch as you mention its polemical content yourself, I would have to think too little of myself to believe that it is addressed at me ... Although you say in your letter that your attack pertains only to the abusers and the chatterers, this distinction is not made in the text.[115]

This was the last letter exchanged between the two. Relations between them were broken off for 20 years, until they bumped into each other quite by chance while on holiday in Karlsbad in the autumn of 1829. They were friendly enough to one another then. Schelling never made any criticism of Hegel in public during his life, but his silence crumbled after Hegel died in 1831. In the Munich Lectures of 1833–34, he began to criticise his former friend. Those who went to Schelling's lectures in 1838 wrote of the contempt with which Schelling spoke of Hegel's philosophy – as we shall see later.

Although he was very hurt by Hegel's perceived attack, it jolted him into making further changes to his philosophical system. This is doubtless because Hegel had hit his mark. Schelling's philosophy contained some painfully unexplained areas in 1807, as discussed above. However, there were also other factors encouraging change. Schelling moved to the Bavarian capital, Munich, in 1806, where he became Vice President of the Academy of Sciences (where Jacobi was President) and, in 1807, President of the Academy of Arts. Here he came under the influence of Franz Baader, 'the one great Roman Catholic intellectual who greatly influenced Schelling', and whose wide-ranging interests included Aquinas and Meister Eckhart.[116] This influence 'opened the passage from bright, transcendental systems to unexplored metaphysical abysses'.[117] He also began to see the connection between religion, philosophy and politics: he wrote to Windischmann in April 1806, 'Since Jena, I have learned that religion, public faith and life in the state form the point around which everything else revolves ...'[118]

Munich was a hugely important move for Schelling. As Fuhrmans writes, Schelling was easily influenced, especially when he encountered a new world. Munich was such a new world. His move there 'meant that Schelling entered a new *spiritual* (*geistig*) space, which can be characterised as one which had been specifically formed by Christianity. It is the Catholic Munich, so deeply linked to Christian usage, whose fluid will soon be felt in his works.' Furthermore, 'in Jena,

---

115 Schelling, Letter to Hegel, 2 September 1807.
116 O'Meara, *Romantic Idealism and Roman Catholicism*, pp. 80 and 81.
117 *Ibid.*, p. 73.
118 Letter to Windischmann, 16 January 1806, in Fuhrmans, *F. W. J. Schelling, Briefe und Dokumente*, Vol. 3, p. 294.

Schelling was the leader; now he will be led.'[119] It was in Munich that Schelling introduced into his philosophy a raft of explicitly Christian themes including the personal God, evil, the fall, salvation and immortality and that he recognised more and more clearly the inability of idealism to accommodate the demands of the Christian faith.[120]

Baader introduced Schelling to the work of Protestant and Catholic mystics. After 1806 the rumour began to spread that Schelling had actually become a Catholic: Goethe became worried about these reports, since Schelling was being considered for a post in Jena in 1816, where he wanted to become a professor of both philosophy and theology, and the sage of Weimar regarded it as a bar to Schelling's appointment.[121] Although Schelling never did convert or try to convert to Catholicism – he denounced the rumours as a lie in a letter to his devout Lutheran mother in 1815[122] – he never hid his admiration for Catholic mysticism or his (in some respects typically Romantic) enthusiasm for the medieval period. Politically, the move eventually brought Schelling to represent Catholic Bavaria against (Hegel's) Protestant Prussia.

---

119 Horst Fuhrmans, *Schellings Philosophie der Weltalter* (Düsseldorf: L. Schwann, 1954), p. 80, emphasis on '*geistig*' in original.

120 Brito, *Philosophie et théologie dans l'oeuvre de Schelling*, p. 11; Horst Fuhrmans, *Schellings letzte Philosophie* (Berlin: Junker und Dünnhaupt, 1940), pp. 26ff. and 36ff.

121 Xavier Tilliette, *Schelling, Une Philosophie en devenir* (Paris: Vrin, 2nd edn, 1992) Vol. 2, p. 130 including note 19.

122 O'Meara, *Romantic Idealism and Roman Catholicism*, p. 90.

Chapter 4

The Metaphysics of Evil

'Ich bin der Geist, der stets verneint.'
(I am the spirit who always says No.)

Mephistopheles, in Goethe's *Faust*

Many commentators agree that the *Freedom* essay of 1809 represents a turning point in Schelling's philosophy, and that it has a crucial religious element. Horst Fuhrmans writes, 'Schelling's change (*Wende*) in 1809 was very great; indeed, it was almost like a rupture (*Bruch*).'[1] Emilio Brito finds that the *Freedom* essay is 'a work of transition'.[2] Marc Maesschalk confirms that the new attention devoted to human freedom – especially the description of man as a 'central being' (*Zentralwesen*), and the insistence that human freedom represents a real choice for good or evil which has real historical consequences – indicates 'a renewal in (Schelling's) anthropological approach'.[3] Xavier Tilliette writes, 'The philosophy which Schelling elaborates during the years of mourning and of studious retreat [after the death of his wife, Caroline, August Wilhelm Schlegel's sister, in 1809], inaugurated by the celebrated *Freedom* essay, is a Christian Gnostic speculation, inspired by Böhme, Oetinger and neo-Platonism.'[4] Another commentator has argued that the *Freedom* essay is written not in dialogue with Kant and Spinoza, but instead with mystics and theologically minded thinkers like Baader,[5] who was the chief conduit for Böhme's thought. (Baader's lectures on Böhme fill two volumes, and he often used to call Böhme his real teacher.[6]) While there were certainly strong neo-Platonist elements, however, we shall observe that it is Schelling's new and striking philosophy of evil, elaborated in this essay, which would cause him to adopt increasingly orthodox religious positions.

---

1   Horst Fuhrmans, *Schellings Philosophie der Weltalter* (Düsseldorf: L. Schwann, 1954), p. 79.

2   Emilio Brito, 'La Création ex "nihilo" selon Schelling', *Ephemerides Theologicae Lovanienses*, 60 (1984): 304.

3   Marc Maesschalk, *L'anthropologie politique et religieuse de Schelling*, Editions de l'Institut supérieur de Philosophie, Louvain-la-Neuve (Paris: Vrin and Leuven: Peeters, 1991), p. 12.

4   Xavier Tilliette, *L'absolu et la Philosophie: essais sur Schelling* (Paris: Presses Universitaires de France, 1987), p. 24.

5   Thomas O'Meara, *Romantic Idealism and Roman Catholicism: Schelling and the Theologians* (Notre Dame and London: University of Notre Dame Press, 1982), p. 79.

6   Hans L. Martensen, *Studies in the Life and Teaching of Jacob Böhme*, trans. T. Thyr Evans (London: Rockliff, 1949), p. 19.

Martin Heidegger – who was fascinated with Schelling and who regarded him as one of the few great philosophers after Kant – was convinced that the *Freedom* essay not only gave extremely valuable insights into the question of freedom, but also that it was central to understanding Schelling's philosophy as a whole. In both his famous 1936 lectures on the *Freedom* essay, and in the less well-known 1941 lectures on the same subject, Heidegger opined that the *Freedom* essay was the summit of the metaphysics of German idealism. (This doubtless explains why the second series of lectures on Schelling's 1809 essay is simply entitled, 'The Metaphysics of German Idealism.'[7]) It may also explain why in 1930 Heidegger gave a lecture with the same title as Schelling's essay, 'On the Essence of Human Freedom', which he subtitled, 'An Introduction to Philosophy'. Heidegger called Schelling 'the truly creative and by far the deepest thinker of this whole period in German philosophy. He is this to such an extent that he pushes German idealism from within, to go beyond its own fundamental positions.'[8]

If this remark is merited, it was surely because Schelling conceived the question of freedom to be fundamentally ontological. Schelling was not concerned with the freedom of the will, but with the ontological implications of the relationship between (human) freedom and being. He was, in other words, separating himself from a long philosophical tradition which had construed freedom as self-coherence or autonomy, the thought of modernity. He did this by identifying freedom with the capacity to conform to, or to pervert, the divine order, when he affirmed that human freedom was the freedom to do good or evil.

Schelling's successive systems up to 1804 were vitiated by their failure genuinely to accommodate human freedom. Despite their increasingly pronounced religious elements, they remained too rationalist, too logical and too systematic for that. He attempted to square the circle in different ways at different times, but the problem he faced was always the same: first, the distinction between human freedom and other activity in the universe was not clearly drawn and, second, the possibility of genuine freedom leading to genuinely unpredictable results – which tear through any logical system – was usually suppressed.

The specifically neo-Platonist influences on Schelling, which came principally from Christian mystics like Giordano Bruno and Jakob Böhme, had forced him to abandon the over-optimistic, harmonizing approach to the relationship between the Absolute and the finite which had characterised the Nature Philosophy and the Identity Philosophy. Henceforth the concept of 'the fall' was to preoccupy him greatly. But it was in the *Freedom* essay that, describing the emergence of being in the most detailed and speculative manner, Schelling affirmed for the first time, as he was to do throughout his later philosophy, that the creation occurred as a result of a

---

7   Heidegger, Martin, *Die Metaphysik des deutschen Idealismus. Zur erneuten Auslegung von Schelling: Philosophische Untersuchungen über das Wesen der menschlichen Freiheit und die damit zusammenhängende Gegenstände* (*Gesamtausgabe*, Vol. 49) (Frankfurt am Main: Klostermann, 1991).

8   Heidegger, Martin, *Schellings Abhandlung über das Wesen der menschlichen Freiheit (1809)* (Tübingen: Max Niemeyer, 1971), p. 5.

groundless act of God – as a result of God's absolute freedom – and not as the result of any logical process.

In the first stage of his philosophy, Schelling had been trying to depict the world as a real self-development, in opposition to the prevailing conceptual rationalism of the time. He had wanted to conceive of the world as a living totality of happening, an attempt he sometimes termed 'objective idealism'. But he had also (at least in the very early period) spoken of the highest destiny of man as being 'the destruction of our personality' and of the 'highest moment of being as the transition to non-being, the moment of destruction'.[9] This, as we saw, was in line with the anti-individualist and anti-realist idealism of his time, especially of Fichte.

However, Schelling had also always believed in the existence of independently existing reality, and he had realised that if he failed to prove its existence then no conclusions about ethics, the natural law, or about the teleology of the universe could be sustained: the finality of man was intimately linked to the finality of the universe. This demand for finality and purpose in the world was one of the reasons why Schelling had recourse to a personal God in his ontology.

It is, indeed, the main difference between the early and late Schelling that he came to believe that the Absolute and its existence could not be reduced to mere concepts. Like Hegel, he had come to realise that intellectual intuition was incapable of giving immediate access to the Absolute. The Absolute had to be a true beginning of the real world. The early Schelling had also believed that the Absolute was unthinkable, yet he was so certain of it that he believed he could trace the development from its unity to that of being. Later, though, he came to insist against his own earlier thinking, and against that of Hegel, that one could not get anywhere with intellectual intuition. The fact that Schelling published nothing after the *Freedom* essay in 1809 suggests that this advance left him with questions he found it impossible to answer.

The *Freedom* Essay Itself

There are three essential aspects to this hugely important essay: 1) The distinction between ontological freedom and the traditional conception of free will; 2) the issue of fatalism and its connection with ontological pantheism; and 3) the metaphysics of evil (seen as non-voluntaristic or ontological ethics).

In Chapter 2 it was argued that the notion of 'system' was one of the central preoccupations of German idealism. Schelling made it clear at the beginning of the *Freedom* essay that a philosophical investigation into 'the essence of human freedom' must firstly describe that essence, and secondly establish where this concept has its place in the whole system. In other words, it had to show how freedom was compatible with the whole of being. The tension between freedom (as the beginning which needs no grounding) and system (as a closed context of grounding) was to become the essential tension in Schelling's whole philosophy.[10] The *Freedom* essay therefore pursued the same aim as the Nature Philosophy and the Identity Philosophy

---

9　*Philosophische Briefe über Dogmatismus und Kriticismus* (1795), I/1, 324.
10　Heidegger, *Schellings Abhandlung*, p. 75.

– an explanation of the nature of being. Unlike them, however, it tried to show that freedom was something potentially antagonistic, or at least radically different from, being. It also tried to show not only freedom's essence but also its existence. The concept of freedom had reality, in Schelling's words, only if we *are* free. In order to understand 'being free' we must therefore not only understand the concept 'free' but also the meaning of 'being', and not just the concept. This is not only because we are investigating the relationship between being and freedom but also because, in order to define something, we need to know both what it is and that it is.

Schelling started the *Freedom* essay discussing the difficulty of reconciling freedom and system.[11] Freedom was groundless yet system demanded that everything be grounded: a system of freedom seemed a contradiction in terms.[12] Schelling responded to his own challenge by saying that it all depended on what was understood by 'system'. He also insisted, in an interesting tacit admission of the primacy of being over concept, that the existence of a system of freedom could be denied, precisely because the fact of individual human freedom was indisputable, as was the fact of the existence of the world.[13] Since human freedom did exist, then it must exist in some relationship to the world – and therefore there must be a system.

Schelling introduced God straight away by mentioning that such a system must exist at least 'in the divine understanding'.[14] This implies that it is the duty of human reason to interpret that reality, rather than to prescribe its laws to it. Schelling was implicitly inverting Kant and Fichte: it is not our knowledge which conditions man's relationship to being, but being which conditions knowledge. His reference to Sextus Empiricus[15] showed that he was distancing himself from those 'grammarians' (that is, the rationalist or analytical philosophers against whom he was writing) who thought that the structures of being could be reduced to those of language. The outcome, he argued, would be either philosophical schemes which, in pursuit of reason, rendered the world meaningless (for example, Fichte's metaphysical nominalism) or ones which rendered it lifeless because too conceptual.

This last point is key. Schelling insisted that the search for the link between the concept of freedom and a view of the world as a whole ('*eine ganze Weltansicht*') remained as necessary as ever. Without this, or with excessive conceptualism, he felt that philosophy would sink into uselessness, and that the concept of freedom would remain vague. The task of resolving the question was therefore the fundamental question of philosophy, the one which defined the search for knowledge at all levels.[16] Both the flight into the irrational, and the belief that everything is explicable with the same rules, avoided the true difficulty, which was to find the right ground or basis (*Boden*) upon which the struggle between freedom and necessity could be

---

11   *Philosophische Untersuchungen über das Wesen der menschlichen Freiheit und die damit zusammenhängende Gegenstände* (1809), I/7, 336.
12   *Ibid.*, I/7, 336.
13   *Ibid.*, I/7, 336–7.
14   *Ibid.*, I/7, 337.
15   *Ibid.*, I/7, 337.
16   *Ibid.*, I/7, 338.

grasped, developed and carried out. The question of freedom was the question of being as a whole.

Schelling broached the question of pantheism, a question at the heart of a philosophical debate at the time. He wanted to show that the system he was proposing did not mean straightforward pantheism, but rather that being was part of God's revelation, and that it was thus connected with him and sustained by him although not equivalent to him. Things in the world enjoyed a derivative divinity, not an absolute one. As Kolakowski has emphasised, extreme pantheism is equivalent to atheism: to say that the world is God amounts to saying that there is no God, since it leaves no room for the creation of the world as a separate entity from God and resembles instead the ancient Greek view that the universe is itself eternal.[17] (This is why the Catholic Church has always condemned the doctrine, and it is significant that Father Emilio Brito argues that Schelling's later philosophy was compatible with the anti-pantheist canons in Vatican I and Pius IX's *Syllabus of Errors*.[18]) Schelling, as we know, was deeply influenced by the quasi-mystical worship of Nature which he inherited from Giordano Bruno, but, as the *Freedom* essay and subsequent works will show, he succeeded in preserving the difference between God and His creation.

The principal philosophical problem associated with pantheism, however, is the problem of evil. Schelling's main aim in the *Freedom* essay was to address this. As Kolakowski again writes, 'In the established tradition of monotheism, moral evil, although of course not caused by God, and lacking an ontological foundation, was real and at least partially unredeemable. The being could not but be good, yet the ill will of men and demons, unavoidably enacting their freedom or self-determination, was a genuine energy directly challenging God's order and plans. But there is no place for such an energy within the pantheists' vision.'[19]

The reason why Schelling identified 'system' with pantheism is that pantheism seeks to explain the whole of being in terms of logical consequences which flow from the existence of God. Spinoza's system was the best example of this. How, in such circumstances, could human freedom be conceived at all, and how can it be conceived as independence from God?

Schelling wrote that, on any reasonable analysis, pantheism would be acceptable if it meant only that all things are immanent in God (for all being things are indeed immanent in the ground of being). While he accepted that this might seem fatalist, he also drew attention to the fact that many people have been drawn to pantheism 'because of the most living feeling of freedom'.[20] In general, we have a feeling of our own freedom, that we can do things; yet the unconditionality of our freedom seems to stand in opposition to the unconditionality of God. The only solution to the dilemma seems to be to posit man as being in God. In other words, the more man feels his own freedom, the more he is conscious of his own being, and the more he is forced to place himself at the very heart of that being: he cannot consider himself outside being, or as nothing. Schelling was to argue that this, the fundamental feeling

---

17 Kolakowski, *Religion, If There is No God* (London: Fontana, 2nd edn, 1993), p. 104.
18 Emilio Brito, 'La Création ex "nihilo" selon Schelling', p. 319, note 122.
19 Kolakoswki, *Religion*, p. 105.
20 *Über das Wesen der menschlichen Freiheit* (1809), I/7, 339.

of human freedom, could lead to the belief in the unity of being, because to have the feeling that freedom is a fact assumes something about the whole of being. This is why freedom formed the centre of the system, and thus why the whole *Freedom* essay turned on the relationship between fatalism and pantheism.

Schelling thus examined three kinds of pantheism, and it is was by rejecting all of them that he opened the way for his new conception of it.[21] What Schelling wanted to show was that it is not pantheism, nor the theology in pantheism, but instead the underlying ontology which brought the danger of fatalism and the exclusion of freedom. He wanted to prove that the pantheistic notion of immanence rendered a fatalistic understanding of the world merely possible, but not necessary. It was false, he said, to think that pantheism meant the identity of things with God.[22] He declared that the falsehood flowed from a mistaken understanding of the law of identity, and of the meaning of the copula 'is' in judgments,[23] in other words on a false understanding of the law of identity and of the meaning of being. By correcting these mistakes, he hoped to show why pantheism, far from eradicating freedom, was predicated on the basic experience of it.

Schelling argued that a statement of identity between a subject and a predicate, 'A is B', does not always express mere sameness, or even an immediate connection between two things. If we say, 'This body is blue', we clearly do not mean that the body is of essence blue, that the body in that and through that by which it is a body, is blue.[24] The statement says nothing about the essence of the body. If we ignore the true meaning of 'is', therefore, it will be impossible to understand the meaning of 'God is all'. The theological question of pantheism thus becomes a question about the meaning of 'is', or about ontology.

Schelling said that one of the first lessons taught by Greek philosophy had been forgotten, namely that subject and predicate are *antecedens* and *consequens*.[25] By saying this, they expressed the true meaning of the law of identity. This, he said, was the meaning of the claim that subject and predicate are *implicitum* and *explicitum*.[26] Thus he tried to show that God coincides with all beings, not in the sense of an indistinct stew but in that of a harmonious and creative difference. If something is a subject, it means that it grounds the possibility of the predicate's being. 'Subject' is that which *underlies* the predicate. If God is all, therefore, he is so as the ground of all being. Identity, therefore, was not empty sameness, but living and creative: to deduce truth from statements of identity was to bring forth that which is latent.

In other words, Schelling argues that, far from pantheism being incompatible with freedom, understood in the right way, man's basic intuition of freedom actually demanded and led to pantheism. The intuition of freedom convinces man that he belongs to being and to the 'life of God'.[27] Schelling described pantheism as the

---

21   *Ibid.*, I/7, 340–44.
22   *Ibid.*, I/7, 340.
23   *Ibid.*, I/7, 341.
24   *Ibid.*, I/7, 341.
25   *Ibid.*, I/7, 342.
26   *Ibid.*, I/7, 342.
27   *Ibid.*, I/7, 339.

theory of the immanence of all things in God: being depends on God. He argued that this dependence did not limit the autonomy or freedom of that on which it is dependent.[28] In other words, the search is for a form of dependence which allows the dependent thing to be free.[29] For there to be a son, there must be a father; but the dependent thing, the son, does not need to *be* that which is his ground, the father.

The particular ground and consequence which Schelling had in mind was God and man: man was dependent on God as the absolute ground of his being, and yet he was free. Schelling was here trying to resolve two things which, as Kolakowski says, may be more easily compatible than might at first appear: neo-Platonist emanationism and the Christian doctrine of creation *ex nihilo*. 'Established Christian theology', Kolakowski writes, 'assumes that to be is to participate in the source of Being and that created things, whether bodies or spirits, though not parts of God, are of Him; their existence is contingent, not independent.'[30]

Indeed, said Schelling, it would be contradictory if the dependent thing were not autonomous, for then there would allegedly be a consequence with no consequent.[31] Moreover, things which are included and conceived within other things were not necessarily nothing as a result: an eye is possible only within a body but it has a life of its own. This general truth was all the more true of God: God is not the God of death, but of life. 'It cannot be understood how the most perfect being would enjoy the most perfect machine.'[32] Above all – and here Schelling was again rejecting mechanism, as in the Nature Philosophy – however we imagine things coming from God, they cannot do so mechanically, nor can it be a matter of the creator placing things in existence which are nothing by themselves.[33]

> The progression (*die Folge*) of things out of God is a self-revelation of God. But God can only reveal Himself in that which resembles Him, in free beings which act out of themselves.[34]

The compatibility between such a remark and Christian metaphysics is only marginal: on the one hand, the Christian obviously does hold, with Schelling, that the creation is God's revelation, and that man was created in God's image, as a free being. On the other hand, the concept of 'progression' sounds neo-Platonist.

Schelling thought he had shown that 'derivative absoluteness'[35] was possible, and that pantheism in this sense was therefore compatible with human freedom. It was significant – and compatible with Biblical metaphysics – that Schelling rejected the idea that the only possible system of reason was one which mixed creation with the creator together in blind necessity.

---

28 Ibid., I/7, 346.
29 Ibid., I/7, 345.
30 Kolakowski, *Religion*, p. 139.
31 *Über das Wesen der menschlichen Freiheit* (1809), I/7, 346.
32 Ibid.
33 Ibid.
34 Ibid., I/7, 347.
35 Ibid.

In order to grasp this, one must bring to mind the reigning spirit of an earlier age. Then the mechanical ways of thinking, which reached the summit of ruthlessness in French atheism, had taken in virtually all minds; even in Germany, people began to see and to declare this way to be the actual and only philosophy.[36]

In Germany, he said, this had led to a foolish view that the head and the heart could be separated. Schelling was always vigorous in his attacks against Romantic *Schwärmerei*,[37] and this thought was later to lead to the break with the fiercely anti-rationalist Jacobi who believed that reason was essentially powerless to come to any knowledge of God at all.

Instead, he said, one had to look deeper at Spinoza's errors. Spinoza had used an abstract concept of being as eternal substance, which indeed was how he described God. Spinozism thus ignored the living and even the spiritual. His mistakes were thus not theological, but ontological: he abolished freedom not because he was pantheist but because he was mechanist and determinist.[38] Spinoza's system was like Pygmalion's statue: it needed the life of reality to be blown into it.[39] Schelling thought he could provide the necessary breath with his conception of the essence of being (the meaning of 'is') as creative. 'God is all things' meant, 'God sustains the being of all things' or 'God underlies all things'. Being and the basic bond of being ('is') was not mechanical, but was to be conceived as will-like, or spiritual. We shall see later that he even equated it with 'love', for love also unites that which is different.[40]

Schelling, in other words, was trying to overcome modern mechanism not by fleeing from reason – or even, says he, from idealism – but instead by the proper use of both. He believed that the errors of mechanism would be overcome only with rigorous philosophy, not by seeking refuge in 'moods'. He saw his philosophy as an attempt to overcome the split between realism and idealism by combining the two.[41] He believed that idealism had grasped the essence of human freedom – as self-sufficiency and self-determination – but that its essentialist ontology has prevented it from grasping the fact of it.

We have already said that idealism interprets being according to the idea, or thought. Idealism is the doctrine of being in which the subject is the basic reality. The nature of idealism therefore depends on the nature of the 'I', and on the relationship between it and the 'object'. Kant took this reasoning a step further and made the true essence of the I not 'I think' but 'I am free', or 'I give myself my own law'. According to transcendental idealism, therefore, being in itself is freedom.[42] As Schelling himself said,

---

36   *Ibid.*, I/7, 348.
37   *Ibid.*
38   *Ibid.*, I/7, 349.
39   *Ibid.*, I/7, 350; on mechanism see also I/7, 397.
40   *Ibid.*, I/7, 408.
41   *Ibid.*, I/7, 350.
42   Heidegger, *Schellings Abhandlung*, p. 111.

The idealistic concept is the true consecration for the higher philosophy of our time, and especially for its higher realism.[43]

In other words, as idealism developed from Descartes onwards, the concept 'idea' modulated from representation (*Vorstellung*) to the appearing to itself of being in absolute knowledge. Absolute being, the being-in-itself of being, came to mean the determination of one's self out of the law of one's own essence, or to be free. Being in general meant to be in itself and for itself, or to will oneself. This is why Schelling said that there was no other being than willing.[44]

But here comes the true difficulty: if the essence of being is freedom, as Hegel, Kant and Fichte all argued, then what is human about human freedom? What distinguishes man's being from being in general? Even if being can be assimilated to thought – or will, or freedom, or whichever other anthropomorphic concept one takes – how does this assimilation allow us to define *human* freedom as something distinct? Or are humans – as the idealists' blood-brothers, the materialists, thought – in fact indistinguishable from the rest of being? That none of the previous philosophers had been able to answer this question explained why all of them, including Kant (for whom the essence of the individual human was the most universal and non-individual thing of all, abstract reason), failed to provide ontologies which could account for individual human freedom. How was one to escape from idealist ontologies in which there is no space for man or human individuality?

Idealism and the Problem of Evil

The answer, Schelling said, was that one has to define human nature. Kant's categorical imperative had been merely formal. The same was ultimately true of Hegel's and Fichte's ethical systems, even though they tried to overcome Kant's shortcomings: despite Hegel's attempt to construct a less abstract theory of the human self, and of value, neither he nor Fichte said quite what the essence was, out of which man was supposed to determine himself. As Schelling says,

> In order to show the specific difference, i.e. the definition of human freedom, mere idealism is not enough.[45]

Not only had idealism been unable to define human freedom, it had not even tried. This is no coincidence, for idealism holds that being *is* reason: that ultimately reality has the same structures as reflexive human thought. There is little specific about humans, therefore. Schelling believed that only he who had truly tasted freedom would feel the urge to understand the whole of being as analogous to it,[46] but this still meant that human nature and human freedom remained to be experienced and

---

43 *Über das Wesen der menschlichen Freiheit* (1809), I/7, 351.
44 *Ibid.*, I/7, 350.
45 *Ibid.*, I/7, 352.
46 *Ibid.*, I/7, 351.

defined. But if this was the case, then the whole idealist project would have to begin again. This is why Schelling wrote,

> Idealism gives us on the one hand the most general, on the other hand the merely formal definition of freedom. The real and living concept of freedom is, however, that it is the capacity for good and evil.[47]

It is the central claim of this book that this single affirmation of Schelling's here blows apart the whole idealist tradition and, with it, the bulk of optimistic philosophy since the seventeenth century. Its magnitude cannot be overestimated. As Schelling himself says,

> This is the point of the deepest difficulty in the whole doctrine of freedom, which has always been felt, and which does not concern this or that system but more or less all of them.[48]

The reason why Schelling's statement here is so important is that all significant philosophical systems since the seventeenth century had understood freedom as the capacity to be rational. No other philosopher of this period had made evil central to freedom: rather they attempted to suppress evil in order to ensure their diluted versions of freedom. To put it another way, evil was in any case largely absent from their basically secular schema. In one fell swoop, with this definition of freedom, Schelling introduced indeterminacy and will into the idealist system: the key concept was not reason, but genuinely indeterminate will, and a will, moreover, which operates with respect to the outside world (being). This shift from the rational to the genuinely voluntary is of the first importance. There can be no doubt that this definition, motivated by Schelling's acute feeling for what Xavier Tilliette has called 'the tentacular powers of evil',[49] constitutes one of the most arresting and decisive elements of his whole philosophy.

The definition of freedom in terms of good and evil opens a vast new area of philosophical and ontological enquiry. If previous modern philosophers had not thought of freedom with reference to evil, this is reflected in (and is perhaps a result of) the fact that there is no space in their ontological scheme for it. If the enquiry into the reality of freedom thus becomes an enquiry into the ontological status of evil, then the metaphysics of freedom also becomes a metaphysics of evil. It is clear that the introduction of a miraculous human capacity to do genuine evil will shatter any system based on rationality, necessity and optimism.

Christian apologists are by and large in agreement that the problem of evil and the question of human liberty are intimately linked, for they agree that the latter causes the former. Many Christians, however, succumbed to the pantheist temptation, and came to see even evil as part of an overall good. In doing so, they often appeared to reduce the seriousness of evil, dissipating it away into a cosmic bonhomie.

---

47 *Ibid.*, I/7, 352.
48 *Ibid.*, I/7, 352.
49 Xavier Tilliette, *Schelling, Une Philosophie en devenir* (Paris: Vrin, 2nd edn, 1992), Vol. 2, p. 479, note 34.

As we have seen, however, traditional Christian teaching is crucially different from the Oriental religions on this point. In Christianity, evil has no ontological status because being is basically good. As Schelling himself is to say, evil wages a war against being. Luther came very close to an Oriental or Gnostic position, to the extent that he thought man was intrinsically evil as a result of his bodily status. Traditional Christianity, however, has insisted that man's separation from God is moral, not ontological: the fault lies in man's free rebellion against God's law, not in his bodily nature and certainly not in the structure of the created world itself.

Christians have often discussed the devil in explaining human evil. According to Jewish and Christian tradition, Lucifer rebelled against God through pride and was cast out of heaven as a result. Augustine was drawing on this long tradition when he said that human evil was a perverted spirit, and that evil was a result of perversion, not nature, and of 'a voluntary falling away from the good'.[50] The Devil was a being who 'did not stand fast in the truth':[51] 'He refused to accept reality and in his arrogant pride presumes to counterfeit an unreality.'[52] This is why Christians have agreed, 'The logic of the devil is the logic of revolt.'[53] The Council of Trent itself argued (against Luther, obviously) that evil came from the malice of the spirit, not from the body, that the passions belonged to the superior parts of the soul, and that they were all the more dangerous as a result.[54] Indeed, Augustine laid the ground work for all subsequent Christian ethics, to the extent that he showed how evil resides neither in matter nor in creation, but in the deliberate free and undetermined choice of man, a choice which is against 'nature' or being.[55]

It is for this reason that, in the *Freedom* essay, Schelling was already convinced that the problem of evil upset all systems: the existence of evil destroyed the possibility of finding a 'system' in the sense of a rational–logical autonomous body of premises and conclusions which could explain being, unless evil itself was held to be rational. Consequently, the introduction of evil as that which perverts or destroys being – for this is how Schelling was to analyse it – would fundamentally destroy the idealist project, which was to establish criteria for morality and being in a way that was self-referential to the individual. With Schelling's definition, freedom could no longer be defined as giving oneself a law out of one's own essence.

Obviously, the essence of being would have to be grasped more deeply if evil was to be included within it. The most obvious problem which evil poses is for any system which sees God as immanent in all being. Being cannot be immanent in God if there is evil; for then God, too, would have evil within Him and would therefore not be perfect.[56] The same difficulty persists if we merely attribute to God the grounding or the allowing of evil, for grounding or allowing is almost the same as authorship.[57]

---

50   St Augustine, *City of God*, Book XII, Chapter 9.
51   *Ibid.*, Book XI, Chapter 13.
52   *Ibid.*
53   Jean Vaquié, *Abrégé de Démonologie* (Vailly-sur-Sauldre: Sainte Jeanne d'Arc, 2nd edn, 1988), p. 26.
54   *Ibid.*, p. 56.
55   St Augustine, *City of God*, Book XII, Chapters 2 and 3, 6 and 9.
56   *Über das Wesen der menschlichen Freiheit* (1809), I/7, 353.
57   *Ibid.*

Another alternative is to deny the reality of evil, by calling it a lesser degree of perfection. (This was Spinoza's and Aquinas' argument, the latter comparing evil to a lack, as blindness is the lack of sight.)

Alternatively, we might consider evil as distance from God. However, this only puts the question on hold, if all being ultimately flows from God.[58] If the cause of things lies in God, then God would be the cause of their distance from Him, and thus of evil.[59] Nor will Manicheism do, for this is merely to destroy reason by throwing oneself into the arms of complete dualism, something against which Schelling fought all his life. Such a solution also risks destroying reason, which is the ability to unify, and to conceive of being as one.

The key point is that Schelling was abandoning the neo-Platonist view that evil was a lack, or that it was the result of finitude. On the contrary, he was emphatically saying that it was the result of human freedom. Concomitantly, Schelling ceased to regard the finite world as intrinsically evil, for that would reduce human evil (and human freedom) to nought. When he considered the various systems of evil on page 355 of the *Freedom* essay, Schelling said quite clearly, 'In the system of emanation, all actual opposition between good and evil disappears.'[60] He made it clear that he was specifically attacking Plotinus for saying that that which is at the bottom of the ontological ladder was evil because it could not produce anything lower.

Because human freedom was the capacity for good and evil, Schelling concluded that evil must have a root which is independent from God.[61] This required finding within God something which is not God. God had to be conceived more deeply, reasoned Schelling, for He was more real than most idealists allowed. Giving voice to the profound realist sentiments which were never far below the surface in Schelling (and which were henceforth to come to the fore), returning to a more theologically orthodox vein, and distancing himself from those Catholic Kantians who thought that God revealed Himself principally in morality, Schelling declared:

> God is more real than a mere moral world order, and he has other, far livelier forces within Him than that ascribed to Him by the deficient subtlety of abstract idealists. The repugnance for that is real, and that which thinks that the spiritual tarnishes itself with all contact with reality, must naturally be blind to the origin of evil. If idealism does not have a living realism as its basis, it will become just as empty and as abstract a system as those of Spinoza and Leibniz, or any other dogmatic thinker. The whole of modern European philosophy since its beginning (Descartes) has this deficiency in common that nature is not present for it, and that it lacks a living ground.[62]

As Heidegger remarked, the sort of idealism which makes God into a purely spiritual being in order to make Him perfect leads to a dilution of the very essence of God;

---

58   *Ibid.*, I/7, 354.
59   *Ibid.*, I/7, 355.
60   *Ibid.*
61   *Ibid.*, I/7, 354.
62   *Ibid.*, I/7, 356.

and this is because in general such thinkers do not have an adequate concept or feeling for being.[63]

> If a philosophy lacks this living basis – which is usually a sign that even the ideal principle in it was originally rather weak – then it loses itself in systems whose abstract concepts like aseity, modifications and so on stand in stark contrast to the fullness and the living force of being. But there where the ideal principle really becomes powerful, but cannot find the mediating and reconciling basis, it engenders a sad and wild fanaticism, which breaks out into self-laceration or, like the priests of the Phrygian Gods, into self-emasculation, which is completed in philosophy by the abandonment of reason and knowledge.[64]

Only fanaticism or nihilism can fill the gap left by the denial of being.[65] It is not fanciful to draw ethical or political conclusions from this, traditional realists having always insisted on ontological realism (on the inherence of objective values in concrete reality) as the only basis for objective morality.

These are exciting statements. However, despite undermining significant elements of idealism, Schelling still also retained important elements of it. In particular, he still believed that freedom was the essence of being. The metaphysics of evil somehow had to be accommodated within this scheme of being. Not only that, but, as we shall see, man is the summit of creation: evil is thus the definitive characteristic of that summit. Schelling's response was that contemporary Nature Philosophy made a distinction between essence or being (*Wesen*) inasmuch as it exists, and essence or being inasmuch as it is the mere ground of existence (*Existenz*).[66] In other words, for every existing thing a distinction had to be made between its ground and its existence. The ground was the basis on which – or rather, out of which – beings stepped out when they exist. Existence was the revelation of the ground.

Although Schelling was no irrationalist, the relationship between the ground and existence he posited here was not a logical one. 'Ground' did not mean a logical ground, from which there flowed a consequence, but a ground in a more literal sense, meaning 'basis' or 'foundation'. In the exchange with Eschenmayer in 1810, Schelling called the ground '*Fundament, Unterlage, Grundlage, Basis*'.[67] Ground was the ground or basis of existence, and was even equated with matter on one occasion in the *Freedom* essay; later, Schelling compared it to the 'nothing' out of which Augustine said the world was created.[68] He tried to explain himself thus:

> This relationship (between ground and existence) can be explained as being analogous to that between gravity and light. Gravity precedes light as its eternal dark ground, which is itself not *actu*, and it flees into the night, while light (the existing) rises like the dawn.[69]

---

63 Heidegger, *Schellings Abhandlung*, p. 124.
64 *Über das Wesen der menschlichen Freiheit* (1809), I/7, 356–7.
65 Ibid., I/7, 357.
66 Ibid.
67 Letter to Eschenmayer, April 1812, I/8, 173.
68 *Über das Wesen der menschlichen Freiheit* (1809), I/7, 373, note 2.
69 Ibid., I/7, 358.

Both gravity and light belong to nature. Light comes out of the darkness, as existence out of the ground, and it reveals that which was hidden; but the darkness remains and supports the light. The light is the lawful and rational, the darkness is chaotic and unformulated. Light and darkness were essential components of being for the pre-modern understanding. Man was believed, especially since the Enlightenment, to stand in the light; his being was that of the light of reason.

The language may be highly metaphorical but the implications are extremely important. The passage quoted above represented the definitive abandonment by Schelling of any belief that the creation was a fall or a catastrophe. His cosmogony here was therefore the very the opposite of that in *Philosophy and Religion*: there was no longer any loss or collapse, but rather an elevation of being towards the light, the truth and God and into existence. This was a very important change.

What Schelling was expressing here, in far clearer language than before, was how he understood that 'real-idealism' which, according to Horst Fuhrmans, is in fact the correct term to describe Schelling's philosophy from its very beginnings.[70] Schelling even suggested that 'the interpenetration of realism and idealism', which he said had been his goal since his earliest writings,[71] was analogous to the key Christian doctrine of the Incarnation:

> Idealism is the soul of philosophy; realism is its body, and only the two of them together makes a living whole. The latter can never provide the principle, but it must be ground and means in which the former realises itself, *and takes on flesh and blood.*[72]

It is difficult to think of a more explicit nod towards traditional Christian metaphysics than this, and Schelling seemed to have understood that he was groping his way back to an ontological scheme which could explain the Incarnation of God as man.

Schelling rejected the doctrine of immanence, if it meant a dead conceptualisation of things in God.[73] Instead, he proposed the notion of becoming as the only one which properly corresponded to the nature of things. God's being, too, was referred to as a becoming, out of the ground into existence, and in Him the ground and the existent were logically and temporally simultaneous. Things were not statically conceived in God, he affirmed, they were in a state of becoming in Him.[74] They could not – absolutely considered – *become* in God, since they were infinitely different from Him. To be different and separate from Him, therefore, they had to have a different ground from Him. Things could not become in God insofar as He is existing and fully Himself; they could only become in God in that which was not God Himself, that is, the ground of His existence.[75] Thus the ground was that in and out of which things became in the world. Schelling wrote,

---

70 Horst Fuhrmans, Introduction to Reclam edition of *Freedom* essay, p. 21.
71 *Über das Wesen der menschlichen Freiheit* (1809), I/7, 355.
72 *Ibid.*, I/7, 356, emphasis added.
73 *Ibid.*, I/7, 358, end.
74 *Ibid.*, I/7, 358–9.
75 *Ibid.*, I/7, 359.

If we want to bring this closer to a human level, we can say this is the longing felt by the eternal One to give birth to Himself. It is not the One itself, but it is eternal with Him.[76]

The concept of longing is entirely heretical, and it emphasises how often Schelling mixed orthodox theological concepts with heterodox ones. Here, his writing sounds suspiciously like the myth of the Upanishads, according to which the Absolute felt lonely without creation. Plotinus also held a similar view. In the Judeo-Christian view, by contrast, the creation is a totally free, willingly undertaken, act of giving. Schelling's purpose in using the concept of longing was to show how desire lies at the foundation of being itself, how it informs its very structure (later in the essay, 'longing' is to modulate into 'love'). Schelling said that this ground was will – the will to bear God, the ungroundable unity – but it was a pre-conceptual will, without understanding. In the world as revealed, everything seemed lawful and ordered but underneath there was chaos which seemed as if it could break through at any moment.[77] This was the ungraspable basis of the reality of things, and it was out of this incomprehensible ground that understanding is born.[78]

Schelling compared the ground to Platonic matter, a formless sea striving towards the light of the understanding.[79] Only God lived in pure light. Despite the highly mystical nature of these speculations, Schelling's insistence on the ground (the 'real') as the basis of empirical reality was in opposition to absolute idealism, which denied that there was being before thought. Schelling was here saying that being was the union of two principles, the ideal and the real, the latter being informed by the former.

The question then was still, 'Why does God create something, man, which has the capacity for evil?' The answer is that God revealed Himself in something which resembled Him in his freedom, man. Although ontologically separate from Him, man sprang from God's very being, although he was not God himself. It is standard Biblical metaphysics to emphasise the metaphysics of creation, and God's revelation in that creation – even though God's ultimate revelation was, obviously, of Himself as Christ, a very important point which Schelling unfortunately omits. St Augustine underlined the ontological priority of the Creator, especially *vis-à-vis* our liberty which is created, but, as Tresmontant insists,

> The fundamental mystery of creation is this creation of a liberty which is itself invited to be creative, co-creative (that is, with God). ... What is most difficult to grasp in Christian metaphysics and theology, because it is the masterpiece of everything, is this coexistence, this co-creation, the cooperation of two creative liberties, that of God, which is ontologically primary, and that of man, which is raised up to God.[80]

---

76 *Ibid.*
77 *Ibid.*, I/7, 359.
78 *Ibid.*, I/7, 359–60.
79 *Ibid.*, I/7, 360.
80 Claude Tresmontant, *La métaphysique du christianisme et la naissance de la philosophie chrétienne: problème de la création et de l'anthropologie des origines à Saint Augustin* (Paris: Seuil, 1961), pp. 67 and 70.

Schelling affirmed that God revealed Himself because He longed to. The ground was like human longing which demanded a 'nameless' good.[81] Being without understanding, the ground had no speech, and it could not give a name to its longing. In God, this longing was the longing for revelation, that is, for that inner reflexive representation through which, because there is no other object for Him, God considered Himself in His own image.

> This representation is the first in which God, absolutely considered, is realised, although only in Himself, it is in the beginning within (*bei*) God, and is the God engendered in God Himself. This representation is simultaneously understanding – the word of that longing, and the eternal spirit which feels the word and the eternal longing in itself, moved by love, which it is itself, speaks out the word, so that now understanding together with longing becomes freely creative and all-powerful will, and which comes to form in originally lawless nature as in its element or as its implement.[82]

Schelling was heretically implying that God somehow needs the world in order to reveal Himself: it is a theosophic or Gnostic idea to say that the Absolute becomes conscious of itself, and to say that God needs creation in order to become conscious of itself and thus become absolute spirit.[83] On the other hand, he was being orthodox when he said that God is moved by love, and that love motivates the longing. Spirit is, therefore, not the highest: love is. (Later, Schelling was to affirm this explicitly.[84]) Schelling developed a theory of creation to sustain this metaphysics of charity, which in turn sustained certain ontological and epistemological positions. In Schelling's description of the creation, God creates a unity, and speaks out the Word of creation, *legein*, *lesen*. The Word is the naming of that unity which has been gathered together.

The Nature Philosophy had shown how matter and soul interact, and now Schelling explained creation as the transfiguration of the dark principle into light.[85] The light shines into the darkness, and by speaking out the word, the unformed ground gathers itself to unity. Although separate, the ground and existence are linked by the eternal bond which Schelling called 'soul'. It is clear – although not much else is in this difficult passage – that Schelling was trying to show that the lawfulness of creation is a result of the understanding having formed something out of the dark ground.

Although the idea that the creation occurs as a result of a split within the Absolute[86] – between the ground of God's existence and His existence – is thoroughly heretical, it is clear that Schelling saw the creation as a matter of informing formless matter, which he sometimes called 'nothing'. He wanted to argue that, because creation reposes on the interplay of two forces, all beings and all of nature contain dark

---

81   *Über das Wesen der menschlichen Freiheit* (1809), I/7, 360.
82   *Ibid.*, I/7, 361.
83   Tresmontant, *La métaphysique du christianisme*, p. 33.
84   *Über das Wesen der menschlichen Freiheit* (1809), I/7, 405–6.
85   *Ibid.*, I/7, 362.
86   *Ibid.*, I/7, 361.

and light principles within them.[87] The first principle was that through which things are separated from God, or that through which they are merely in the ground. This principle is the self-will of creation. Because this dark principle has not come to union with the light (the principle of understanding) it is blind, selfish will. Against this there stands the universal will of the understanding, the principle of light, which needs the first principle and subjects it as an instrument.[88] Man, of course, is the summit of this creation.

> In man there is the whole power of the dark principle and in him there is also the whole force of the light. In him there is the deepest abyss and the highest heaven, or both centres. The will of man is the kernel, hidden in eternal longing, of the God who is only in the ground; it is the divine regard locked in the depths which God saw when he took the will to nature. In him (in man) God loved the world ...[89]

This is why the new doctrine of the creation was so important. In spite of all the Gnosticism and theosophy, Schelling was here clearly saying that the world did not come about because of a catastrophe, but because of a free and loving decision by God. This love reached its peak in his decision to create something free like himself, man. The creation was therefore emphatically not the result of some 'geometrical necessity' but of 'freedom, spirit and self-will'.[90] Freedom, indeed, like life, was God's supreme gift. Evil did not come about until man misused that freedom: it was certainly not inherent in the physical world itself.

Here, then, Schelling espoused traditional Biblical metaphysics. Man was the summit of creation, and he showed the meaning of it.[91] His liberty was not one gift among many, but the defining fact about creation's supreme product. God can create another being which is called to become god-like itself, to the extent that it is free.[92] Indeed, it was precisely Schelling's insistence that the created world was ontologically separate from God that the accusations of pantheism, formulated by Reinhold and later Jacobi, were unfounded. As Tresmontant says, 'The metaphysics of Christianity is a metaphysics of the creation, but also of liberty.'[93]

It is only in man, moreover, that the divinely ordained and rightful order of the universe can be inverted. The unity of the light and the dark is developed in man but it is only in man that the dark principle can be perversely raised to the level of the understanding.[94] Only man can reverse the rightful order of the two principles of creation: 'This is the possibility of good and evil.'[95] (The notion that man has a light and a dark principle within him, which he struggles to keep in the right order and under control, is strongly reminiscent of Plato's portrait of the human soul as a

---

87   Ibid., I/7, 362–3.
88   Ibid., I/7, 362–3.
89   Ibid., I/7, 363.
90   Ibid., I/7, 376.
91   Tresmontant, *La métaphysique du christianisme*, p. 654.
92   Ibid., p. 652.
93   Ibid., p. 68.
94   *Über das Wesen der menschlichen Freiheit* (1809), I/7, 363.
95   Ibid., I/7, 364.

charioteer with two horses, one good and the other bad, in the *Phaedrus*.) Man can raise the particular will up to the place where the universal will should be:[96] he can invert, or rather pervert the natural order of things, overthrowing divine unity, and this ability is man's capacity for evil.[97] It is as if man had become a counter-God. By contrast, when man keeps his particular will in the ground so that the divine relationship of things remains, he preserves divine will and order and thus does good.

Human freedom did not consist in 'liberating' oneself from the iron laws of mechanical necessity in the real world, as Descartes and Kant would have it, but rather in this terrible capacity for perversion of the order of being. Schelling made it clear that he believed that modern philosophy ('dogmatism') had been unable to grasp the essence of evil because it had no understanding of personality, 'that is, of selfhood raised to spirituality, but instead only the derivative concepts of finite and infinite'.[98] It is of the first significance that Schelling's metaphysics of evil should be based upon the notion that freedom consists in man's relationship to being and God, rather than to himself. As many of the early Church fathers insisted, evil spirits turn away from God. They turn their thoughts away from that which is intelligible – true being – and, abusing their faculties, take pleasure instead in the contemplation of their own bodies.[99] This turning away is a Platonic theme, but Christianity is more dogmatic: man's sin is not just a matter of 'distance' from God, or of a neglect of what is true in favour of the bodily passions, but rather a *crime*, an act of deliberate disobedience and rebellion.

Schelling too spoke of evil in a much more vivid way than a neo-Platonist. His notion of evil was far more akin to the Biblical notion of a crime. He was quite clear about the importance of this:

> All other notions of evil leave the understanding and the moral consciousness unsatisfied. They basically all rest on the destruction of evil as a positive opposite, and on the reduction of it to the so-called *malum metaphysicum* or the negative concept of the imperfection of nature.[100]

In Schelling's analysis, evil was a matter of conscious choice in favour of evil things: it was not the result of a lack of knowledge. Schelling used the analogy of physical illness, in which he made use of contemporary medicine – especially as interpreted by Franz Baader – to show that evil was like illness in consisting of an inversion or perversion of the natural order, an analogy of obviously Biblical inspiration.

But Schelling also used this argument to define the nature of evil. This is one of the most striking parts of the essay, for he equated evil not with matter or nature, but with mind. Unlike the Gnostics or the neo-Platonists, therefore, he did not consider the world of created matter, or even the human body, to be evil or even the cause of evil; he did not think that the way to salvation lay in knowledge. On the

---

96 *Ibid.*, I/7, 364.
97 *Ibid.*, I/7, 365.
98 *Ibid.*, I/7, 370–71.
99 Tresmontant, *La métaphysique du christianisme*, pp. 679–80.
100 *Über das Wesen der menschlichen Freiheit* (1809), I/7, 367.

contrary, he insisted that the problem of evil depended not on God, but on man's freedom. Schelling insisted that it was not in the nature of evil to be merely a lack or a limitation.

> It is the understanding which gives the principle of evil, even though it does not thereby become evil ... even the simple reflection that it is man, the most perfect of all visible creatures, that is the only one capable of evil, shows that its root cannot lie in lack or deficiency. In the Christian view, the devil is not the most limited creature, but the most limitless.[101]

Schelling even took St Augustine to task for describing evil as a privation. As Marc Maesschalk writes, 'Evil acquires its consistency in Schelling's thought (*Freedom* essay, VII 370 and 371) as an inverted relation. At the centre of this inversion, there is not so much the attraction or the seduction of the sensory, nor even the weakness of the flesh, but rather the totalitarian spirit (*Stuttgarter Privatvorlesugen*, VII 468 and 476) which wants to divert all truth to its own ends.'[102]

The self-will which raises itself up to the universal will wants to impose its own perverted order in place of the divinely ordained one. This perversion is a full-blooded and conscious negation of the divinely-ordained order of being. In animals, the dark principle operates just as much as in man, but an animal can never invert the natural principles in the way man can.[103] For Schelling, evil was spiritual. To err from the good did not require a lack of mind, it required a perverted mind. This is why Schelling called evil a 'lie' in the *Freedom* essay: you cannot lie unless you know the truth and knowingly reject it.[104] He believed that all other explanations of evil were intellectually unsatisfactory, for they denied its fullness.[105]

When using his analogy of illness, Schelling wrote that illness was the true image of 'evil or sin'. He thus equated the two. But the word 'sin' is meaningful only in the context of religious faith: Schelling was seeking to make theology philosophical and philosophy theological and, in doing so, turning against two centuries of philosophical secularism. Indeed, Schelling himself pointed out that his insistence on evil was what we might call 'politically incorrect' for his time.

> The opinions which our age has on this point – an age which is far more trivial (*leicht*), and which has driven philanthropism so far that it denies the very existence of evil itself – have not the slightest connection with such ideas.[106]

If evil is chosen, willed or desired, as Schelling affirmed that it is, then this implies, contrary to the rather excessively optimistic idealist tradition, that human reason is not infallible. Further, the idea that a Kantian thief is merely irrational in desiring to keep his loot, is inadequate according to this view, for evil is more than a logical mistake.

---

101   *Ibid.*, I/7, 368.
102   Maesschalk, *L'anthropologie politique et religieuse de Schelling*, p. 27.
103   *Über das Wesen der menschlichen Freiheit* (1809), I/7, 372–3.
104   *Ibid.*, I/7, 366.
105   *Ibid.*, I/7, 367.
106   *Ibid.*, I/7, 371.

This doctrine is also contrary to those systems of theogony – such as that espoused by Schelling in *Philosophy and Religion* – according to which metaphysical history is cyclical, with souls returning to the One after having been separated from it. In Plotinus, for instance, everyone is saved. On the contrary, as Christianity has always insisted, salvation is not inevitable; perdition is possible; and the possibility of the individual's refusal to collaborate in God's creation is inherent in human liberty itself.[107]

Schelling said that idealism was the only school of thought which had put freedom where it belongs. 'The free action flows immediately from that which is intelligible in man', said Schelling, giving what he believed to be a more accurate gloss of Kant than Kant himself had given.[108] For man to be able to determine himself, he must do so out of his essence; but this essence must itself already be determined. The essence out of which an individual determines himself could not, argued Schelling, be some undetermined general thing, such as reason, but had to be the intelligible essence of this particular man. Moreover, each individual was also personally responsible for that essence: Schelling argued that man chooses his own nature.[109]

In other words, Schelling was trying to modify Kant by clearly giving each man an individual essence, rather than by dissolving individuality away into the universality of reason. Schelling tried to say that the choice of one's essence (character) occurs at the moment of creation, when individuals leave what Schelling explicitly refers to as the golden age.[110] From this primeval choice flowed the individual's nature, and all the actions which he accomplishes. Those (he did not mention them, but he meant Calvinists) who sought to place the choice for good or evil in God, condemning some by predestination to hell and others to heaven, had extinguished all freedom from their system.[111] Schelling also believed in a kind of predestination – a man's free actions flow necessarily from his nature – but he insisted that each man had somehow chosen his own nature.

In the orthodox Christian view, predestination is of course ruled out. God provides the means for men's salvation by giving His only son to be martyred on the cross. Christianity is a deeply individualistic creed: salvation is individual, not collective. However bizarre his views seemed, Schelling's insistence, first, that the alienation of man from God is moral, not metaphysical (man can choose good or evil) and, second, that each individual makes his choice (albeit at the moment of creation) meant that he was clearly not in the same camp as Plotinus or Hegel.

Schelling argued that if man allows evil to act through him, he raises selfish will to the status of universal will instead of making it into a basis or an organ.[112] If in man the dark principle of selfhood is infused with light, and at one with the light, then God, as eternal love, as really existing, is the bond of forces in him.[113] Good

---

107 Tresmontant, *La métaphysique du christianisme*, p. 67.
108 *Über das Wesen der menschlichen Freiheit* (1809), I/7, 384.
109 *Ibid.*, I/7, 385.
110 *Ibid.*
111 *Ibid.*, I/7, 387.
112 *Ibid.*, I/7, 389.
113 *Ibid.*, I/7, 389–90.

could be worked only with 'divine magic'[114] – was this a nod towards the Catholic doctrine of grace? Evil, by contrast, was falsehood, and the enemy of all creation. It tempted man with non-being, and is the product of pride. Schelling wrote,

> Thus the beginning of evil is when man steps out of actual being into non-being, out of truth into the lie, out of light into darkness, in order himself to become creative ground, and with the power of the centres which he has within him, to reign over all things.[115]

This passage recalls what St Augustine wrote on the Devil – that he rebelled against God and the truth.[116] Schelling was at pains to show the violence of evil: the 'non-being' of which he wrote here was not a mere lack but instead a virulent denial of the truth. It is an attack on creation itself. Schelling wrote,

> Flagrant sin does not fill us with regret as weakness or incapacity does, but with fright and horror, a feeling which can only be explained because sin strives to break the word, to soil the ground of creation, to profane the mysteries.[117]

Evil was therefore the conscious choice of perversion. Like Mephistopheles in Goethe's Faust – *'Ich bin der Geist, der stets verneint'* – evil wants to destroy and to enjoy its destruction, to say 'No' to everything, and to push being into unbeing. For Schelling, when man was evil, he was the anti-God. In other words, evil could only be understood in the context of what can only be called a religious view of the world. Schelling was convinced that evil was not unfaithfulness to oneself, as Kant would have it, but instead impiety towards God and His creation.

In the *Freedom* essay, Schelling elaborated on his view of religion itself, in terms which were practically lifted word for word from the 1804 *System*.[118] He wrote in the essay that a good man is one who does immediately what is right without pausing to make a conscious Kantian choice about it.[119] He specifically said that the original meaning of 'religion' was 'being bound', from *religio*. He said that Cato never did the right thing out of mere respect for the law, but because he could not have acted in any other way. This strength of character is the kernel out of which blossoms true individual dignity: 'The highest is by definition not always the most general',[120] Schelling said in an explicitly anti-Kantian remark. Faith was not merely a matter of holding certain things to be true, but a fundamental trust, an absolute confidence in the divine which excluded all choice. However, Schelling did not subscribe to Schiller's doctrine of the *'schöne Seele'* (beautiful soul) which was a common way of attacking Kantianism at the time. He believed that the doctrine of the *schöne Seele* simply reduced morality to taste.[121]

---

114 *Ibid.*, I/7, 391.
115 *Ibid.*, I/7, 390.
116 St Augustine, *City of God*, Book XI, Chapter 13.
117 *Über das Wesen der menschlichen Freiheit* (1809), I/7, 391.
118 *System der gesammten Philosophie* (1804), I/6, 558.
119 *Über das Wesen der menschlichen Freiheit* (1809), I/7, 392.
120 *Ibid.*, I/7, 393.
121 *Ibid.*

But how did God view the reality of evil? Is His revelation the result of blind necessity, or is it a free act? Did He will evil, and, if so, how is this will to be assimilated to His perfection? It is very significant that Schelling attacked those who treat God as a 'logical abstraction':[122] if He were such, he says, then His self-revelation would flow out of Him only as a result of logical necessity. God would be only the highest law out of which all things flow, without personality and consciousness. By saying this, Schelling was again distancing himself from Spinozist or neo-Platonist theories. Schelling contrasted this with his own idea of God as a personal and living unity of forces. Indeed he attacked Fichte and Spinoza by name as representatives of 'pure idealism' who, just like the 'pure realists' make God into an impersonal concept.[123] On the contrary, and as Bruaire emphasises, Schelling insisted that God was a person, a free being who manifests Himself in freedom.[124] Schelling argued very strongly that he understood creation to be the result of a free act of God:

> The will of love [unlike the will of the ground] is simply free and conscious, precisely because it is this [that is, love]; the revelation which follows from it is action and deed. The whole of nature tells us that it [that is, nature] is in no way there merely because of a geometrical necessity; there is not just pure reason which is in it, but personality and spirit ... otherwise the geometrical understanding which has reigned for so long would long since have penetrated it ... Creation is not something which is just there, it is an act. There is nothing which follows from general laws, but instead God, that is, the person of God, is the general law, and everything which happens, happens because of the personality of God; not according to an abstract necessity ...[125]

This emphasis on a personal, loving and creating God, which Schelling was to develop more deeply in his later work, especially in the *Weltalter* (the 1827–1829 Munich lectures) which is hugely important for its Christian ontology, also enabled Schelling to introduce another crucially important theological element into his system: that of a 'humanly suffering God'.[126] 'Without the concept of a humanly suffering God,' he wrote, 'which is common to all the mysteries and spiritual religions of antiquity, the whole of history is incomprehensible. Even Holy Scripture differentiated between periods of revelation, and posited in the distant future the time when God would be all in all, that is, when he would be entirely real (*wirklich*).'[127] It is obvious that the strongest expression of a suffering God is the Cross, and, as Schelling was to make clear in the later philosophy, the meaning of history to which he referred here was that love is the foundation of all being.

Schelling argued, therefore, that the 'system' with the question of whose existence the *Freedom* essay began, was in the divine understanding. God was not just a system: He was life. All existence needed to be conditioned in order that it be personal, and God's was no exception. Were there no selfishness, there would only

---

122 *Ibid.*, I/7, 394.
123 *Ibid.*, I/7, 395.
124 Claude Bruaire, *Schelling ou la quête du secret du l'être* (Paris: Seghers, 1970), p. 48.
125 *Über das Wesen der menschlichen Freiheit* (1809), I/7, 395–6.
126 *Ibid.*, I/7, 403.
127 *Ibid.*, I/7, 403–4.

be death, and the good would be somnolent: there was no life without a struggle. The good without operative selfhood was no good at all. If God had decided not to create anything for fear of evil, then evil would have won over the good and over love. Indeed, if God had abolished the will of the ground, he would thereby have abolished the conditions for His very own existence and personality.[128] It was the very aim of creation for evil to be banished into non-being, and for independent things to come back to God.[129] Conversely, evil needed to (ab)use the good in order to be evil. The end of revelation was thus for evil to be pushed out, away from the good, and to be declared non-being. For love was the highest – higher, even, than spirit.[130]

It is with this declaration – that mind is not the highest – that Schelling, perhaps unwittingly, sounded the death-knell for German idealism. If love lay at the origin of being, then logic did not. It was perhaps inevitable that this death-knell should be sounded by a metaphysical tract which, despite some neo-Platonist and Gnostic (that is, proto-idealist) elements, was based on some of the most important elements of traditional Church metaphysics, which are in turn indissolubly linked to an ontology and an epistemology which are both inimical to idealism. To put it bluntly, if creation is the free gift of God, and if man is the highest being of creation who can use his reason and his freedom to apprehend the good, then his cognitive and reasonable faculties must be capable of telling him how the world really is. In such a scheme, it would be perverse to conceive of him as shut up in his private sense-perceptions. As Marc Maesschalk remarks,

> The theogonic drama just sketched shows, through its final historical meaning, the impotence of the concept to produce for itself the self-mediation of the Absolute in nature and in history ... Schelling thus opposes the monism of Fichtean and Hegelian idealism, which are incapable of positing an absolute, irremediable separation provoked by the liberty of man and irreducible to the necessary (dialectic) process of the Idea in history.[131]

Since Schelling's concept of freedom was precisely not derived from reflections on the opposition between man and nature, it both separated man from the world and also included him in it. Those philosophies which had tried to bridge the gap between man and the world – perhaps by making the real world disappear as a real and different entity – conversely destroyed human freedom.

Schelling paused at this point in the essay to come back to the central point, the distinction between ground and existence. It is clear that he wanted to avoid dualism, but how then could the two principles of ground and existence be resolved? There had to be a common middle ground between them. 'What else can we call it but *Urgrund* or even better *Ungrund*', he asked.[132]

This is the point at which Schelling definitively broke with Biblical metaphysics too. His suggestion that there was something anterior to God – that God was not the

---

128 Ibid., I/7, 403.
129 Ibid., I/7, 404.
130 Ibid., I/7, 405–6.
131 Maesschalk, *L'anthropologie politique et religieuse de Schelling*, p. 101.
132 *Über das Wesen der menschlichen Freiheit* (1809), I/7, 406.

Absolute and that indefinable chaos preceded Him – comes from ancient Oriental cosmogony, not from Christianity. Meanwhile the idea that the Absolute is not pure simplicity, but rather contains the ground of its own existence, comes from Jakob Böhme.[133] Schelling argued that there must be a common essence or being which preceded all duality, existence and ground. It had to precede all opposites, so these could not be present in it. It could not even be identity, but only absolute indifference. It could have no predicates, but was not therefore nothing. Real and unreal, light and dark, good and evil, could never be predicated as opposites of the *Ungrund*. Indeed, without this absolute indifference, there would be no difference and no duality of principles: far from being a merely logical difference, that between ground and the existent was a real one.

Schelling affirmed that the essence of the ground, like that of the existent, could only be that which preceded all ground, and was therefore the *Ungrund*. It could only be such, however, if it divided into two eternal beginnings. The *Ungrund*, which he described as 'the Absolute', divided itself so that life, love and personal existence could be.[134] Love bound things together which could exist separately. The primordial *Ungrund*, indeed, which came before the ground, was the love which is all in all. The one being therefore divided itself into two operative beings, ground and existence. Only God was the unity of the two.

Schelling believed that he had developed a system which included freedom and evil in a way which was neither dualistic nor which negated or mitigated the nature of evil. In his system, every concept had its place. He concluded that a system which contradicted faith could never be true: religion and reason were strictly compatible. Reason, however, was not the source of heroism or the progress of mankind, as everyone claimed.[135] It was only in personality that there was life; and all personality reposed on a dark ground. Understanding could come out of the ground only by dialectic and science. Philosophy was animated by the dialectical unity of love and wisdom, as her name suggested. It was only by studying the world and nature that we could decipher the revelation of God; and the study of this was the true object of religion and of philosophy.

The *Freedom* essay, in other words, represented the beginning of Schelling's move towards more traditional Christian ontological positions. There was still a long way to go in his development, but the doctrine of evil as revolt was a crucial turning-point. The essay represented a decisive break with the kind of secular, self-contained systems of thought for which his contemporaries and idealist predecessors were famous, and from which contingency was effectively banished. In contrast to them, Schelling had insisted that human freedom was a capacity for good and evil, and this introduced a genuine element of unpredictability into the history of the world. In this sense, his system was not like theirs, for the true possibility of evil as rebellion represented a rupture for that kind of system.

---

133 On the influence of Böhme on Schelling's *Freedom* essay, see Frederick O. Kile, *Die theologischen Grundlagen von Schellings Philosophie der Freiheit* (Leiden: E.J. Brill, 1965), especially Chapter 3, 'Jakob Boehmes Einwirkung auf Schelling', pp. 28ff.

134 *Über das Wesen der menschlichen Freiheit* (1809), I/7, 408.

135 *Ibid.*, I/7, 413.

Schelling disliked systems in this sense. He quoted Leibniz, who wrote, 'I have found that the majority of sects are right in a good amount of what they affirm, but less so in what they deny.'[136] Schelling's feelings on this matter were close to one of the supreme concerns of traditional ontological realists, who find systematism prone to detachment from reality. In methodological terms, realists consider systems to be mistaken because they pretend to offer an understanding and a knowledge of the whole of reality based on a set of self-evident axioms. Even if such a principle were true, it would engender only a partial understanding of reality, and would also be liable to exclude all other perceptions of reality. It is this which makes the will to system so arrogant, a product of the sin of pride. This, realists fear, leads either to moral relativism or to authoritarianism: either everything goes, because right and wrong are not believed to exist outside the human mind, or rigid systems of positive morality have to be arbitrarily promulgated in order to fill the void. Without the fixed point of objective reality which the mind can apprehend, ontological nihilists rush in where angels should fear to tread. A more modest approach to the richness and facticity of being is more seemly.

And yet, the doctrine of the ground and existence, which was so central to Schelling's ontology, gives us cause to ask whether Schelling answered his own initial question ('Why does the Absolute go out of itself?'), or whether he merely postponed answering it by pushing the explanation into the mysteries of the *Ungrund*. He did, after all, insist in the *Freedom* essay that there could be such a thing as a system of freedom, providing that one did not think of system in too simplistic a way. The creation of the world may arise from the interaction of the ground and existence, but what is the cause of this splitting of the *Ungrund*? This was never made clear. Indeed, as Heidegger said, this left Schelling with an unexplained dualism. If so, then he failed to overcome Kant; and if creation was unexplained, then he failed to create a system. Are the structures of being therefore ultimately incapable of systematisation after all? If they are, then Schelling failed where the idealist project itself failed, in the attempt to create a self-grounding system of reason.

Or did Schelling achieve victory by turning a defeat into a strategic withdrawal? Surely it is normal that we can say nothing about the Absolute. Can the Absolute be included in a system of reason if we can say nothing reasonable about it and if reason must always remind itself that it belongs to the finite? As his thinking developed, and as the *Freedom* essay showed, Schelling increasingly insisted on the absolute and unthinkable priority of freedom – God's freedom – over everything else. In the essay case, however, Schelling seemed to finish by endorsing Kant, who similarly posited freedom as a necessary but inarticulable foundation for the possibility of reason and thought itself. After all, Kant himself had written, 'Unconditional necessity which we, as the last bearers of all things, need so indispensably, is the true abyss for human reason.'[137]

---

136 Quoted in *Über die Natur der Philosophie als Wissenschaft* (*Erlanger Vorträge*, 1821–25), I/9, 213.
137 Kant, *Kritik der reinen Vernunft*, 3. Hauptstück, *Das Ideal der reinen Vernunft*, 5. Abschnitt, *Von der Unmöglichkeit eines kosmologischen Beweises vom Dasein Gottes*, B 641;

Schelling quoted this very passage in the *Introduction to the Philosophy of Revelation*.[138] He did indeed come very close to Kant in his conviction that the Absolute was inarticulable. The difference was that he tried to apprehend something of this mystery, and to comprehend it within his philosophy, something which Kant rejected as impossible by definition. In the ethical domain, moreover, Schelling's philosophy, from the *Freedom* essay onwards, was also to be very anti-Kantian: morality was not defined in terms of man's relation to his own essence or to the moral law, but rather in terms of man's relationship to God and the order of the universe.

Meanwhile, although his later work revealed a certain rapprochement with Kant's concept of the inaccessible transcendent, Schelling displayed an increasing focus on, and an increasingly firm rejection of, the Hegelian and Fichtean idea (which he had himself earlier espoused) that the world was a logical or necessary progression from God or the Absolute. Schelling's theory of the creation became more and more Christian and anti-Hegelian. For him, the creation was a totally free act of God: it did not proceed from any necessity whatever, and certainly not from a Hegelian dialectical necessity. Creation existed only because God had willed that it exist, and the act of creation could not 'be conceived in any way through mere reason or *a priori*'.[139] Attacking Hegel elsewhere, Schelling wrote, 'The realisation (of God's word) is a freely chosen act which absolutely interrupts logical consequence.'[140] It is difficult to be clearer than this.

Schelling's later thought, then, turned on the same question of the progression of the finite world from the Absolute. He kept trying to give theological and ontological (not logical) reasons for the creation of the world, of which the *Ungrund* in the *Freedom* essay was but the first attempt. In the *Weltalter* he made a vain attempt to find a sufficient cause for God's act, but by 1827 he had concluded that the common mistake of all previous philosophy had been that it assumed a 'merely logical relationship of the world to God'.[141] We shall examine the implications of this statement in the last two chapters of the book.

Kant and Hypocrisy

An important source of inspiration for the *Freedom* essay, especially for the account Schelling gives of evil, is Kant's *Religion within the Bounds of Pure Reason*. Although there certainly are similarities between the two works, the differences help us to understand Schelling's position more clearly.

A 613, p. 543 in Immanuel Kant, *Werke*, Vol. 2, ed. Wilhelm Weischedel [Wiesbaden: Insel, 1956]).

138 *Einleitung in die Philosophie der Offenbarung* (1842–43), II/3, 163.

139 *Ibid.*, II/3, 303.

140 *Zur Geschichte der neueren Philosophie* (Münchener Vorlesungen) (1833–34), I/10, 159.

141 Schelling, *System der Weltalter* (1827–28), 14. Vorlesung, ed. S. Peetz, (Frankfurt am Main: Klostermann, 1990), p. 57.

To the extent that Kant wrote a lot about evil – and about the good and evil principles in man – there are some apparent similarities. On closer inspection, however, it appears that the Kantian vision is different. Kant's definition of freedom was not 'the capacity for good and evil' but rather the capacity 'to determine oneself out of the laws of one's own essence'.[142]

Secondly, and crucially, the Kantian code of ethics was logically separate from religion. Just as Frederick the Great had built the palace of Sanssouci ('without a care') to escape being pestered by priests and women, so Kant wanted his moral system to be independent of any interference by clerics or God. 'Morality in no way needs religion', Kant declared in the very opening sentence of the book's preface. Morality needed the idea of no higher being: indeed, said Kant (and this is a classically Lutheran thought), it would be contrary to morality itself to act in pursuit of an extraneous goal such as eternal life.

Schelling, by contrast, held a specifically religious view of morality and human freedom. They were defined in terms of man's relationship to God. Schelling equated evil with revolt against the divine order, or perversion of it, and it is for this reason that he used the explicitly religious term 'sin' to describe it. Leszek Kolakowski has lucidly explained why religion cannot be reduced to morality: 'Whoever says seriously, "I have sinned", does not mean merely that he has committed an act which is contrary to a law, but also that he has offended against God; his words are not meaningful unless they are referred to God and thus to the whole area of faith ...'[143] Thus, Schelling's definition of liberty, as we have seen, was not one in which the decisive issue was the relation of the self to the self but instead that of the individual to God.

Thirdly, Kant emphasises 'the radical, inborn evil in human nature'[144] in a way Schelling does not. Man was 'evil by nature',[145] wrote Kant, whose famous *bon mot* about man as a crooked timber he used at least three times.[146] Schelling was less Lutheran in this respect.

Let us examine the area of greatest similarity with Schelling, which was Kant's statement that evil consisted in inverting the correct order of the two principles in man, self-love and reason.[147] Kant wrote,

> The difference between a man who is good or evil does not lie in the difference between the motivating force which he brings into his maxims (not in their substance) but rather in

---

142 Ibid., p. 3 (*Vorrede zur ersten Auflage*).
143 Kolakowski, *Religion*, p. 168.
144 Kant, *Die Religion innerhalb der Grenzen der bloßen Vernunft*, Erstes Stück, III, Reclam edition, p. 39.
145 Ibid., Reclam edition, p. 38.
146 In Kant, *Die Religion innerhalb der Grenzen der bloßen Vernunft*, III. Stück, Erste Abteilung, IV; in Kant, *Metaphysik der Sitten, Einleitung in die Rechtslehre*, para E; and in Kant, *Ideen zu einer allgemeinen Geschichte in weltbürgerlicher Ansicht, Sechster Satz, Werke*, ed. E. Cassirer (Berlin, 1913), Vol. IV, p. 158.
147 Kant, *Die Religion innerhalb der Grenzen der bloßen Vernunft*, Erstes Stück, III, Reclam edition, pp. 43–4.

the subordination of them (in their form) ... Consequently the man is evil only insofar as he inverts the moral order of motivating forces, by taking them into his maxims.[148]

For Kant, evil occurred when man brought self-love into his maxims, and this in turn was a result of perversion (*Verkehrtheit*) of the heart.[149] Such perversion was caused by the fragility (*Gebrechlichkeit*) of human nature, its inability to be strong enough to follow the right principles. It was a result of the impurity (*Unlauterkeit*) in man's motivating forces.

This was close to Schelling but crucially different. For Schelling, evil consisted in man's wilful perversion of the order of the universe: it was not merely the consequence of misdirected desire. For Kant, falsehood, impurity and deception – in short, hypocrisy – was what prevented the good from developing within people, and the goodness or evil of a person's heart depended on its capacity to take the moral law into its maxims. For Schelling, by contrast, evil waged a deliberate and pitiless war against the very basis of being itself.

The differences are even clearer in the light of Kant's explicit rejection of the very thing which Schelling was describing when he discussed evil:

> The maliciousness (*Bösartigkeit*) of human nature is therefore not also evil (*Bosheit*) if one takes this in the strict sense of the word, that is, as the intention (*Gesinnung*) to take evil as evil as a motivating force into one's maxims (for this is diabolical); but rather wrongness (*Verkehrtheit*) of the heart ...[150]

This is precisely what Schelling did mean by evil: he made it explicitly clear in the *Freedom* essay that he did consider human evil to be precisely diabolical.

Schelling, St Augustine and Aquinas on Evil

Frequent references have already been made to St Augustine, whose work exercised an undeniable influence on Schelling. Indeed, Schelling mentioned him twice in the *Freedom* essay. Like Schelling, Augustine wrote a book on freedom (*De libero arbitrio*) and, like Schelling, Augustine drew inspiration from Plotinus (whom Schelling also quotes). Both men, indeed, were led back to Christian orthodoxy by neo-Platonism. The question of sin was as much at the heart of *De libero arbitrio* as in the *Freedom* essay. Augustine insisted there that the origin of evil did not lie in God but in man: to do evil was to submit one's will to one's passions, and to prefer one's personal satisfaction to the eternal law. Augustine explained that sin consisted in overturning the divine order and that it was the result of a perverted and disordered soul. Augustine insisted that evil did not lie in things, but in the bad use man made of them; and that only will could turn man's spirit away from the right path.[151] Like Schelling, Augustine was to push his enquiry to the point where

---

148 *Ibid.*, p. 44.
149 *Ibid.*, p. 45.
150 *Ibid.*
151 St Augustine, *De Libero Arbitrio*, I, XVI, 34.

human reason must fall silent, and he concluded that there existed a reality which was superior to human reason.[152]

However, the more arresting similarities are perhaps those with Aquinas. A contemporary commentator has discussed the similarities between the question of evil as it is treated by Schelling and the Angelic Doctor.[153] St Thomas considered that the essence of will (*voluntas*) was to tend towards the good (*bonum*) and to desire it. Indeed, will was will insofar as it did this.[154] Similarly, the good was good insofar as it was desired by the will: each side of this equation was purely analytic. (Indeed, all things tend to the good in St Thomas, but only that which has knowledge of its aim can tend towards it by itself.[155]) Formally, therefore, the will cannot will evil. Will desires good in itself, *bonum simpliciter*. As a spiritual force, will was fundamentally determined by God, just as intellect was: both participated in the first truth which is God.[156]

St Thomas thus distinguished spiritual from non-spiritual will, and he employed the surprising term 'divine' to qualify man's reasonable nature. As such the objects of our will and intellect were transcendent and universal: the perfect and unchanging good dwelt within us and animated our spiritual appetite. The divine principle determined the spiritual will of man immutably. This sounds suspiciously pantheist or mystical, and indeed in his time St Thomas (like Schelling!) was suspected of being a pantheist.[157] But Aquinas stepped back from making the final plunge into pantheism by showing how man can be both spirit (infinitely determined) and also a creature (finitely determined).[158]

He did this by distinguishing between man's essence, which is *quodammodo* (in some way) divine, and his existence, which can never be perfect. Man can never make his perfect essence real. This failure or inability did not lie in the essence itself, which remains perfect and divinely determined, or indeed in any accidents of this essence. It lay rather in the difference between essence and being. Clearly, in any creature, there is a difference between essence and existence – only in God are the two the same – but with spiritual beings (that is, man) the difference between essence and being lies at the very heart of its act of being as such. As Welte writes, 'The spiritual creature indeed "is" its own being through its essence as spirit, as it can perfect that being on its own in knowledge and desire.' Thus in knowledge and striving the difference must appear between eternal essence and deficient being.[159]

Man was thus driven to his own realisation by himself: he was driven by an inner principle, not by something outside him. Every act of a man's life was determined and made possible by the divine principle which characterises every spiritual being

---

152   *Ibid.*, II, VI, 14.
153   Bernhard Welte, *Über das Böse, Eine thomistische Untersuchung* (Freiburg im Breisgau: Herder, 2nd edn, 1986).
154   Aquinas, *De Veritate*, Quaestio XXII, Articulus 5.
155   Aquinas, *De Veritate*, Quaestio XXII, Articulus I, paras 2 and 3.
156   Welte, *Über das Böse*, pp. 10–14.
157   Emilio Brito, 'Schelling et la bonté de la création', *Nouvelle Revue Théologique*, 108/4 (July–August 1986): 505.
158   Welte, *Über das Böse*, pp. 15–19.
159   *Ibid.*, p. 20.

as such. However, this action of the divine principle was incomplete, as man is a creature: were he not, then his actions would have divine clarity and perfection. Thus man always remains in hesitant indeterminacy with respect to that which he is in virtue of his nature. Men are de-coupled from the ground of their actions and thus from themselves.[160] (Christians obviously consider that men have their ground in God, which is why Schelling is at his most Christian when he associates religiosity with utter commitment to the good, without choice. A man for whom it is impossible not to do the good he knows, said Schelling, is religious and conscientious to the highest degree. It is obvious that this notion of 'conscientiousness' is utterly at variance with Kant's, for it is grounded in God and not in human autonomy.[161])

Here, indeed, lies the ground of evil: in the relationship between the spiritual and infinite ground and essence of the will to its own finite reality. A spiritual creature is necessarily deficient because the finite spiritual will can never be certain of itself and of its own essential ground in its acts, and yet it can never be dissociated from it either.[162] The togetherness of these two differing determinations makes evil possible. Welte writes, 'A purely infinite will could only be good, a purely finite will however can be neither good nor evil in the real sense of the words.'[163] Man, by contrast, who was neither, could cease to will that which he always and necessarily wills in his essential ground, that is, the good. He could will things of which he knows, in his essence, that they are not good.[164]

There are clear similarities between this and what Schelling wrote on page 364 of the *Freedom* essay, as Welte shows (even if he skims over the slight difference between the Thomist distinction, which is between essence and existence [*esse*], and Schelling's, which is between essence or being [*Wesen*] inasmuch as it exists, and essence or being inasmuch as it is the ground of existence.) As Welte writes, keeping in mind the very different angles from which the two philosophers have come to such similar conclusions,

> Schelling recognises, like St Thomas, that the ground of evil is not to be found in the concept of freedom as pure indeterminacy; he recognises like him that the spirit, wherever it is, is as such a 'spirit in God'. Schelling also recognises, in a totally analogous way to St Thomas, that there is a duality in the human spirit, a difference of itself to itself, through which alone the finite spirit differentiates itself from the infinite. And in *this* difference he sees the possibility of good and of evil, that is the ambiguous possibility of the spirit to be one with itself and with its ground, but also to fall away from both.[165]

And as Bernhard Casper also shows, the Thomist analysis – as emphasised, was the case with Schelling – is characterised by the fact that the question of evil is analysed in terms of man's relationship to God. What the two philosophers have in common is

---

160 *Ibid.*, p. 22.
161 *System der gesammten Philosophie* (1804), I/6, 558; *Über das Wesen der menschlichen Freiheit* (1809), I/7, 392.
162 Aquinas, *De Veritate*, Quaestio XXIV, Articulus 7.
163 Welte, *Über das Böse*, p. 22.
164 Aquinas, *De Veritate*, Quaestio XXII, Articulus 6
165 Welte, *Über das Böse*, p. 26.

precisely that they see the phenomenon of man's responsibility is rendered possible only by the infinite–finite constitution of man, and that the freedom to do good and evil cannot be separated from the question of man's relationship to God. As Schelling makes clear, evil can be accomplished only by a personal act. The main difference between Schelling and Aquinas, however, as Brito points out, is that Schelling is far more interested in demonology than St Thomas. Evil for the latter is more a matter for the metaphysics of creation, and less of anthropology or demonology.[166]

---

166 Brito, 'Schelling et la bonté de la création', p. 507.

Chapter 5

Christian Cosmogony and the End of Idealism (Schelling's Development from Stuttgart to Munich, 1810–27)

Freiheit ist unser und der Gottheit Höchstes.
(Freedom is the highest thing that we and the Godhead possess.)

Schelling[1]

Stuttgart Private Lectures (1810)

It was in the Stuttgart Private Lectures (*Stuttgarter Privatvorlesungen*) that Schelling developed many of the themes which were incipient in the *Freedom* essay. In those lectures, neo-Platonist elements were still strong, but in keeping with his more realist approach, Schelling was by now rejecting the notion that a philosophical system should be invented. Instead, he said that the system existed – in God's understanding – and that therefore it was up to man to find it instead of to construct it.[2] In a suitably and perhaps proto-Hayekian attack on the constructivism of his enemies, he called the desire to invent such a system oneself 'highly illiberal'.[3]

Schelling made his religious position clear by saying something very important about his idealist predecessors. Unlike the dogmatic system of Leibniz and Wolff, which only brought in God at the end, he said that the Absolute (God) was the principle of the whole of his philosophy and that it 'lives and moves in God'.[4] Schelling also accepted – unlike Hegel – that the unconditional could not be proved, any more than a geometrician needed to prove the existence of space before practising his science. 'In the same way,' he said, 'philosophy does not prove the existence of God, but instead recognises that it would not even be present without an absolute or God.'[5] Being, in other words, precedes thought; and thought does not need to be – indeed, cannot be – presuppositionless.

In seeking to explain the creation of the world, Schelling wrote even more clearly in these lectures than before that the creation was a free act. 'There is therefore an

---

1   Schelling, *Urfassung der Philosophie der Offenbarung, Vorlesungen aus dem Jahre 1831/1832*, ed. W.E. Erhardt (Hamburg: Meiner, 1992), p. 79.
2   *Stuttgarter Privatvorlesungen* (1810), I/7, 421.
3   *Ibid.*
4   *Ibid.*, I/7, 423.
5   *Ibid.*, I/7, 423.

explanatory ground of the world in the freedom of God,' he affirmed explicitly.[6] We can say, therefore, that freedom, which was always Schelling's central preoccupation, pushed him to adopt a Christian ontology. Schelling significantly nuanced the notion of 'longing' which he had introduced in the *Freedom* essay: 'God Himself is linked to nature through voluntary love, He does not need it, and yet does not want to be without it.'[7] This statement removed the last traces of Orphism from his thought.

This freedom with which God created the world was to become Schelling's obsession in the later period. His emphasis on it clearly undermined the anonymous inevitability of the Hegelian dialectic. As Josef Anton Stüttler emphasises, 'Nowadays, thought has freed itself too much from the groove of idealism to be able to credit the novelty of this difficult breakthrough (that is, by Schelling). The whole structure of decades of effort seemed threatened with the undermining of its foundations by one of its own masters: the *beata necessitas boni*, the last driving force of German idealism, suddenly stood faced with the free creating God.'[8] (By *beata necessitas boni* Stüttler means the essential driving element of the whole dialectic occurrence in Hegel's system of absolute idealism.) Again and again – in the last version of the *Weltalter* for instance – Schelling was to return to the story of Genesis in order to grasp the act of liberty by which the world first came into being.

There are two schools of thought about Schelling's later writing: those who think that Schelling completed or perfected idealism, and those who think he went beyond or even destroyed it by returning to a truly Christian philosophy.[9] As we shall see later, when we return to the emphasis on creation as a free act, the argument here is that the latter view is right.

On the other hand, Schelling claimed that the notion of creation *ex nihilo* needed to be nuanced. He said that it was as a result of a misunderstanding of the notion of non-being that the idea of creation out of nothing arose. In reality, he said, creation occurred out of non-being, not out of nothing. Investigation into this, the concept of non-being, was the 'cross of all philosophy',[10] the very phrase he had used in the *Freedom* essay. In other words, although the general direction of Schelling's thought was clear, his attenuation of the truly free nature of the creation meant that, in the Stuttgart Lectures, he still did not manage to think of the act of creation as truly *ex nihilo*. Nonetheless, he used the distinction between not-being and nothing to emphasise his peculiarly powerful concept of evil: evil, he said, was (like illness) against nature. It was therefore the quintessential non-being, from one point of view; on the other hand, it also had 'a terrible reality'.[11]

---

6   *Ibid.*, I/7, 429.
7   *Ibid.*, I/7, 453.
8   Josef Anton Stüttler, 'Das Gottesproblem im Spätwerk Schellings', *Scholastik*, 36 (1961): 73–83.
9   The former position is taken by Walter Schulz, *Die Vollendung des deutschen Idealismus in der Spätphilosophie Schellings* (Stuttgart and Köln: Kohlhammer, 1955) and the latter by Horst Fuhrmans (even though he does not like Schelling's late philosophy). Emilio Brito also takes the latter position.
10 *Stuttgarter Privatvorlesungen* (1810), I/7, 436.
11 *Ibid.*, I/7, 437.

Schelling said that the more absolute we make God, the more He loses personality and becomes abstract. This was wrong: instead we had to emphasise the analogies between Him and a man.[12] Indeed, he argued that the whole process of creation was nothing other than the personalisation of God.[13] Schelling repeated the analysis of personality which he first presented in the *Freedom* essay: man, like God, had two principles in him, a dark one and a light one. The process of self-development consisted of bringing the dark principle into light. Just as consciousness begins when we realise that there are these two principles in us which can divide, so God's consciousness begins when he separates Himself from Himself and conceives of an opposition within Himself. Creation is the bringing forth of the higher, the divine, into that which was shut out.[14] The dark principle in God is matter, which is the unconscious part of Him: His main purpose is achieved in man.[15]

What we see here, in other words, is a renewed comprehensive rejection of the kind of Orphism we encountered in *Philosophy and Religion*. Schelling also rejected the impersonal and monistic systems he had elaborated before 1804. (As we have seen, *Philosophy and Religion* itself represented an important step towards a more traditional Christian position, and away from logical–ontological monism, for in that work appeared for the first time the notion that the creation was an event.) Creation was not only the result of a free and loving decision by God, but also a raising up out of darkness into light. God's love drew creation up towards Him and became fruitful as a consequence.[16] Man's relationship to God was like that of a flower to the sun: by the operation of its rays, it grows up out of the dark earth towards the light.[17] The 'night in which all cows are black' is transfigured into daylight full of colour by the Word of God: *lux in tenebris lucet*.

The maintenance of things in being required precisely this maintenance of the right order of light and dark principles. Creation, in other words, was neither a malediction nor a fall. Time was a gift, not something to be escaped from, and in emphasizing this, Schelling was turning against Plato, Hegel, Fichte, Spinoza and the whole mystic tradition which once interested him. Above all, as Marc Maesschalk notes, this is because the Gnostic or mystic tradition is incompatible with the immediate experience of liberty in real, daily life.[18] Such theories are, therefore, in the strictest sense, unethical. Similarly, Schelling's repeated affirmation that man is the summit of creation, and that he is that which gives it its meaning, showed that the purpose of the Absolute was achieved only through revealing itself in history. The sense of the Absolute was not to be found in abstract, other-worldly contemplation.

Schelling made significant references to Holy Scripture. Although elements of mysticism certainly remained – the notion that the creation was a 'letting down' of God by Himself, or a contraction, (*'dieser Akt der Einschränkung oder*

---

12   *Ibid.*, I/7, 432.
13   *Ibid.*, I/7, 433.
14   *Ibid.*, I/7, 434.
15   *Ibid.*, I/7, 435.
16   *Ibid.*, I/7, 453.
17   *Ibid.*, I/7, 457–8.
18   Marc Maescchalk, *L'anthropologie politique et religieuse de Schelling*, p. xxvii.

Herablassung Gottes'[19]) is cabbalistic, for instance – and although Schelling's continuing interest in mysticism has been rightly commented on widely,[20] as Father Tilliette argues, Schelling's reading of the Bible 'protected him from Gnosticism and conjured away the bewitchment of Böhme'.[21] Christian Danz also insists that in the later philosophy (that is, after the *Stuttgart Lectures*) all traces of Gnosticism were eradicated,[22] leaving the field open for traditional Christian doctrines. As he approached the later philosophy, Schelling was to insist that philosophy should not only not be in contradiction with faith, but that it should even take certain dogmas of faith – especially freedom and providence – as its very axioms.

Political Overtones

Schelling believed that, like nature itself, man must struggle out of darkness into light. He must push the darkness in himself down and away, and call in the light of the good, the true and the beautiful to take the place of the perversion of evil.[23] Because of man's sin, the world had lost its originally happy unity. Among other things, Schelling concluded, 'The state is the result of the curse cast upon man.'[24] This is a clearly Augustinian thought, recalling what is said in *The City of God* about the state. It was precisely because man had abandoned the unity of God that he needed to subject himself to a physical unity. While the state was necessary, said Schelling, the unity it promoted was always only temporary and precarious: other, moral forces were needed to sustain ethical life. The state could not do so itself, even if people sometimes believed otherwise.

Schelling made a specific attack on the inherent authoritarianism of 'the French Revolution and Kantian concepts' – a conjunction of terms which is music to a conservative ear – and he also attacked Fichte for his own despotic political philosophy. Indeed, Schelling began to see more and more clearly that modern contractarian political philosophy – that is, that current of thought which severed the foundations of the state from any transcendent or eternal values, placing them instead merely in the needs and desires of men – could be a source of despotism. In 1807 he had argued against social contractarianism, saying that it attempted to derive rights within society from philosophical presuppositions which explicitly ignored society (such as Rousseau's state of nature):

---

19 *Stuttgarter Privatvorlesungen* (1810) I/7, 429.

20 See notes 1 and 2 in Marc Maesschalk, *L'anthropologie politique et religieuse de Schelling*, Editions de l'Institut supérieur de Philosophie, Louvain-la-Neuve (Paris: Vrin and Leuven: Peeters, 1991), p. 192 for an extensive bibliography.

21 Xavier Tilliette, *Schelling, Une Philosophie en devenir* (Paris: Vrin, 2nd edn, 1992), Vol. 1, p. 636, note 14.

22 Christian Danz, *Die philosophische Christologie F.W.J. Schellings* (*Schellingiana*, Vol. 9, ed. Walter E. Erhardt) (Stuttgart-Bad Cannstatt: Frommann-Holzboog, 1996), p. 83.

23 *Stuttgarter Privatvorlesungen* (1810), I/7, 459.

24 *Ibid.*, I/7, 461.

> Upon this maddest of claims of absolute egoism there has been built a science, quite foreign to the ancients, a so-called Natural Right, which gives to everyone the same right to everything without any internally binding duties, but with only outward force; a doctrine which knows no positive actions but only interdictions and limitations, in which everyone pleases himself by contemplating his basic rights, in order better to enjoy what remains for him in self-satisfying isolation. From this sad source of contemptible selfishness, and enmity of all against all, arose the state through human agreement and mutual contract.[25]

For Schelling, it was unacceptable that the state be philosophically founded in this way. If there were no divine principle behind it, then the state operated in a moral vacuum. It was impossible therefore to will it, to love it, or even to be virtuous within it. It made a nonsense of all morality. In his view, furthermore, virtues could develop only in a public space, not in private (as Kant had thought). Instead, the philosophy of the modern state was predicated on the view that states can do without virtue, and instead they can just mechanically restrict and control people's actions.

There is no doubt in Schelling's mind that rationalist philosophy was responsible for political revolutions, and that the attempt to create states based on merely mechanical conditions, and without a transcendent reference point, could end in tyranny.

> Thus it is quite natural that at the end of this period, in which people spoke of nothing but freedom, the most logical minds who followed the idea of a perfect state have finished up by advocating the worst forms of despotism (for example, Fichte's *geschlossener Handelsstaat*).[26]

This is very much in keeping with the criticisms of Fichte outlined in Chapter 2. Above all, Schelling went on, revelation was that which elevated man from his downcast state.[27] Schelling's analysis of the two principles in the universe led him to adopt an ethical system with strikingly Greek overtones. Virtue, like being itself, said Schelling, required limitation in order to exist. Moral merit consisted in overcoming one's own will, and in mastering one's selfhood. Indeed, good could only be good if it included evil within it which has been overcome.[28] Human liberty was not just domination of the subjective principle, as Kant thought, nor acceptance of the objective principle, as Spinoza and Hobbes had argued, but rather the fruitful interplay of the constant tension between both.

Similarly, understanding itself existed only after a victory over madness and the irrational. 'The basis of understanding itself is therefore madness.'[29] It was only by transfiguring the non-being into being – by undertaking an act analogous to the creation itself – that goodness and understanding came about. In other words, it is only when limited by being or God that human freedom can be properly understood and made valuable. Once again, Schelling drove home the crux of the matter: freedom was to be described ontologically and with reference to God, not just with reference

---

25 *Über das Wesen deutscher Wissenschaft* (1807), I/8, 10–11.
26 *Stuttgarter Privatvorlesungen* (1810), I/7, 462.
27 Ibid., I/7, 423.
28 Ibid., I/7, 467.
29 Ibid., I/7, 470.

to causality: 'The defenders of freedom generally think only about how to show the independence of man from nature. But they forget man's inner independence from God, his freedom with respect to God, precisely because this is the most difficult.'[30] Precisely because man was on the cusp between the non-being of nature and the absolute being of God, he was free from both – for good or ill.

Evil

It is evil which convinces us of the existence of freedom, said Schelling. 'For evil is nothing other than the relative non-being (*das relativ Nichtseiende*), which erects itself to being and pushes out true being (*das wahre Seyende*). It is from one point of view a nothing, from another a highly real being (*ein höchst reelles Wesen*).'[31] Leszek Kolakowski has had the same thought. Emphasizing how evil is primary in human experience, he writes,

> In an experience which is not enlightened by divine wisdom, good and evil ... do not appear ... We owe the moral distinction to our participation in taboos. And the distinction appears in experience as a result of those of our acts which violate a taboo and *thus bring disorder into the world*. In other words, we really know what is good by knowing what is evil and we know evil by doing it ... And the first evil I know is the evil in me ... In the experience of failure, in seeing Being defeated by nothing, the knowledge of Being and of good emerges. By becoming evil myself I know what evil is and I know what good is.[32]

As in the *Freedom* essay, Schelling insisted that evil arose from the perversion of order. Error was not lack of spirit, but rather 'perverted spirit'.[33] Evil did not come from the body: the body is like a flower from which either honey or poison can be drawn. On the contrary,

> Evil is in some senses the most purely spiritual, for it wages the fiercest war against all being (*Seyn*), indeed, it tries to destroy the very ground of creation. Anyone who is slightly acquainted with the mysteries of evil ... knows that the highest corruption is the most spiritual, that in it everything natural and sensory – even pleasure itself – disappears, and that the demonic-devilish evil is far more foreign to pleasure than is good.[34]

Once again, Schelling's powerful depiction of evil has great philosophical importance, as well as carrying great conviction on a human level. Evil is not a lack of faith to oneself, but rather to God. It is not a result of the weakness of the will, but rather of intensely strong, perverted will – in short, of hubris or demonic possession. It is not even the pursuit of pleasure. Schelling even recalled the myth of the angels who, led by Lucifer, had rebelled against God. He explicitly said that their act was

---

30   Ibid., I/7, 458.
31   Ibid., I/7, 459.
32   Leszek Kolalowski, *Religion, If There is No God* (London: Fontana, 2nd edn, 1993), pp. 187–8, emphasis added.
33   *Stuttgarter Privatvorlesungen* (1810), I/7, 468.
34   Ibid., I/7, 468.

analogously hubristic to man's own rebellion: both rebellious angel and rebellious man wanted to be 'master of the world without God, out of his own power'.[35] As we saw earlier, this is precisely the diabolical concept of evil which Kant ruled out. It recalls Saint Ambrose's assertion that evil is not a living substance (as the Manicheans held) but rather the perversion of a soul which has left the true path of God.[36] Schelling, indeed, was firmly in the Augustinian and Thomist traditions in denying that evil has any real being (it wages a war against all being), but he refused to reduce it to a simple privation, as Leibniz had done.

The most strikingly Christian element in the Stuttgart Lectures was the explanation of the historical and philosophical sense of the Incarnation at the end. Having described the full horror of evil, Schelling explained that it was not eternal. Through the 'perfect incarnation (*Menschwerdung*) of God' the rupture in the world, brought about by human sin, was healed.[37] The Church succeeded the state as the institution which brought about external and internal unity. The 'contraction' of God is not, therefore, a matter of God abandoning Himself to history, but rather of divine condescension in which He remains the master of time. Humanity was not the centre of history, as the moderns thought, God was. It is this thought which was to introduce the decisive change from Schelling's 'negative' to his 'positive philosophy'.[38]

Difficulties with Idealism

Schelling argued that, like Spinoza, Leibniz had got caught up in a one-sided account of being. His ontology had been absolutely idealist and the only force was representation. Schelling said that materialism was the other side of the same coin, for it regarded matter as dead and deprived of spirit: this is exactly the argument made by the Church against both idealism and materialism. By contrast, said Schelling, matter is vivified and made alive by the divine. (The notion of God breathing life into matter is obviously lifted from religious tradition: 'Credo ... in Spiritum Sanctum, Dominum, *et vivificantem*.') Even worse, said Schelling, was mechanism of the mind: he referred to (unnamed) French materialists, but he might just as well have mentioned Hobbes. The one-sidedness of their vision was as bad as that of absolute idealists like Fichte and perhaps Kant. Although Kant was open to different interpretations, he said, Fichte was clear: he interpreted the whole universe as I. There was, according to Fichte, nothing outside us at all: there was just the subjective I.[39] In terms which mirror very closely the Church's traditional opposition to Kant, Fichte and idealism, Schelling described this philosophical development as 'a process of decomposition' which had been initiated by the absolute dualism posited

---

35   *Ibid.*, I/7, 479.
36   St Ambrose, *Hexameron*, I, viii, 31, PL, XIV, 140: see Claude Tresmontant, *La métaphysique du christianisme et la naissance de la philosophie chrétienne: problème de la création et de l'anthropologie des origines à Saint Augustin* (Paris: Seuil, 1961), p. 686.
37   *Stuttgarter Privatvorlesungen* (1810), I/7, 484.
38   Maesschalk, *L'anthropologie politique et religieuse de Schelling*, p. 103.
39   *Stuttgarter Privatvorlesungen* (1810), I/7, 445.

by Descartes.[40] By separating mind from body, Descartes had set modern thought off on the wrong track.[41] This initial Cartesian step was itself the result of the mistakes of modern metaphysics, according to which everything had to be learned anew from the point of view of thought which was certain of itself. It introduced a metaphysics which was foreign to any reflection on the Absolute. As Marc Maesschalk glosses, 'This is the drama of the *Aufklärung* [Enlightenment] which is in fact the first time the death of God is thought – the isolation of man in a world where he seems to be the only bearer of meaning, faced with purely repetitive nature and an uncertain history.'[42]

This is about as traditional critique of Enlightenment philosophy as one could imagine. Schelling had begun to sound like the great twentieth-century Thomist, Etienne Gilson: 'These ideas of Holy Scripture', he wrote – referring to his own remark that 'everything was made through God' – 'were proscribed because they were not understood, as it is indeed generally the mystery of Enlightenment thinkers (*Aufklärerei*) … that they have made a virtue out of the limited nature of their intellectual faculties.'[43] Had not Gilson introduced his great book, *L'être et l'essence*, with the cutting phrase, 'Everything happens, throughout history, as if fear of the first principle of wisdom were itself the beginning of wisdom.'[44] Schelling's whole purpose in the Stuttgart Lectures – a purpose conceived in the *Freedom* essay and developed in the late philosophy – was to return from this dead modern philosophy back to traditions which had been obliterated by modern thought.

The Ages of the World (1811–27)

As time went on, the Gnostic (and thus idealist) elements were progressively eradicated from Schelling's philosophy. With the *Weltalter* (*The Ages of the World*), Schelling accomplished the breakthrough which was to lead him to the philosophy he was to call 'positive'. Intellectual intuition was finally abandoned as a means of reaching the Absolute. Human reason, feeling, will and liberty were said to require not a God remaining in his absolute separateness but instead a living God who had created man in His image. Schelling's emphasis on this was one of the most traditional aspects of his thought.[45] Schelling felt an ineradicable need to know God as He is.[46]

Neither science nor sentiment will be satisfied with a God who is not, because He is Being itself (*er ist das Seyn selbst*), who is not living, because He is Life itself, who is not

---

40   *Ibid.*, I/7, 444.
41   *Ibid.*, I/7, 443.
42   Maesschalk, *L'anthropologie politique et religieurse de Schelling*, pp. 86–8.
43   *Stuttgarter Privatvorlesungen* (1810), I/7, 442.
44   Etienne Gilson, *L'être et l'essence* (Paris: Vrin, 1994), p. 9.
45   Emilio Brito, 'L'anthropologie chrétienne de Schelling', *Revue théologique de Louvain*, 18 (1987): 12.
46   Xavier Tilliette, *L'absolu et la Philosophie: essais sur Schelling* (Paris: Presses Universitaires de France, 1987), p. 167.

conscious, because He is pure consciousness. They both demand a God who is there in a manner different from his essence (*Wesen*), who is not just knowledge according to his essence but who expressly and particularly knows, and whose operation is not contained in his essence but rather in the deed, that is, in a manner different from his essence.[47]

It is clear that God cannot be a person if he is identical with His creation. It is also clear that making God a person radically separates any philosophy from heathen pantheism. Although reason demands that God exist, the concept of God is not described by rational knowledge, for God is greater than human reason.

It is for this reason that Schelling concluded the 1811 *Weltalter* with an explicit appeal in favour of 'realism' as opposed to 'idealism':

> Realism undoubtedly has the advantage over idealism. Whoever has not recognised the priority of realism wants development without previous development; he wants the bloom and the fruit which comes from it without the hard shell which encloses it. Just as being (*das Seyn*) is itself the force and the strength of the eternal, so is realism the force and strength of all philosophical systems. Even in this respect it is true that the fear of God is the beginning of all wisdom.[48]

Schelling emphasised again that creation was God's free act. 'Everybody recognises that God created beings which are exterior to Him, not in virtue of a blind necessity, but with the greatest liberty.'[49] The world did not come into being as a result of a logical process or as the result of a collapse in the Absolute. 'God freely created the world – by which no logical fact is expressed, but rather a deed is given ... If we assume a factual relationship of God to the world, then we cannot assume a merely logical one and *vice versa*.'[50] Theologians who assumed such a logical relationship, said Schelling, had blundered with their very starting-point, the concept of God.

On the contrary, as Fuhrmans points out, Schelling showed that the creation had introduced no change in God: it was simply the expression of God's liberty.[51] This view also encouraged Schelling to abandon his previous pantheism. Indeed, by this, the time of the last version of the *Weltalter*, Schelling was arguing that the idea of God – His essence – was not, after all, one of pure identity with Himself, nor one of absolute solitude, but instead simply the freedom to create. 'God's action does not consist in positing Himself (he does not need that) but rather in positing something else.'[52] Like Aquinas, Schelling insisted, 'God's being is the cause of all other being.'[53]

---

47   *Die Weltalter* (1811), I/8, 238.
48   *Ibid.*, I/8, 344.
49   *Ibid.*, I/8, 210.
50   Schelling, *System der Weltalter* (1827–28), 3. Vorlesung, ed. S. Peetz (Frankfurt am Main: Klostermann, 1990), p. 11.
51   Horst Fuhrmans, *Schellings Philosophie der Weltalter* (Düsseldorf: L. Schwann, 1954), p. 349.
52   Schelling, *System der Weltalter* (1827–28), 34. Vorlesung, p. 153.
53   *Ibid.*, p. 152.

This in turn forced him away from the key theme of his earlier philosophy, namely the immediacy of the relationship between the finite and the infinite. As Maesschalk writes, 'It is liberty which succeeded in smashing the conceptual straightjacket of idealist panlogism.'[54] Jankélévitch agrees: 'The "incarnation" of the Absolute is not a natural function of the Absolute; more and more, Schelling comes to regard *Einbildung* as an *event*.'[55] Whatever Schelling himself may have said to the contrary, Jankélévitch continues, transcendental idealism knew nothing of this.[56] Horst Fuhrmans concurs: 'Idealist dialectics, convinced that being in all its forms can be developed from the divine without any gap, came into antinomy with the Christian doctrine of the freedom of the divine. To have grasped *this* antinomy is, I believe, the hour of birth of Schelling's later philosophy.'[57] Finally, as Emilio Brito points out, Schelling's theological notion of creation becomes the very axis on which the whole later philosophy turns.[58]

God's being was thus the foundation for all being. He is the Lord,[59] the giver of life. Like Aquinas, Schelling placed heavy emphasis on God's goodness as the cause of creation, something which distinguishes Schelling from Hegel – as Franz Baader saw at the time – for the creative action of Hegel's God is motivated only by the need to realise Himself as spirit, and not by any love.[60]

The great lesson of the *Weltalter* was therefore the discovery of the absoluteness of the beginning, and of the fact that the relationship between God and the world was historical and not logical. It is also of the first importance that Schelling made clear his linear conception of time, in opposition to the cyclical notions of time he associated with logical philosophy, and which we analysed in Chapter 1 as belonging in the 'Oriental' category. He established that unless the world is understood as lying in temporality, then no linear progression of time could be conceived, and everything was in eternal return because the cosmos itself was eternal.

This led Schelling to remind us that philosophy should study the existing temporal world as it is, in order to extract truth from that study. It should not develop systems which assume that truth inhabits some separate eternal realm, like mathematics. In other words, philosophy should turn away from the essentialist ontologies and mathematical systems examined in Chapter 2 and elsewhere. Only by doing this could philosophy break through the barriers of this world – for if this world is eternal, then it presumably cannot. The world is contingent and temporal, and we should accommodate ourselves to that fact (not least because it is the will of God)

---

54 Maesschalk, *L'anthropologie politique et religieuse de Schelling*, p. 194.

55 Vladimir Jankélévitch, *L'odysée de la conscience dans la dernière philosophie de Schelling* (Paris: Félix Alcan, 1933), p. 4.

56 *Ibid.*, p. 5.

57 Horst Fuhrmans, 'Dokumente zur Schellingforschung', *Kant-Studien*, 47 (1955/56): 276.

58 Emilio Brito, 'La Création ex "nihilo" selon Schelling', *Ephemerides Theologicae Lovanienses*, 60 (1984): 298ff.

59 Schelling, *System der Weltalter* (1827–28), 24. Vorlesung and ff.

60 Franz von Baader, *Sämtliche Werke* (Leipzig, 1855), Vol. 9, p. 334; quoted by Emilio Brito in 'La création chez Hegel et Schelling', *Revue Thomiste*, 87 (1987): 265.

and look for meaning in the given, rather than seeking to prove that everything exists logically.

> Time is the starting point of all investigation in philosophy, and there can be no explicable development without a definite explanation of time. The past cannot be conceived without it, and before the pulse of time beats with life again, science will not find its liveliness either ... Thus we will never achieve satisfactory results if we regard things which are there (*die vorhandenen Dinge*) as necessary. Everything is only a product of time and we do not know the simply true, but only that which that time allows to which we are restricted (*eingeengt*). We are beginning to understand that eternal truths are in fact nothing other than propositions which have been extracted from present circumstances ... It is philosophy in the true sense of the word when the whole organism of things can be deduced from the times of the this world (*von den Weltzeiten*).[61]

We saw in Chapter 1 how time was a positive element in the Christian tradition, as the medium of intelligibility, and that it is not conceived as a consequence of degradation or as the badge of an illusory world. Oswald Spengler captured brilliantly this positive Christian assessment of time by pointing out that there are clocks on church spires, but not on minarets. As Siegbert Peetz shows, this theory of time has four consequences: that philosophy is not to be likened to geometry (that it is not a pure *Vernunftwissenschaft*); that philosophy is not about propositions whose opposites are impossible; that a philosophical system should be modelled more on music than mathematics; and that the world should be studied in its entirety, and especially in terms of the relations of one thing to another, rather than in terms of individual propositions which can be treated individually.[62] These are all realist and anti-rationalist thoughts.

Schelling ceased to understand the creation as a process of (God's) personalisation, and instead started to understand it as the act of a person, God. This element is absolutely key: because of it, the *Weltalter* are a testimony to Schelling's rapprochement with Biblical tradition. It is only with a personal God that Schelling can think of the Absolute as 'both absolute and historical, both infinite and finite, both transcendent and immanent'.[63] As Josef Anton Stüttler so rightly remarks, 'In the free creative act of God, God raises the ideally being into reality. In this, Schelling comes much closer to the Christian understanding of the relationship between God and the world: God sees in eternity the being of the world as a possibility in his divine essence; but he only raises it in time into reality with the free creative act. Thus the real world is not the eternal correlate of God. Through perception of this, Schelling effects a further abandonment of the pantheism of the earlier philosophy: God is now the free creator, the master of being.'[64]

---

61   Schelling, *System der Weltalter* (1827–28), 4. Vorlesung, p. 16.
62   Schelling, *System der Weltalter* (1827–28), p. xi.
63   Manfred Durner, 'Zum Problem des "Christlichen" in Schellings "Weltalter" und Spätphilosophie', *Philosophisches Jahrbuch*, 89 (1982): 25–38.
64   Stüttler, 'Das Gottesproblem im Spätwerk Schellings', p. 79.

Munich Lectures (1833–1834)

Descartes

It was these considerations about the origin of the world which led Schelling to make his great critique of transcendentalism and idealism, contained principally in the Munich lectures of 1833–1834. He attacked the problem at its root, namely the idealist attempt to derive being from thought. 'In the *cogito*', Schelling wrote, 'Descartes thought that he had recognised being and thought to be immediately identical.'[65] This is precisely the traditional realist objection to Descartes.[66] Schelling said that in fact, the 'cogito' established only my – perhaps transitory – being as something which is thinking. I do not think all the time, and even when I do, it only proves that I exist in a certain way, that is, not unconditionally.[67] Descartes had therefore not established the unconditional being of the self: the being which I ascribe to myself with the *cogito*, he said, was just as doubtful and as conditional as that which I apply to things: 'One might as well say, "I doubt the existence of things, therefore they exist (or at least, therefore they do not not exist at all)"'.[68]

These statements represented a fundamental challenge to idealism: first, because they denied the absolute certainty, and the logical and ontological priority, of 'I am'; second, because they concluded that not everything can be proved and grounded in a logical manner by human reason, without ungroundable assumptions. As Gilson was to say, when he wrote that 'the innermost spirit of Cartesian philosophy is mathematism', Descartes' idealism was itself responsible for the materialism of the eighteenth century. 'The first attempt to prove the existence of the material world was the first step towards denial of its existence.'[69]

In other words, there are three issues between Schelling and Descartes. First, Schelling did not think that the *cogito* proved my unconditional existence. Second, Schelling thought that there must be pre-reflexive identity – that is, that which exists before the thinking subject reflects – in order for there to be truth and knowledge. Being, in other words, preceded thought. Third, Schelling rejected the rationalistic assumption that, armed with a few certain truths, everything can be proved.

This led him to launch an attack on the ontological argument. Descartes had used that argument to lever himself out of the solipsistic pit into which his method had lowered him. Philosophy, said Schelling, was still grappling with the misunderstandings which Descartes had thereby created. It is significant that Schelling referred to the Scholastics (especially Aquinas) in support of his claim that the ontological argument is problematic, saying correctly that the Scholastics

---

65 *Zur Geschichte der neueren Philosophie* (Münchener Vorlesungen) (1833–34), I/10, 9–10.
66 Jean Daujat, *Y a-t-il une vérité?* (Paris: Téqui, 1974), p. 194.
67 *Zur Geschichte der neueren Philosophie* (1833–34), I/10, 10.
68 *Ibid.*, I/10, 11.
69 Etienne Gilson, *The Unity of Philosophical Experience* (London: Sheed & Ward, 1938), p. 186.

were suspicious of it because it implied that God was a blindly existing being with no freedom.[70]

Schelling attacked the ontological argument by saying that existence did not add to the perfection of a concept. Instead, the question was whether those perfections *existed*. Also, whereas Descartes had concluded that God necessarily exists, Schelling said that logically his conclusion ought to have been that God can exist only necessarily if He does exist.[71] Schelling says that Descartes has not proved that God exists.[72]

In general, Schelling took issue with Descartes' view that there were two sorts of logical connection between being and thought: first, that any thinking thing could be sure of its own existence, and, second, that any thinking thing could prove God's existence. (He also held that extended things were quite distinct from our thoughts about them, and that God bridged the gap between mind and matter.) In contrast, Schelling came to argue that the structures of being and thought were far from identical. (This, indeed, is the essence of his theory of freedom and the death of all idealism.) He held that dialectics constructed a system of being – a scheme laying down what can or cannot be – but that it did this only because it abstracted from existence itself, and that therefore it knew nothing about what does or does not exist.

This view is what Schelling came to disparage as 'negative philosophy': that which dealt only with concepts and not with really existing things. The later Schelling was to conclude that existence could not be grasped by thought alone, but the first signs of this idea can be traced back to the Nature Philosophy, when he said that the knowledge of facts came only from experience.[73] Schelling certainly had no desire to call God's existence into question, nor even to say that it was doubtful; instead, his view was that logical concepts were an inadequate tool with which to examine the question of the existence of anything.[74]

Nothing, said Schelling, was more foreign to God's nature than the idea that He exists blindly and necessarily. If God existed blindly, then He would have no power over His own being. He would be decidedly unfree – a dead, impersonal force. The concept of the necessarily being (*des nothwendig Seyenden*) thus led not to a living God but to a dead one. The ontological argument took us only to some abstract absolute, not to God Himself.[75] It was a crucial part of Schelling's ontology, as well as of his emphasis on God as the master of being and as the absolutely free creator of the world, to reject the ontological argument in its Cartesian form.

In other words, here, in a few succinct pages, Schelling sketched his own philosophical development. By distinguishing 'God as a necessary being' from 'God as necessarily the necessary being', he had come to realise that the attempt to slip in

---

70   *Zur Geschichte der neueren Philosophie* (1833–34), I/10, 14 and 20.
71   *Ibid.*, I/10, 15–16.
72   *Ibid.*, I/10, 15f.
73   Emil L. Fackenheim, 'Schellings Begriff der positiven Philosophie', *Zeitschrift für philosophische Forschung*, VIII (1954): 323.
74   *Zur Geschichte der neueren Philosophie* (1833–34), I/10, 18.
75   *Ibid.*, I/10, 20 and 21.

ontological necessity under the cover of logical necessity had to fail, since the two domains were separate. Reason could get the measure of existence on its own, for reason was human. But existence could be brought into being only by God. It is for this reason that Schelling said that the Scholastics had been right to be sceptical about the ontological argument. Indeed, his rejection of the ontological argument seemed to mirror exactly the rejection of it by Aquinas as described by Etienne Gilson: even if we allow that we can understand that God 'is a being greater than which cannot be conceived', the fact that we understand this definition means only that God exists for our understanding, not that he exists in reality. There is no contradiction between admitting that God cannot be conceived as not existing and God not existing.[76]

Schelling also attacked Descartes for establishing the notorious dualism between mind and body. It had led to Descartes' conception of matter as utterly dead, and of the *res extensa* as spiritless. Similarly, Descartes' idea of mind was that it was completely immaterial. All this was contrary to experience, for nature was patently alive. Moreover, how could mind and matter operate upon one another if they were as different as Descartes claimed? By tearing apart what in fact belonged together, Descartes' influence had been very damaging – 'in all parts of human life and even in religion.'[77]

Although Descartes had been right to accept as true only that which is obvious and clear, he had been wrong in that he did not seek what was first in itself, but rather only what was primary for *me*. He posited God, said Schelling, but he never grasped Him.[78] This led philosophy off into Baconian empiricism, on the one hand, and into rationalism on the other. 'What both schools have in common is the tearing apart of Scholasticism', Schelling wrote.[79] Being expressly anti-Scholastic,[80] both Bacon and Descartes had understood knowledge to come from the movement of the thing,[81] instead of from the subjective movement of the concept, as Scholasticism had maintained: it was precisely the Cartesian notion that ideas were representations (on which he built his whole system) that had made the subject utterly passive. Descartes had said that the mind received impressions like a piece of wax receiving an imprint, and that it was not active in knowledge as the Scholastics had maintained. The same misunderstanding of the difference between transitive and immanent activity led Kant to make the equal and opposite error from Descartes: for him, the subject was the formal cause of knowledge. The only way out of this is to stop thinking of knowledge as a transitive activity: it does not consist in a transitive relation between object and subject, but in the immanent activity of the subject which is capable of knowing, an activity in which it perfects itself.

---

76   Etienne Gilson, *Le thomisme* (Paris: Vrin, 6th edn, 1989), p. 63.
77   *Zur Geschichte der neueren Philosophie* (1833–34), I/10, 28.
78   *Ibid.*, I/10, 29.
79   *Ibid.*, I/10, 30.
80   *Ibid.*, I/10, 32.
81   *Ibid.*, I/10, 30.

Spinoza

Spinoza had seemed at first to provide an improvement on the Cartesian system, because he started with God as the necessarily existing being, or substance, through which everything else had its existence. But Spinoza's God was without will or understanding, he was just the blindly existing. Schelling said specifically that Spinoza's God was dead,[82] and that his God was just substance and not free cause.[83] Spinoza's substance, moreover, may have been a subject–object, but it was one in which the subject got completely lost. He did not show the necessity of how things flowed from God, nor the difference between extension and thought. Schelling's view was that thought could not exist if there were not things to think about.

Leibniz, by contrast, developed a system of pure spirituality. But like Spinoza, he offered only an inadequate account of evil, according to Schelling who warmed to a crucial and much-loved theme.[84] For Spinoza, evil was substantially the same as good, only less perfect and less positive. For Leibniz, evil just came from limitation. 'And yet something more than just limitation must belong to matter,' retorted Schelling, 'for of all creatures it is precisely the most perfect, that is, the least limited, which is capable of evil. The devil is not the most limited, but rather the most limitless creature.'[85]

Once again, in other words, Schelling returned to his powerful concept of evil to overturn rationalist philosophical systems. A genuine concept of evil, he believed, was incompatible with the simple, optimistic self-contained systems of rationalism. He knew that the *a priori* dialectic was simply smashed apart by the sovereign freedom of God.[86] He also made an implicit attack on Kant – and other rationalists – for unwittingly abolishing God's freedom by trying to understand it in purely moral terms. This was a crucial passage:

> Whoever is slightly acquainted with our times knows that the claim (that God can do only that which is good) destroys (*aufhebt*) freedom in God under the appearance of moral necessity. It is the last call of rationalism which imagines that it can be exclusively moral at the same time, even while opposing what is positive in revealed religion. This is in fact a state of opposition to all that is positive in philosophy.[87]

There was, in other words, no religion within the bounds of pure reason, and no philosophy either. Schelling insisted that our view of the world could not be dissociated from the question of its beginnings. Was it created, did it begin at a specific point, or was there an infinite causal link stretching back forever? Schelling insisted that we could not pursue philosophy without answering these questions.[88]

---

82   *Ibid.*, I/10, 20.
83   *Ibid.*, I/10, 36.
84   *Ibid.*, I/10, 56.
85   *Ibid.*, I/10, 57.
86   Horst Fuhrmans, *Schellings letzte Philosophie* (Berlin: Junker und Dünnhaupt, 1940), pp. 79 and 84.
87   *Zur Geschichte der neueren Philosophie* (1833–34), I/10, 58.
88   *Ibid.*, I/10, 61–5.

Or rather, he said that philosophy had been pursued without answering them and that it had simply become ever more rationalistic as a result. This had led it to forget being. The ontological argument, for instance, may tell us about the nature of God, but it did not tell us whether God exists, whence the Scholastics' suspicion of the argument.[89]

It was also significant that Schelling took Descartes to task for the political implications of his ontology. In the *Stuttgart Lectures*, Schelling had advanced some clearly anti-rationalist and conservative political positions. Here, too, he described the age in which he was writing as 'an age which is politically torn apart',[90] and he attributed part of the blame for this to the 'revolutionary element' introduced into philosophy by Descartes.[91] These were all eminently traditional and conservative sentiments.

Kant

If creation was a gift which provided a context in which man could reconcile himself with God, then being could not be unintelligible. It was therefore no coincidence if Schelling attacked Kant – while congratulating him for having set philosophy back onto a subjective track, from which it had been diverted by Spinoza.[92] Schelling was merciless in his attack: he recalled that Kant had called Berkeley *schwärmerisch* (woolly-minded and Romantic) but that 'being *schwärmerisch* is philosophically better than that which finishes in a total non-thought or un-thought, like Kant's theory of sensory perception. This ends with two utterly incomprehensible things: the incomprehensible establishment of the representing in us, which is required to represent in space and time that which is outside all space and all time; and the equally incomprehensible outer world, of which we know neither that it is nor how it operates upon us, nor what necessity or interest it has in operating on us in order to cause the representation of the sensory world.'[93]

Schelling explained that his own theory was much more realist. 'These concepts are in the represented objects themselves. Our judgement that this or that is a substance or a cause is not merely subjectively, but rather objectively valid. Things can be as little thought of without these concepts as they can be looked at without space.'[94] In other words, said Schelling, one should conclude that there is *Verstand* in things themselves, but Kant did not do this. Schelling was coming close to a classic Aristotelian realist position. As Walter Kasper has commented, Schelling's form of thought, like that of Catholic theology, holds that human thought by definition moves between the infinite and the finite: 'Man can think only in this double-movement.'[95]

---

89   *Ibid.*, I/10, 65–6.
90   *Ibid.*, I/10, 59.
91   *Ibid.*, I/10, 59–60.
92   *Ibid.*, I/ 10, 73 and 89.
93   *Ibid.*, I/10, 81.
94   *Ibid.*, I/10, 82.
95   Walter Kasper, *Das Absolute in der Geschichte, Philosophie und Theologie der Geschichte in der Spätphilosophie Schellings* (Mainz: Grünewald, 1965), p. 425.

Schelling wrote that Kant reduced ultimate reality to *nothing*. One is reminded here of what Leszek Kolakowski has called 'horror metaphysics', which sets in when philosophers 'make the very concept of existence useless ... If nothing truly exists except the Absolute, the Absolute is nothing; if nothing truly exists for myself, I am nothing ... If the world is an illusion, then other people are automata.'[96] Similar concerns have been forcefully expressed by Gilson.[97] Indeed, Schelling himself was later to refer explicitly to 'horror' (*Schrecken*) as the natural reaction of one who realises that he has developed a purely essentialist ontology, and that one thus has no 'vessel' in which to put the 'content' of being.[98]

Kant tried to ground understanding of the world in something utterly incomprehensible. His main purpose had been to rule out metaphysics as being beyond the human ken, and this, said Schelling, was wrong. The result was that the Kantian critique was 'empty and useless'.[99] Kant had been wrong, said Schelling, to put mind outside nature: mind could understand nature only by understanding itself as part of it. As Maesschalk shows, it is precisely this, Schelling's evolution away from an anthropology of the One and the many, and towards a *religious* anthropology, which forced him to break with idealism, including transcendental idealism.[100]

Schelling emphasised the sheer poverty of absolutist and rationalist reason without faith. He rejected Kantian agnosticism because criticism reduced God's revelation to a supposition of pure reason. Kant had left the question of God open, making Him a thinking extended substance that regulates our experience of the world.[101] Like Spinoza, Kant was also guilty, Schelling said, of making liberty foreign to the world. Fichte had then picked up the subjective baton and made it the cornerstone of his whole system: Fichte's claim that everything came about only because of the I flattered human self-importance.[102] In fact, Fichte's *Ich* was unfree, because its creation of the world was blind and necessary, not the result of free will.

By contrast, Schelling said that he himself had tried to show how the world is there for me. The perception of self-consciousness in 'I am' depended on the existence of the outside world. The world could not have been created by me. It could be known only by being there together with the I. There was 'an inseparable connection (*ein unzerreißbarer Zusammenhang*) between the I and an outside world which was necessarily represented.[103] Schelling said that he had initially tried to show this by explaining the history of how the I came to itself, and that these were his first steps to get back to the objective after Fichte. 'It was an attempt to reconcile Fichtean idealism with reality.'[104]

---

96   Leszek Kolakowski, *Metaphysical Horror* (Oxford: Blackwell, 1988), p. 21.
97   Gilson, *The Unity of Philosophical Experience, passim.*
98   *Abhandlung über die Quelle der ewigen Wahrheiten* (1850), II/1, 590.
99   *Zur Geschichte der neueren Philosophie* (1833–34), I/10, 89.
100   Maesschalk, *L'anthropologie politique et religieuse de Schelling*, p. 25.
101   *Zur Geschichte der neueren Philosophie* (1833–34), I/10, 81 and 82.
102   *Ibid.*, I/10, 92.
103   *Ibid.*, I/10, 93.
104   *Ibid.*, I/10, 95.

In order to reestablish the objective, said Schelling, philosophy had to descend deep into nature. Thus he defended the Nature Philosophy.[105] But his passionate interest in the objective eventually led him to abandon the anthropocentrism which characterises so much modern philosophy. Indeed, as Schelling became persuaded of man's status as a fallen creature, and of the resulting ontological deficiency of the finite world, he became concomitantly aware of the limitations of human reason as of the claims which were made for it by the rationalists. This led him in a conservative ontological direction. Deliberately using vocabulary borrowed from the *Freedom* essay, Schelling described his own philosophical development, explicitly linking his ontological discoveries with the change in his political views:

> It became clear that limitless freedom, untamed by any lawfulness, led to a hopeless and desperate view of history. Here, where the highest and mostly tragic dissonance appears, in which the misuse of freedom teaches us the necessity of calling ourselves back, here man sees himself obliged to recognise something which is greater than human freedom.[106]

This last line was a direct dig at Kant, for whom duty came precisely only from the moral law as apprehended by the autonomous (free) human self. It was also an implicitly religious and anti-Enlightenment remark. Philosophy brought knowledge precisely of a subject which is above man and human selfhood, and to which everything is ultimately subordinate. This 'thing' was the master of the real and ideal world.[107] Schelling, in other words, had completed his journey out of anthropocentric idealism and had arrived back at a consciousness of God.

He had also arrived at a deep awareness of being, and of the rationalistic shortcomings of idealism. At this point, indeed, his attack on idealism could hardly have been more orthodox from a Christian–realist point of view. He stated in a few lines what was to be the backbone of his positive philosophy. Speaking of the genuine action and development of God's work in the natural world, Schelling wrote of its treatment by modern idealism:

> But an eternal happening is no happening at all. Thus the whole representation of that process and that movement is illusory in itself, and in fact it is one in which nothing has happened. Everything has merely occurred in thought, and this whole movement was in fact nothing but a movement of thought. That philosophy should have grasped this: in order to do so, it puts itself beyond all possibility of contradiction, but precisely in doing this it renounced all claim to objectivity. In other words, it had to recognise itself as a science in which there is no question of existence, that is, of what really exists, nor thus of knowledge in this sense. It deals only with relationships which objects take on in pure thought ...[108]

Because existence was that which is positive, 'posited (*gesetzt*), ensured and maintained', said Schelling, this – the philosophy which ignores it – should be called 'negative philosophy'. As we shall see, the turn towards positive philosophy

---

105   *Ibid.*, I/10, 106.
106   *Ibid.*, I/10, 116.
107   *Ibid.*, I/10, 117.
108   *Ibid.*, I/10, 124–5.

was an essential element in Schelling's lifelong pursuit of a satisfactory definition of freedom: unlike Kant, who confined freedom to the intellectual and not the sensory realm, Schelling was insistent that freedom of the will would be an empty concept if philosophy did not turn to the place where freedom was real, namely to experience.[109] Experience was also the domain in which the concept of God received its true meaning, for religion was perfected only in its experienced happenings.

Hegel

Such considerations formed the basis for and indeed the essence of Schelling's magisterial attack on Hegel, that for which his philosophy is most arresting. His dispute with Hegel was the definitive fact about his philosophy: having started in 1809, the differences between them became the key point about his later philosophy. Anti-Hegelianism became Schelling's stock in trade.

We saw in Chapter 2 that Hegel's aim had been to establish a system in which reason would be totally self-grounding. He wanted philosophy to be a presuppositionless science and wanted to turn Cartesian doubt and Kantian criticism on to the structures of thought itself. Hegel's starting-point was thus not the Cartesian *cogito*, but instead the more impersonal conviction that thought is. He began with the simple being of thought. He tried to arrive at the notion of that which is common to all that is by making an abstraction from all the differences between beings, that is, from all the determinations which are proper to each thing.[110]

As we also saw in Chapter 2, traditional realism affirms that being is the first determination of all, and not that it is that which is most indeterminate. We also saw that the desire to attain in our knowledge of the world the kind of direct truth that we have in mathematics leads paradoxically to systems which in fact cut themselves off from being completely.

It is clear that Hegel's *Logic* did move entirely within the realm of thought, and that its very purpose was to undercut or forestall any realist objection about independent reality.[111] Pippin writes, 'The *Logic* is idealist in its function and goal, and that at least means that thinking about the relations between the thought determinations of the *Logic* and "reality" cannot be construed as a problem of "correspondence". For Hegel, any "reality" side of such a dyad is just another thought determination. "Truth", he says, "is the agreement of a thought content with itself." [*Wissenschaft der Logik*, 86].'[112] Indeed, Hegel himself never denied the cyclical nature of his philosophy, which Schelling was to attack, but rather justified it as a simple fact which corresponded to what really happens.[113]

---

109 Danz, *Die philosophische Christologie Schellings*, p. 155.
110 Daujat, *Y a-t-il une vérité?*, p. 43.
111 Robert B. Pippin, *Hegel's Idealism: The Satisfactions of Self-Consciousness* (Cambridge: Cambridge University Press, 1989), pp. 92 and 98.
112 *Ibid.*, p. 187.
113 Manfred Frank, *Der unendliche Mangel an Sein, Schellings Hegelkrikitk und die Anfänge der Marxschen Dialektik* (Frankfurt am Main: Suhrkamp, 1975), p. 161.

It was this search for absolute indeterminacy – pursued in the name of completely self-constituting reason – that led Hegel to undermine the law of identity. If pure being disappeared into nothing, then the idea must be abandoned that everything is what it is and not another thing. Being and nothing were no longer very different from one another. In fact, they became indistinguishable: as Schelling says, in Hegel, 'between being and nothing, there is no opposition, they do nothing to one another.'[114] This is the very opposite of Aristotelian logic.

Hegel's purpose was to give a richer content to Kantian idealism, which he regarded as excessively conceptual and abstract. He did this by proposing a reform of the notion of the concept, and an account of how the concept progressively acquired determination from its initial utter indeterminacy. He claimed that it did this by a process of contradiction or negation. This brought the principle of contradiction, instead of the principle of identity, into the centre of Hegel's ontology. Hegel did, indeed, find the laws of *Verstand* too constricting, and rejected the need to stick to the law of identity.[115] He preferred eternal flux instead:

> *Pure being and pure nothing are therefore the same.* The truth is neither being nor the nothing (*das Nichts*) but being in nothing and the nothing in being ... In the same way truth is not its lack of difference but that it is not the same, that it is absolutely different but also unseparated and inseparable and immediately *everything vanishes into its opposite*. Its truth is therefore this *movement* of the immediate disappearance of one into the other; *the becoming* (*das Werden*) of the immediate disappearance of the one into the other; *the becoming*: a movement in which both are different but through a difference which has just as immediately dissolved.[116]

Thus, as Walter Kasper says, Hegel's dialectics abolishes the rule of non-contradiction in positing the identity of identity and non-identity.[117] Houlgate says (reading Hegel), 'We have to think of pure being and nothing in terms of one another.'[118] It is precisely this attitude which Etienne Gilson attacked when he criticised the essentialist tradition which began with Plato and culminated in Hegel: 'One can be certain of finding oneself in the Platonist tradition whenever the notions of existence and nothingness are brought down to purely essential notions of the same and the other ... the radical opposition between being and nothing is effaced by the distinction between that "which really is" and that which "is not really". Being receives that variable value which it always has in an ontology of essences.'[119]

Hegel concluded from this (rather like Spinoza) that it was only by saying what something is not that we can say what it is: the determination of identity becomes indistinguishable from the determination of difference. The ultimate concepts,

---

114 *Zur Geschichte der neueren Philosophie* (1833–34), I/10, 137.

115 Stephen Houlgate, *Freedom, Truth and History: An Introduction to Hegel's Philosophy* (London and New York: Routledge, 1991), pp. 55–7; Charles Taylor, *Hegel* (Cambridge: Cambridge University Press, 1975), p. 116.

116 Hegel, *Wissenschaft der Logik, Erstes Kapitel, C. Werden, Einheit des Seyns und Nichts*. Emphases original.

117 Kasper, *Das Absolute in der Geschichte*, p. 429.

118 Houlgate, *Freedom, Truth and History*, p. 54.

119 Gilson, *Le thomisme*, p. 55.

therefore, are not the principles of identity or non-contradiction, but instead the principles of difference and contradiction. Hegel's notion of the self-determination of spirit led him to say that the whole of philosophy consisted in positing (*setzen*) that which is already implicit in a concept.[120] This in turn implied that fully presuppositionless thought could not begin with any conceivable distinction between thought and being at all. Hegel insisted that reality was not given, and his *Logic* was therefore profoundly critical of the ontological aspirations (and assumptions) of any philosophy which does not make the full effort to be fully self-determining.[121] For Hegel, being was not just there-ness: it was conceived as dialectically structured self-determination and self-generation. The existence of nature was not just a contingent fact but rather the result of the gradual unfolding of reason: being was rational, because to be was to be self-determining, that is, rational. Indeed, developing reason was the very substance of existence itself, and this is why Hegel said being was to be understood as absolute *Geist*.[122]

Schelling recognised that Hegel thought the concept was everything, and that it could encompass the whole of history as well as things like the proof of the Holy Trinity. Hegel started with the concept of pure being, and Schelling attacked him for this – much as Hegel had taken Schelling to task in the Preface to the *Phenomenology* – by saying that it was an inadequate concept. In particular, the movement Hegel described was, according to Schelling, no real movement at all. Schelling, therefore, attacked his late former friend exactly where the traditionalist realists attack him too: on his identification of being with nothingness. He said this was typical of negative philosophy, first because it ignored what true being is, and second because its logical ('negative') system could not explain why the Absolute should go out of itself.

> That Hegel nonetheless attributes immanent movement to pure being means nothing other than that the thought which begins with pure being feels the impossibility of remaining with this, the most abstract and the most empty, by which Hegel himself explains pure being. The necessity to go beyond this has its cause in the fact that the thought is used to a more concrete being, more full of content (*inhaltsvolleres*): it cannot be satisfied with the meagre fare of pure being, in which only a content in general, but none in particular, is thought. In the final instance, it is only because there is in fact a richer and fuller (*inhaltsvolleres*) being, and that the thinking mind is itself such a thing; and so it is not a possibility which lies in the empty concept itself, but rather one which is in philosophizing itself, and one which is forced up by its remembrance, which does not allow it to remain with pure abstraction.[123]

Hegel's concepts therefore lacked all life and all reality. (Later, Schelling was to say that the use of purely logical concepts, instead of ones which are grounded in reality, was like wanting to use lead soldiers in a real battle.[124]) By analogy with his rejection of the ontological argument, Schelling held that thought did not know

---

120 Hegel, *Enzyklopädie der philosophischen Wissenschaften*, I, para 88 (1).
121 Houlgate, *Freedom, Truth and History*, pp. 72–3; p. 74.
122 Houlgate, *Freedom, Truth and History*, pp. 177–80.
123 *Zur Geschichte der neueren Philosophie* (1833–34), I/10, 131.
124 *Philosophie der Mythologie, Erstes Buch, Der Monotheismus*, II/2, 93–4, note 1.

without experience whether necessity exists in reality. We have already seen that this Hegelian view is predicated on a misguided attempt to arrive at a notion of pure being by making an abstraction from all things which are, and from the erroneous conclusion that this means that being is the most indeterminate thing of all.

Instead, Schelling argued, being was that which has the potential for thought and knowledge within itself, and of which thought and knowledge are the direct manifestation. This is why Schelling said that one is thus driven beyond Hegelian abstraction by the fact that there is a fuller and richer being, a fact of which we are aware because the thinking mind is such a being. We are led to being and existence not by an empty abstract concept, but by the richness and reality of thought itself. There was no such thing as pure being without an object (*Gegenstand*). Indeed, when Hegel thought of pure being, he was in fact thinking of nothing, and he was therefore trying to deduce becoming from nothing.[125]

> In fact, one cannot contradict these sentences or declare them to be false; because they are sentences from which you can get absolutely nothing. It is like trying to carry water in the palm of your hand: you get absolutely nothing. The sheer work of trying to hold fast onto something which cannot be held fast, because it is nothing, here takes the place of philosophizing. One can say the same thing for the whole of Hegel's philosophy.[126]

Schelling's criticism was acid. All that Hegel reached was a general concept of becoming, but not any particular becoming.

> The transfer of the concept of process onto dialectical movement, where no struggle at all is possible, but only a monotonous, soporific progression, belongs to that misuse of words which for Hegel is an important means of hiding the lack of true life in his system.[127]

Hegel's system represented the apogee of simple withdrawal into pure thought. Schelling's point was that being could not be reduced to consciousness or to the concept one has of it. Being simply escapes the sphere of the concept, as Manfred Frank puts it, and Schelling is unique among the idealists for making this point.[128] In fact, this makes him no longer an idealist.

Schelling concluded his traditionalist critique of Hegel by attacking rationalist philosophies, like Hegel's, for whom God was nothing but an abstract conclusion reached at the end. Hegel tried and failed, said Schelling, to account for free creation. In fact, Hegel's God became captured by world-historical processes: he was a never-resting God. Schelling reproached Hegel for digging the grave of God's liberty. In words which betray Schelling's horror of the futility and nihilism inherent in Hegel, he called Hegel's God, 'The God of eternal continuous doing, of relentless unrest, who never finds the Sabbath, he is a God who only ever does what he has already done, and therefore can never create anything new ...'[129] As Walter Schulz rightly says, 'In these words, Schelling indicates that an eternal happening is senseless and

---

125 *Zur Geschichte der neueren Philosophie* (1833–34), I/10, 133.
126 *Ibid.*, I/10, 135.
127 *Ibid.*, I/10, 137.
128 Frank, *Der unendliche Mangel an Sein*, p. 140.
129 *Zur Geschichte der neueren Philosophie* (1833–34), I/10, 160.

nihilistic, for in it nothing really happens, what comes out is only what already once was, there is no meaningful action into the future.'[130] At least in Schelling's world, the creation happens.

Schelling's attack on the constancy and circularity of God's efforts in Hegel's system was not fortuitous: it was an attempt to torpedo the whole Hegelian system by destroying its very basis – the idea that truth is contained only in the whole. Hegel thought of the Absolute as a process, and he believed that he could deal with the central question of the transition from the infinite to the finite by arguing for the identity of thought and being within a self-contained philosophical system. With the phenomenology of spirit as with human history, the sense was known only in the whole, a proposition which, it was argued in Chapter 2, can open the way to the relativism Schelling spent his life attacking. On the contrary, Schelling held that even if something came to truth only at its end, it would have to be already familiar with itself at the beginning, or else there could be no recognition.[131] This was the significance of Schelling's adherence to the principle of identity, and of his insistence on the Absolute's pre-reflexive identity with itself.

Schelling therefore perpetrated a kind of tear in the seamless system of Hegel's *Phenomenology*, because the decision made by God to create the world, like the decisions made by individuals for good or evil, are absolutely free and therefore unpredictable. 'To tear the absolute away from the dialectic and to place it in its own freedom, against Hegel and against all idealism – *that* was Schelling's preoccupation to which all his later questioning was directed', says Fuhrmans.[132] Hegel is too solipsistic, and his attempt to ground an entire system on thought in fact leads to the suppression of the individual. As Tilliette argues, Hegel's elimination of the real world as an object of individual experience produces a narrowness and partiality of vision in which the superior notions of ethics and religion have no place.[133] Hegel handed reality over to logic and thereby destroyed it.

Schelling's lifelong central preoccupations, in other words – the creation and the nature of God's action in reality – were what drove him to abandon the structures of Hegelian idealism. Whereas Hegel reflected only on the internal structures of liberty, Schelling attempted to reflect on the sources of that liberty – which he regarded as an irruption and as a divine spark – as well as on its purpose or teleology.[134] The concept of teleology, indeed, was obviously central to a truly religious view of reality. Schelling reproached Hegel for fleeing from the question of the origins of human liberty, and of thus ignoring its true nature. Hegel had thought he could find the richness of existence in the structures of pure reflection, while existence itself remained a pure fact, inaccessible to thought. Hegel, as Schelling insisted, could

---

130 Walter Schulz, *Der Gott der neuzeitlichen Metaphysik* (Pfullingen: Neske, 1957), p. 104; quoted by Andrew Bowie, *Schelling and Modern European Philosophy* (London: Routledge, 1993), p. 176.
131 Bowie, *Schelling and Modern European Philosophy*, p. 177.
132 Horst Fuhrmans, 'Ausgangspunkt der Schellingschen Spätphilosophie', *Kant-Studien*, 48 (1956/57): 302.
133 Tilliette, *L'absolu et la Philosophie*, p. 123.
134 Maesschalk, *L'anthropologie politique et religieuse de Schelling*, p. xx.

conceive of *Seyn* only in terms of *Wesen*: indeed, he accused him of being fully ignorant of the difference.[135] In a lovely phrase, Schelling wrote, 'The whole world lies in the nets of understanding or of reason, but the question is precisely how it got into these nets, for there is obviously more in the world than just reason – indeed there is something which strives to break out of reason's limits.'[136]

What Schelling wanted to do was to force Hegel's thought to take account of that which it presupposed, namely existence – 'that which is more than pure reason'. The Hegelian process was dominated by an abstraction whose consequence obliterated the starting-point, the source or the foundation of existence which causes the movement of thought.[137]

The difference between positive and negative philosophy thus crystallised around the notions of existence and of God. Positive philosophy started with the premise, which is fully assumed as transcending logical deduction, that God exists and there is thus such a thing as existence. As Walter Schulz put it, the God of negative philosophy was the result, or end, of a chain of reasoning: the God of positive philosophy, by contrast, was a beginning, a creator.[138] By contrast, as Schelling wrote, '[Hegel's] God is not free from the world, but burdened with it.'[139] As Schelling declared in 1820,

> Here nothing more can be explained by necessity; rather, the transition into being is a free deed ... Here we separate ourselves from the concept of the dialectician. Here is the point where not the concept but only the deed is decisive.[140]

In other words, Schelling concluded against Hegel that thought was incapable of completing itself by itself, much in the same way as the Catholic metaphysicians deny powers of totally autonomous self-legislation *in abstracto* to the unaided reason of the individual. This is why Schelling's influence on Catholic theologians of the period was important. Unlike Hegel, who was distinctly anti-Catholic, Schelling provided his Catholic disciples with a way of conceiving their theology and philosophy in the style of the nineteenth century.[141] Although Schelling was obviously very much part of the idealist current of philosophy which starts with thinking rather than with being, his later development was distinctly anti-Enlightenment and *a fortiori* anti-idealist. The fact that he may not have been completely religiously orthodox on all points was just what contemporary Catholics liked about him.[142] This is why O'Meara calls

---

135 *Zur Geschichte der neueren Philosophie* (1833–34), I/10, 133.

136 *Ibid.*, I/10, 143–4.

137 Maesschalk, *L'anthropologie politique et religieuse de Schelling*, p. xxi.

138 Walter Schulz, *Die Vollendung des deutschen Idealismus in der Spätphilosophie Schellings*, p. 20.

139 *Zur Geschichte der neueren Philosophie* (1833–34), I/10, 159.

140 Schelling, *Initia Philosophiae Universae* (1820–21), ed. Horst Fuhrmans (Bonn: Bouvier, 1969), p. 116; cited in Bowie, *Schelling and Modern European Philosophy*, p. 139.

141 Thomas O'Meara, *Romantic Idealism and Roman Catholicism: Schelling and the Theologians* (Notre Dame and London: University of Notre Dame Press, 1982), p. 5.

142 *Ibid.*, p. 9.

Schelling a bridge between idealism/Romanticism and Roman Catholicism,[143] as opposed to the more Protestant transcendentalism of Kant, Fichte and Hegel.

Jacobi

The final piece of the jigsaw fell into place in Schelling's discussion of Jacobi. For Schelling, being may be an extra-logical fact, but it is also an intelligible fact.

Jacobi had greatly influenced Schelling at the beginning of the century because of his criticism of Spinoza, against whom he directed the familiar charges of atheism and nihilism. He provided the first philosophical critique of modern rationalism, for he maintained that nihilism resulted from Kantian dualism, and from interpreting the whole world according to scientific or causal laws. He predicted that this would open the floodgates to the worst aspects of materialism and scientism, and he demanded that philosophy return to religion instead.

Jacobi drew direct inspiration from Hume's pragmatism in his fight against German rationalism and idealism, and especially from the Humean notion of natural belief in the external world. Jacobi also used Hume to provide a defence of religion: anti-Cartesian and anti-rationalist, Jacobi held that belief in God was as natural as belief in the outside world, but that neither could be grounded in deductive reason – precisely because reason presupposed them. Jacobi concluded – rightly, as we know with hindsight – that Kantianism would have to move on to absolute idealism. Indeed, Jacobi thought all rationalism nihilist. He believed, like Hume, that any philosophy which undermined naive realism could not be believed. He thus challenged philosophy to think of existence other than in terms of an abstract essence.[144]

All these theories would have been grist to Schelling's anti-idealist mill if Jacobi had not, in Schelling's eyes, gone too far. By the time of the Munich lectures, Jacobi and Schelling had fallen out, precisely because Jacobi thought all knowledge was fatalist, so he appealed to feeling and mystical intuition instead. In Schelling's view, this total abandonment of rationalism paradoxically meant that Jacobi was himself a kind of rationalist, who accepted the validity of rationalist arguments, but used mysticism as a means to escape the conclusions. Hence he called Jacobi, somewhat sourly, 'the person from whom one can learn the most in modern philosophy'.[145] By shutting himself off from the proper use of reason, Schelling opined, 'The end of Jacobi's philosophy is thus general non-knowledge.'[146]

In other words, Schelling attacked Jacobi's view that revelation was outside the grasp of reason.[147] Jacobi's rational world was even more arid and hostile to reason than that of the critical philosophers. By banishing all value from real experience, Jacobi ended up with nothing but a vague spiritualism. Schelling reproached Jacobi

---

143   *Ibid.*, p. 11.
144   Jacques Rivelaygue, *Leçons de métaphysique allemande*, Vol. I, *De Leibniz à Hegel* (Paris: Grasset, 1990), pp. 124–9.
145   *Zur Geschichte der neueren Philosophie* (1833–34), I/10, 168.
146   *Ibid.*, I/10, 178.
147   *Ibid.*, I/10, 176.

for sending away precisely that which can give philosophy its true content, namely the real world as God had created it.[148] Positive philosophy must start with a That, the consequence of God's liberty, and religious knowledge did indeed begin with such positivity, of which transcendental philosophy was quite ignorant. Struck by the emptiness of contemporary philosophy in comparison with the 'fullness of revelation',[149] Schelling said instead that there was a kind of knowledge which Jacobi did not want to acknowledge, namely one which included the main dogmas of faith – and especially 'freedom and providence as the cause of the world, the freedom of the human will, individual life after death, and all the other demands of faith'.[150]

He had expressed a similar thought in the *Freedom* essay, when he had written approvingly of Lessing's determination to elaborate revealed truths as rational ones:[151] neither passage was much different from St Thomas Aquinas' and St Augustine's maxim, *credo ut intellegam*, 'I believe in order to understand.' Just as one could not understand Euclid unless one took the first premises and sentences on trust, Schelling said, so 'All knowledge arises from faith.'[152] By contrast, 'In looking, there is no understanding.'[153] Because Schelling knew that the split between faith and philosophy was inevitable after Descartes, and because he rejected Jacobi's blanket conviction that all philosophy led to fatalism and atheism, Schelling was determined to develop a philosophy which understood the reality was intelligible and reasonable.

Although still tempted by certain aspects of mysticism, Schelling insisted that it was wrong to turn away from clear perception and understanding. He declared himself to be fundamentally an empiricist: 'If we had the choice between empiricism and the thought-necessity of exaggerated rationalism, which suppresses everything, then no free spirit could hesitate to plump for empiricism.'[154]

For Schelling, empiricism denied neither supernatural nor moral laws. Philosophy based on the view that the world was the result of the act of creation was a science of knowledge.[155] Schelling attacked 'French philosophy' for taking nothing from the empire of experience other than psychological observations and analyses. He rightly called this 'ideology'. Instead of this, he said it was the German calling to bring positive philosophy and empiricism together.

The significance of the way in which Jacobi and Schelling drifted apart is very great. For Jacobi, 'Motion towards the Absolute implied an intuitive leap of faith.'[156] His philosophy thus illustrated the difference between Protestant and Catholic approaches: although Catholics say that man cannot apprehend God completely, they disagree with Protestants who affirm that human reason is so vitiated by sin that it can have no knowledge of the Absolute at all. It is clear that there are parallels

---

148 *Ibid.*, I/10, 178.
149 *Ibid.*, I/10, 178.
150 *Ibid.*, I/10, 182.
151 *Ibid.*, I/7, 412.
152 *Ibid.*, I/10, 183.
153 *Ibid.*, I/10, 188.
154 *Ibid.*, I/10, 198.
155 *Ibid.*, I/10, 199.
156 O'Meara, *Romantic Idealism and Roman Catholicism*, p. 45.

between the Protestant view and Kantian epistemology (although the cause of our inability to know reality as it is in itself does not come from sin in Kant) and, conversely, between the Catholic view and Schelling's.

Indeed, being strongly mystic, Jacobi had attacked Schelling after the publication of the *Freedom* essay for even trying to describe God.[157] He also accused him of atheism, a charge Schelling returned in 1812.[158] Schelling said Jacobi himself was atheist because his theories culminated in an escapist faith which avoided the problem of how a real God grounded the world's life. O'Meara writes, 'By attacking Jacobi, Schelling hurled himself against the remaining bulwarks of the Enlightenment. Although he only perceived this dimly, he was rejecting religion without reality.'[159] It was this, indeed, which brought Schelling and Baader together: Schelling was becoming realist, both philosophically and religiously, and this brought him closer to the Catholic tradition than the Protestant – even if Baader, who also fell out with Schelling, in whose philosophy he always detected an anti-individualism incompatible with Catholic teaching, was to write witheringly to Hegel that, 'Schelling's early Nature Philosophy was a strong and tasty steak, but now he just brews up a ragout with all kinds of ingredients in it, including Christian ones.'[160]

But the main point for us is this: Schelling concluded his attack on theosophy with a specific attack on the Gnostic notion that knowledge of God is so mystical that it cannot be communicated in speech.[161] Schelling specifically rejected any such tradition, especially when he attacked the mystical notion that 'discursive speech' was useless.[162] These remarks put Schelling at a distance from the theosophical and mystic tradition in which he was earlier interested, and drew him yet closer to traditional realism.

Conclusion: Schelling and the Creation

In the light of all this, it is significant that, two years after the Munich lectures, in the *Darstellung des philosophischen Empirismus* (Portrayal of Philosophical Empiricism) of 1836, Schelling returned to the question of creation, insisting that the liberty of God would be attenuated if a concept of it did not imply liberty from all relationships, even from any possible creation.

In this work, Schelling insisted that God would be free only if he were able to create within Himself any potentialities which may precede the creation. He would

---

157 Fr H. Jacobi, *Von den göttlichen Dingen und ihre Offenbarung* (1811); see Martin Heidegger, *Schellings Abhandlung über das Wesen der menschlichen Freiheit (1809)* (Tübingen: Max Niemeyer, 1971), pp. 81ff.

158 F.W.J. Schellings *Denkmal der Schrift von den göttlichen Dingen u.s.w. des Herrn Friedrich Heinrich Jacobi und der ihm in derselben gemachten Beschuldigung eines absichtlich täuschenden, Lüge redenden Atheismus* (1812).

159 O'Meara, *Romantic Idealism and Roman Catholicism*, p. 88.

160 Franz von Baader, Letter to Hegel, 30 May 1830, in *Sämtliche Werke* (Aalen: Scientia, 1963 [Leipzig: Neudruck der Ausgabe, 1851]), Vol. 15, p. 464–5.

161 *Zur Geschichte der neueren Philosophie* (1833–34), I/10, 186 and 187.

162 *Ibid.*, I/10, 186.

not be free if the act of creation consisted only in bringing those potentialities into reality, especially if they were eternally present within Him.[163] This obviously brought Schelling much closer to the fully-fledged traditional concept of creation *ex nihilo*. As Schelling himself emphasised, 'Creation out of nothing can mean nothing other than *creatio absque omni praeexistente potentia* – creation without any *potentiality* being there before, and without any potentiality having been posited by the will of the creator.'[164]

Having begun to write of 'creation *ex nihilo*' ('*eine Erschaffung aus Nichts*')[165] in the Erlangen lectures of 1820–21, and having also written warmly of '*eine Schöpfung aus Nichts*' ('a creation out of nothing')[166] in the 1827–28 *System der Weltalter*, Schelling also abandoned the idea that that out of which creation was created was just the relatively not-being. He started to call it 'das Nichts' ('nothing') or '*eigentlich nichts*' ('actually nothing') instead. In Genesis, of course, the world before creation was both without form *and void*, while St Augustine made it clear that God made creatures 'out of nothing'.[167] It is obvious that if existence is a result of the free act of God, then it is not the result of some logical process and therefore not deducible by mere human thought. As Maesschalk writes, 'Thought presupposes at its origin more than itself. It thus finds itself incapable of completing itself and it remains separated from its only possible foundation, existence.'[168]

Schelling made it very clear later that his earlier distinction between nothing and non-being was a mistake. Precisely because the notion of absolutely free creation informed the whole of Christianity, said Schelling, it had to be adhered to: the notion of creation out of nothing, he said, presupposed 'that absolutely nothing – no non-being, indeed no potentiality, whether in the Creator or outside Him, can precede fully free creation'.[169] It is important to remind oneself in all this that Schelling's distance from Kant here could hardly be greater, for such speculation is precisely what Kant denied philosophy could make.

Schelling insisted, coherently, that if the potentialities were themselves created by God, then the creation was a matter of His will, not His intelligence.[170] They were not present within Him independently of His will. Even if it has been rightly argued that there were some weaknesses and hesitations on this issue right to the end of his life, Schelling's unabashed emphasis on the utter freedom of the creation is surely the crucial point, especially with respect to Schelling's relationship to idealism.[171]

---

163   *Darstellung des philosophischen Empirismus* (1836), I/10, 282.
164   *Ibid.*
165   Schelling, *Initia Philosophiae Universae*, Erlanger Vorlesung (1820–21), ed. Horst Fuhrmans (Bonn: Bouvier, 1969), p. 152.
166   Schelling, *System der Weltalter* (1827–28), 33. Vorlesung, p. 150.
167   St Augustine, *City of God*, Book XII, Chapter 2.
168   Maesschalk, *L'anthropologie politique et religieuse de Schelling*, p. 107.
169   *Darstellung des philosophischen Empirismus* (1836), I/10, 284.
170   *Ibid.*, I/10, 286.
171   Brito, 'La Création ex "nihilo" selon Schelling', p. 319; Tilliette, *Schelling, Une Philosophie en devenir*, Vol. 2, pp. 381–2; pp. 388–9.

Schelling is clear, unlike Hegel, that the doctrine of creation *ex nihilo* is fundamental to Christian doctrine.[172]

On the other hand, as Brito argues, Schelling was never very happy with the Thomist (and traditional Christian) view that God could have created whichever world he liked. Brito feels that Schelling's view is that God can create or not create the world, but that God does not have fully free reign in deciding what kind of world He creates. God's free choice was identified with necessity, and the negation by Schelling of any alternative to the world as it is created limits to the infinite liberality of God's creative goodness. Yet, as Brito also makes clear, Schelling conceived three very important Christian dogmas: the goodness of creation, the redoubtable power of evil, and evil's ultimate defeat by Jesus Christ.[173]

This is why it seems right to hang on to the main thrust of Josef Anton Stüttler's argument. He draws attention to the similarities between Schelling's *Potenzen* (potentialities) and the *possibilia* of the Scholastics.[174] Despite a slight difference – in the Scholastic tradition, God's creative act is defined as His freely bringing the *possibilia* into reality, while in Schelling it consists more in a free bringing forth of the *Potenzen* in God[175] – the commentator rightly emphasises how different Schelling's doctrine is from that which flows through the whole late idealist tradition in Germany, namely the affirmation that the world is the result of God's coming to Himself. Schelling thought that the world was the result of the free creation of God; it was not the place of His eternal birth. It was precisely Schelling's determination in the later philosophy to conceive of the world as the product of freedom, and not as the result of God's becoming. This notion of creation as a free act is utterly incompatible with the idealist project, which was to search for an absolute beginning and then explain the world through an immanent process of mediation: Schelling had quite clearly broken out of that particular mould, precisely because, for him, freedom meant that which could not be predicted *a priori*. Dialectical necessity is simply blown apart by genuine freedom, whether it be man's or God's. This is why Josef Stüttler concludes that Schelling did not so much complete German idealism as break through it and destroy it.[176] Meanwhile, as Christian Danz rightly emphasises, it is precisely because Schelling came to conceive specifically of Christ as the 'realisation of freedom in history' (because He is Himself unconditional) that the philosopher's quest for the correct understanding of freedom led him, eventually, back to God.[177]

---

172 Brito, 'La création chez Hegel et Schelling', p. 261.
173 Emilio Brito, 'Schelling et la bonté de la création', *Nouvelle Revue Théologique*, 108/4 (July–August 1986): 514–15.
174 Stüttler, 'Das Gottesproblem im Spätwerk Schellings', pp. 76–7.
175 *Darstellung des philosophischen Empirismus* (1836), I/10, 282.
176 Stüttler, 'Das Gottesproblem im Spätwerk Schellings', p. 81.
177 Danz, *Die philosophische Christologie Schellings*, p. 14.

Chapter 6

The Religious Flowering in Schelling's Late Philosophy

> Keen as is a travelling stranger, his degree in his pocket, to continue the studies of his choice, I went straight to the heart of the matter and tried to put my interlocutor [Schelling] onto his own terrain by saying that public opinion was very interested in his project of creating a new philosophy. I asked him to tell me what to think of it. His regard, which had been calm until this moment, became animated and shone with a more lively clarity. He replied with perfect good nature, and with his own desire to give me satisfaction, that he had indeed been working for many long years on a work whose goal was to present the harmony between revelation and philosophy and thereby to give the key to the latter ... Encouraged by this overture and desirous of more exact information, I asked the venerable old man, 'What will be the principle, what will be the dominant note of this harmony?' Thereupon – I can still see it now – Schelling got up, went to his library, took down an old copy of the New Testament in Greek and came back to me holding out the sacred volume. Then he opened it at Romans XI:36 and read himself: 'For of Him, and by Him, and in Him, are all things.' (The philosopher spoke even of this passage as indicating the Trinity.) 'That', he said simply, 'is the fundament and the last word of my philosophy. Holy Scripture gives them to us.'
>
> A. Eschenauer, *Philosophie religieuse: une visite au philosophe Schelling à Berlin en 1851* (Lille, 1862)

Thought and Being in the *Philosophy of Revelation*

This study began with an assessment of the difficult relationship between the Christian religion and German idealism. It ends with an examination of Schelling's late philosophy which is explicitly if not exclusively religious. As Manfred Durner writes, 'Schelling's late philosophy, both in its content and in the structure of its thought, is influenced by the heritage of Christian thought to the highest degree. Its conception would be unthinkable without this relationship to Christianity.'[1] Josef Anton Stüttler writes, 'It cannot be seriously disputed today that Schelling already in the *Weltalter* but also in the *Philosophy of Mythology* and [the *Philosophy of*] *Revelation* effects a clear turn towards Christian thought.'[2] Klaus Hemmerle says, 'Schelling's later work is concerned with God, and precisely not a merely philosophical God but with the God of living religion, with the God of Christian

---

1   Manfred Durner, 'Zum Problem des "Christlichen" in Schellings "Weltalter" und Spätphilosophie', *Philosophisches Jahrbuch*, 89 (1982): 37.

2   Josef Anton Stüttler, 'Das Gottesproblem im Spätwerk Schellings', *Scholastik*, 36 (1961): 81.

revelation.'[3] Josef Kreiml writes that the question of God is '*the* central question' of the late philosophy and that the whole of the late philosophy should be seen as nothing less than an attempt to elaborate a philosophical theology.[4] Surveying the secondary literature, Christian Danz draws attention to the wide consensus that, 'Christology has a central position in Schelling's late philosophy'.[5] Xavier Tilliette writes, 'The positive philosophy is an enterprise of theological content, directed principally against rationalism and idealism.'[6]

Schelling's contemporaries well understood the reason for his appointment to succeed Hegel as professor of philosophy in Berlin in 1841. The new Prussian king, Friedrich Wilhelm IV, wanted to install Schelling in the 'high temple of Hegelianism' (to use Fuhrmans' expression) in order to pursue a conservative cultural and political agenda: in a splendid phrase, he said that he wanted Schelling to combat 'the dragon seed of Hegelian Pantheism, the flat arrogance of know-alls, and the dissolution by law of domestic discipline'.

Schelling was known as a conservative figure. His star had waned as Hegel's had risen, and many commentators regarded him as an object of ridicule. In 1835 (Hegel had died in 1831) Heinrich Heine made fun of a Schelling who, he said, had been dethroned by Hegel and who could now be seen wandering around Munich looking downcast and dejected. Heine declared sarcastically, 'He has become a good Catholic.' For the humorist and cynic, Schelling's decision to creep back into 'the religious stables of the past'[7] was a thoroughly bad thing: 'The old believers can, if they want, ring their bells and sing their Kyrie eleison in honour of such a conversion [that is, of Schelling, supposedly to Catholicism]. It proves nothing for their doctrine, it proves only that a man turns towards Catholicism when he is old and tired, when his physical and spiritual forces abandon him and when he can no longer either play or think.'[8]

Schelling's luck turned with the accession of a new king to the throne of Prussia. His appointment to Hegel's old chair went hand in hand with Prussia's suppression of David Strauss's *The Life of Jesus, Critically Examined*, the book that founded the school of exegesis which holds that the gospels are historically unreliable documents: Strauss had cited Hegel as one of the sources for his work, which was to excite both Ludwig Feuerbach and Karl Marx, and they of course were great enemies of Schelling. Berlin was then in a ferment of revolutionary enthusiasm and many of the people who attended Schelling's first lectures were to go on to become professional revolutionaries or socialists in later life, Mikhail Bakunin and Friedrich Engels in first place. But also in the audience were people from the whole spectrum of the

---

3   Klaus Hemmerle, *Gott und das Denken nach Schellings Spätphilosophie* (Freiburg im Breisgau: Herder, 1968), p. 11.

4   Josef Kreiml, *Die Wirklichkeit Gottes, Eine Untersuchung über die Metaphysik und die Religionsphilosophie des späten Schelling* (Regensburg: S. Roderer, 1989), p. 1.

5   Christian Danz, *Die philosophische Christologie F.W.J. Schellings* (*Schellingiana*, Vol. 9, ed. Walter E. Erhardt) (Stuttgart-Bad Cannstatt: Frommann-Holzboog, 1996), p. 16

6   Xavier Tilliette, *Schelling, Une Philosophie en devenir* (Paris: Vrin, 2nd edn, 1992), Vol. 2, p. 10.

7   Heinrich Heine, *De l'Allemagne*, Vol. I (Paris: Eugène Penduel, 1835), p. 226.

8   *Ibid.*

Berlin intelligentsia: Friedrick Trendelenburg, Schelling's colleague who influenced him towards Aristotle; Friedrich Carl von Savigny, the great Roman jurist; Sören Kierkegaard, Alexander von Humboldt, Jacob Burckhardt, Leopold von Ranke and others. The lectures aroused huge interest at first, precisely because so many people realised what was at stake.

For his part, Engels was in no doubt about the historical significance of Schelling's move to Berlin. 'Ask anybody in Berlin today on what field the battle for dominion over German public opinion in politics and religion, that is, over Germany itself, is being fought,' he wrote, 'and if he has any idea of the power of the mind over the world he will reply that this battlefield is the University, in particular Lecture-hall No. 6, where Schelling is giving his lectures on the philosophy of revelation.'[9] Engels' account of those lectures is vivid and polemical and he drew particular attention to the essence of the battle, which was between Schelling and Hegel. 'Anybody', he wrote, 'will see in the declaration of Hegel's death pronounced by Schelling's appearance in Berlin the vengeance of the gods for the declaration of Schelling's death which Hegel pronounced in his time.' Naturally, Engels sided vigorously with Hegel against what he later called 'the last stand of reaction against free philosophy', that is, Hegelianism. As it turned out, of course, Schelling's 'last stand' proved notably ineffective and Hegel's epigones, the Marxists, were soon to embark on what turned out to be a century of cultural hegemony which seemed to come to an end only with the so-called 'collapse of communism' in 1989–91. To this extent, Schelling is a philosopher on the losing side of history.

If perceptive political observers like Engels noticed immediately what was afoot, this was because Schelling had become not only a politically conservative figure but also a philosophically and religiously conservative one too. His increasing interest in religion went hand in hand with his increasing emphasis on the primacy of existence, that is, with a realist ontological standpoint. Schelling wrote, 'In all reality two aspects can be recognised and stated: *quid sit und quod sit* = what a being (*ein Seiendes*) is and *that* a being is ... Is philosophy just concerned with the *essence* (*Wesen*) of things, and does it have nothing to do with their existence?'[10] No, he replied. *That* things exist, he insisted, we know only by experience, not reason. Experience is thus the ultimate source of knowledge about the world. Explaining Schelling's view, Bowie writes, 'Reason can legislate on what must be the case *if* something exists, but not whether something really *does* exist.'[11] This did not mean that existence was beyond reason, nor that Schelling's approach was irrationalist. Rather, Schelling insisted that being (*Sein*) was the 'inborn content of reason'.[12] Precisely because thinking required being, Schelling attacked modern philosophy for

9   Friedrich Engels, 'Schelling on Hegel', *Telegraph für Deutschland*, 207/208 (December 1841), <www.marxists.org>. The article was signed 'Friedrich Oswald' but Engels admitted his authorship after the publication of *Schelling und die Offenbarung* in 1842, for which he had used the same pseudonym.

10   Schelling, *Philosophie der Offenbarung* (1841–42) (Paulus-Nachschrift), ed. Manfred Frank (Frankfurt am Main: Suhrkamp, 1993), p. 99.

11   Andrew Bowie, *Schelling and Modern European Philosophy* (London: Routledge, 1993), p. 163.

12   Schelling, *Philosophie der Offenbarung* (1841–42) (Paulus-Nachschrift), p. 100.

being only negative and abstract. Any philosophy which moved only in the realm of concepts, like Kant's, could give only a very unsatisfactory account of the world.[13]

The search for knowledge thus implied the search for intelligible being: philosophy assumes being.[14] The that-ness of reality precedes all philosophy, and thus philosophy even presupposes the existence of God, as the fount of all existence.[15] Unlike systems of emanation, for which God is a mere concept arrived at at the end, Schelling said that his system should take God's real existence as its very beginning, as the source of all existence and reason. In a very telling phrase, he wrote that if the potentiality, which was above all being, existed, 'Then existence must be the first principle (*Prius*); the concept comes later.'[16] The ontological argument, and the idealism it underpins, was wrong to see things the other way around.

Fichte, for instance, was too subjective. 'No one can find in Fichte's *Wissenschaftslehre* the slightest trace of objective knowledge.'[17] Nonetheless, Schelling praised him for having at least begun with being, which he had grasped in the act of self-consciousness. This was the point of departure for the succeeding philosophy: 'It was only a small step from this to recognizing the essence of the foundation (*Prius*) of all being (*Sein*).'[18]

The late Schelling was thus able to describe his own trajectory as one of attempting to work within the framework of his predecessors, while at the same time liberating himself from their excessively subjective preoccupations – much the interpretation offered in Chapter 3. Because he had thought he still needed the I as a basis, Schelling explained, he had turned to nature as an object of philosophy, and by the time of the *System of Transcendental Idealism*, he said, the objective nature of his methodology was already visible.[19] This seems a very fair description of his own development.

According to Schelling, his own Identity Philosophy had differed from Fichte's claim that the outside world was non-being or non-subject. He also began to see that such negative philosophy did not deny the existence of objects in the real world: rather, it simply passed the question by. Negative philosophy should say that it does not know whether God or the world exists.[20] Kant had allowed himself to be distracted by the accusation that he was an idealist who denied the existence of things in the real world, whereas in truth his philosophy, being 'absolutely idealist', in fact did not treat the question at all. Schelling said that Kant's attempt to prove the contrary was a mistake: only 'relative idealism' actively denied the existence of things.[21] But because of its negative character, said Schelling, his own Identity Philosophy merely became another form of Spinozism.

---

13 *Ibid.*, p. 109.
14 *Ibid.*
15 *Ibid.*, p. 109.
16 *Ibid.*, p. 110.
17 *Ibid.*, p. 111.
18 *Ibid.*, p. 111.
19 *Ibid.*, p. 112.
20 *Ibid.*, p. 119.
21 *Ibid.*, pp. 119 and 120.

It was Hegel who took the implications of the Identity Philosophy to their logical conclusion. It is comforting, in view of the cosmogonical context in which this study has tried to place Schelling's thought, that Schelling should have specifically used the term 'Orphic' to criticise the Hegelian absolute, in which everything lay hidden and waiting to be revealed.[22] Hegel tried to prove the existence of the Absolute in his *Logic*, said Schelling, but the very title emphasised that his method was purely logical: 'Logic makes no claim to contain anything real within it. Thought is on its own (*ist mit sich allein*) so that it never has the world, but only itself, as content. The richness of the concrete world, says Hegel, is still beyond it. The process takes place within the realm of pure concept.'[23]

The result of this was that, whereas previous philosophy had assumed the real as an *a priori* concept – 'concepts were already made with respect to the real'[24] – subsequent philosophy had lost all relation to reality completely. Its concepts were this 'empty', said Schelling. He sounded more and more like Gilson when he bemoaned the fact that, 'Since the decline of metaphysics which Bacon began, ontology has lost all importance.'[25] Schelling emphasised once again – as this study has affirmed – that his Nature Philosophy was an attempt to counteract this decline of 'metaphysics' and to put thought back into contact with reality.[26] For 'with mere concepts, there can be no real thought'.[27]

Hegel's other weakness, Schelling maintained, was to have described his Absolute as if it were a thing or a person. 'A mere concept can obviously not "decide"', Schelling wrote scathingly.[28] In other words, Schelling was attacking Hegel on his favourite ground, the creation. Schelling insisted that he was not trying to mock Hegel's negative philosophy, but merely to describe its limits: negative philosophy dealt with the world of possibilities, positive philosophy with the facts.[29]

In particular, Schelling attacked Hegel's notion that the development of the world was the development of God, for this would mean that God were less perfect at the beginning than at the end.[30] Negative philosophy or rationalist philosophy (*Vernunftphilosophie*) was neither Christian nor un-Christian, he said. The key was not to have a philosophy for which Christianity was a mere possibility, but rather one which integrated it entirely. Here, indeed, lay the crux. 'Revelation assumes the real God, and a real relationship of human consciousness to God. Pure rational science (*Vernunftwissenschaft*) cannot even include this as a possibility.'[31]

Schelling's view of existence, including God's, was that it was the presupposition of thought and thus beyond thought, but not therefore irrational. 'If we want to attain anything which is outside thought (*irgend etwas außer dem Denken Seyendes*), we

---

22   *Ibid.*, p. 123.
23   *Ibid.*, p. 127.
24   *Ibid.*, p. 128.
25   *Ibid.*, p. 128.
26   *Ibid.*, p. 128.
27   *Ibid.*, p. 129.
28   *Ibid.*, p. 130.
29   *Ibid.*, p. 131.
30   *Ibid.*, p. 132.
31   *Ibid.*, p. 136.

have to go out from a being which is absolutely independent of all thought, which comes before all thought. Of this being (*Seyn*) Hegel's philosophy knows nothing. It has no place for this concept.' Paradoxically, this led Schelling back to something approaching a Kantian position, for 'precisely that which is in God, thanks to which He is that which groundlessly exists, Kant calls an abyss for human reason: for what is this other than that before which reason falls silent, by which it is swallowed up, and against which it is nothing more, and can do nothing.'[32]

Schelling quoted Kant approvingly at this point, for he had realised that freedom was indeed an abyss for human reason. But he said that 'in our times' philosophy had posited this 'as a mere moment in thought, whereas in this thought, which is the deepest of all in human nature, it is a question of that being which is before all thought.'[33] But that before which reason fell silent was being itself. As he said,

> This ultimate thing is that which stands above being, that which no longer goes over into being, it is that which we have named the being (*das Seiende*) ... (It is) that which is most worthy of knowledge ... (it is) that which is to be known in the most perfect way, in the purest knowledge, because according to its nature it is the whole of existing reality, not potentiality, but pure reality, whereas everything else is mixed out of being and non-being, and can therefore be the object only of a knowledge composed of knowledge and non-knowledge, which we call empirical.[34]

Being precedes thought: thought has to recognise itself as subsequent to real existence and as coming out of something unthinkable. Or to put it as Manfred Frank does, 'Idealism explains the manner of being of the real, but not reality itself.'[35] There is a fundamental impossibility of deducing an existing idea from a concept. 'Thought cannot justify its unity with pure being on its own. It is therefore not justified by itself, but rather by another instance.'[36]

It is this thought which caused Schelling to abandon idealism (including transcendental idealism) and to return to realism. As Etienne Gilson glosses, 'The idea of an existence is in no case equivalent to an existence. An existence can be ascertained or inferred: it cannot be deduced.'[37] While negative philosophy culminates in the possibility of real existence, positive philosophy begins with the fact of it.

Rehearsing his familiar attack on the ontological argument, and his belief of the damage caused by Spinozism, which he said affected all modern philosophers, Schelling also attacked the mystical theories of Böhme and Jacobi. 'This is the beginning of the reaction of Orientalism against the Occidentalism of our essentially still Aristotelian philosophy',[38] he said, significantly. This was because of the former's

---

32   *Einleitung in die Philosophie der Offenbarung oder Begründung der positiven Philosophie* (1842–43), II/3, 164.
33   Ibid., II/3, 163.
34   Ibid., II/3, 148–9.
35   Manfred Frank, *Der Unendliche Mangel an Sein, Schellings Hegelkrikitk und die Anfänge der Marxschen Dialektik* (Frankfurt am Main: Suhrkamp, 1975), p. 149.
36   Ibid., p. 150.
37   Etienne Gilson, *Le thomisme* (Paris: Vrin, 6th edn, 1989), p. 61.
38   Schelling, *Philosophie der Offenbarung* (1841–42) (Paulus-Nachschrift), pp. 155–6.

sovereign disdain for any of the data provided by human reason. By contrast, 'The beginning of positive philosophy is the being which comes before all thinking.'[39]

It was precisely in this vein that Schelling said that, in criticizing Hegel, he was speaking not as an idealist but as someone who started with reality: 'Whatever starts in mere thought can only continue in mere thought, and cannot get any further than the idea. That which will attain reality must start with reality.'[40] As Frank says, 'Only when the extra-logical *reality* of the principle is ensured can a dialectical movement attain reality in consequence.'[41]

Indeed, Schelling wrote, 'The last question is always, "Why is there anything at all? Why is there not nothing?" I cannot answer this question with mere abstractions from real being. I must first of all admit some reality or other before I can come to that abstract being.'[42] Unlike Heidegger – who genuinely thought that this question could be put[43] – Schelling seemed to rule out this possibility. Being simply could not be doubted, as he had said in the 1804 *System*.[44] As he emphasised, he did not proceed from essence to being, but rather from being to essence (*vom Seyn zum Wesen*) in the traditional Aristotelian manner. Being, he emphasised, was primary, essence secondary.[45] Indeed, as he said explicitly: 'It is not because there is thinking that there is being, but rather, because there is being that there is thinking.'[46]

We have seen that Schelling argued against Kant that freedom was not practical reason, but the capacity to subvert the natural and divine order of things. In doing so, he maintained, also against Kant, that man was not entirely a creature of reason: reason was not his essence, as Kant thought, freedom was. This freedom was the capacity for good and evil, not the capacity to act rationally. God's creation was certainly not unreasonable, but the fact of it could not be subsumed within the structures of human reason. Human reason could not, of itself, come to a knowledge of being, and could not, therefore, deduce the existence of the world from *a priori* assumptions. For Schelling, essential aspects of the universe were not logical at all.

This was precisely because of God's and man's freedom. The former had created the world out of an act of utterly undetermined freedom; the latter had put the world into a state of disorder. This brought Schelling into straightforward contradiction with one aspect of his earlier thinking. Whereas before he had optimistically seen only the positive side to nature, and had thought that nature's principle of formation was always harmonious and meaningful – the growth of crystals and organic phenomena epitomised this for him – he later came to realise that nature had a destructive force as well. He came to see nature as a dark urge, which was longing and lustful – even if evil itself arose only in man. Nature itself was not evil, but it was certainly no longer a simple *Vorform des Geistes* (prior form of spirit). Instead, man was guilty

---

39 *Ibid.*, p. 156.
40 *Einleitung in die Philosophie der Offenbarung* (1842–43), II/3, 162.
41 Frank, *Der unendliche Mangel an Sein*, p. 168, emphasis original.
42 *Einleitung in die Philosophie der Offenbarung* (1842–43), II/3, 242.
43 Martin Heidegger, *Einführung in die Metaphysik* (Tübingen: Max Niemeyer, 1987), p. 1; see also Bergson's criticism of this question in *L'Evolution créatrice* (Paris, 1907).
44 *System der gesammten Philosophie* (1804), I/6, 155, quoted in Chapter 3.
45 *Einleitung in die Philosophie der Offenbarung* (1842–43), II/3, 159.
46 *Ibid.*, II/3, 161, note 1.

of bringing evil into the world, even if he was only making actual something that had always been potential in nature, the selfish will.

Because he redefined will as a kind of natural urge (*Drang*), Schelling showed that will and reason did not form a single unit. He decoupled one from the other – the very opposite of Kant. In time, this thought was to be used by Schopenhauer and Nietzsche to develop philosophies which attributed total importance to the will, but this was never Schelling's position. On the contrary, he would have disagreed with both of his successors that the understanding was a mere tool in the hands of the will, for this was but Hobbesian theory in nineteenth-century German garb. On the contrary, it is the central claim here that Schelling was reacting against idealism and materialism together, for they are two sides of the same coin. In this sense, he stood between ages, wishing to accord total primacy neither to the will nor to reason.

Instead, Schelling accorded primacy to God. He reminded us that God created man in His own image, but that man turned away from Him. The possibility of the restoration of the original order of things was then introduced by God's incarnation as Christ, and at the end of time that order will be fully restored. Schelling explained that the spirit of love would reign through everything, and the essence of love presupposed separateness and disorder, which only love was capable of overcoming. It is, indeed, striking that Schelling attributed such importance to love in his ontology, a theme dear to both St Augustine and Plotinus. In Biblical metaphysics, the Absolute (God) is *agape* or charity: the metaphysics of creation is unthinkable without a theology of charity. Schelling held that good and evil could not oppose each other if they were not already constituted as opposites, and they would not *be* opposites if they did not reciprocally condition each other, and were thus not ultimately correlated in their being. Schelling designated this concordance or mutual letting-be (of ground and existence) as *Liebe* (love), and he even illustrated the idea with the dubious etymological claim that *vermögen* (to be able) came from *mögen* (to like).

His central point was that God must take on the ground if there is to be creation, as otherwise He remains just pure freedom. Thus, Schelling repeatedly explained God's decision to create the world, and His relationship to it, as one which flowed from love. This was very different from Hegel, who in the Preface to the *Phenomenology*, gave a narcissistic interpretation of the creation: 'The life of God and divine cognition can be characterised as love playing with itself.'[47] For Hegel, love was a symmetrical relationship of mutual dependence in which I can be myself through my reflection in the Other. In Schelling, by contrast, love is a non-dialectical, non-reflexive relationship in which two separate things are united while remaining separate. Given such different concepts of love, it is hardly surprising that Schelling was uneasy with the narcissistic elements in idealism, and that he proposed in their place a philosophy in which man is turned outwards to being and towards other men.

Man was therefore no longer at the centre of the world, as he had been after Kant's anti-Copernican revolution. On the contrary, God was at the centre and man at the periphery, and man had to strive to depend upon God as much he could. Indeed, instead of the apparent clarity of self-consciousness unlocking the mysteries

---

47   Hegel, *Phänomenologie des Geistes*, *Vorrede* (Stuttgart: Reclam, 1987), p. 21.

of the world, the evident fact of human freedom was in fact one of the most difficult things of all to explain. In such conditions, history could never be conceived as the inexorable unfolding of the rational, because although such an unfolding could occur, man was always there to upset it.

Philosophy and Revelation

Schelling alleged that his own philosophy – he called it '*a priori* empiricism'[48] – was based on all experience, including supersensory and metaphysical experience. Because 'only fools say there is no God',[49] the authority on which positive philosophy rested was that of revelation, and on the appearance of the world and of man.[50] Schelling thus insisted that positive philosophy must include Christianity within it, just as it included nature – although it would not be philosophy if it were not there independently of Christianity itself. Schelling claimed that this idea made his philosophy special, but this was also St Thomas Aquinas' position. Aquinas always emphasised that reason could achieve nearly everything independently of faith.[51]

Indeed, Schelling seemed to call explicitly on Scholastic vocabulary when, having discussed being in general, he turned to the question of God's being and quoted the well-known Latin formula: 'In Deo essentia et existentia unum idemque sunt.'[52] Schelling fully subscribed to its thesis: 'The essence (*Wesen*) and thus the concept of God consists precisely in that He *is*', he wrote.[53] Using Latin freely, Schelling trotted off other very Thomist-sounding phrases, one of which in fact is a direct quote from St Thomas' *Tractatus de spiritualibus creaturis*[54]– 'est ipse suum esse ... suum esse est ipse'.[55] He went on, still in Latin, '"In Deo non differunt esse et quod est", the what of God (*das Was Gottes*) consists in being (*Sein*).'[56] These quotations recall the following quotations from Aquinas, even if (unlike the first) they are not direct quotes: 'Deus est suum esse', 'In Deo idem est esse et essentia' and 'Ipsum igitur esse Dei est sua essentia', in the *Summa contra Gentiles*;[57] 'Sua substantia non sit aliud quam suum esse', also in *Summa contra Gentiles*;[58] 'Essentia sua non est aliud quam esse suum', in *De Ente*

---

48 Schelling, *Philosophie der Offenbarung* (1841–42) (Paulus-Nachschrift), p. 147.
49 *Ibid.*
50 *Ibid.*, p. 148.
51 See for instance, Aquinas, *Summa contra Gentiles*, Book 1, Chapters 3, 4, 7 and 8.
52 Schelling, *Philosophie der Offenbarung* (1841–42) (Paulus-Nachschrift), p. 161.
53 *Ibid.*, p. 162.
54 Cf. Aquinas, 'Unde dicimus quod Deus est ipsum suum esse', in *Tractatus de spiritualibus creaturis*, Articulus I, Responsio, ed. Leo W. Keeler (Rome: Pontifica Universitas Gregoriana, 1946), p. 11.
55 Schelling, *Philosophie der Offenbarung* (1841–42) (Paulus-Nachschrift), p. 162.
56 Schelling, *Philosophie der Offenbarung* (1841–42) (Paulus-Nachschrift), p. 162; cf. Schelling, *System der Weltalter* (1827–28), ed. S. Peetz (Frankfurt am Main: Klostermann, 1990), p. 105.
57 Aquinas, *Summa contra Gentiles*, Book 1, Chapter 22.
58 Aquinas, *Summa Contra Gentiles*, Book 2, Chapter 52.

et Essentia;⁵⁹ 'Deus est idem quod sua essentia', in *Summa Theologiae*;⁶⁰ and 'Deus non solum est sua essentia ... sed etiam suum esse,' also in *Summa Theologiae*.⁶¹

Schelling credited Spinoza with having subscribed to this *a se esse* of God, but criticised him for never getting any further. He insisted again and again that existence did not flow of necessity from God, but rather that the act of creation was free. God was not blindly being, as the ontological argument suggested, but rather that which can be (*das Seinkönnende*). This, indeed, was '*principium divinitatis*'. 'The Godhead consists in its mastery over all being, and it is the highest task of philosophy to attain the master of being by beginning with that which simply is (τό ὄν).'⁶²

Although this author believes that he is the first to have tracked down the direct quote from Aquinas, there are several other commentators on Schelling who have noted the highly Scholastic tone of the later philosophy. Manfred Frank has commented on the 'richly Scholastic' nature of Schelling's writing in the later period;⁶³ Adriano Bausola has said of the positive philosophy that, 'The distance from the traditional perspective of the Scholastic type is not too great.'⁶⁴ Others have commented on the Aristotelian influences on Schelling in Berlin.⁶⁵ Indeed, throughout the later philosophy, Schelling made favourable references to Scholastic metaphysics, and especially to its pre-Cartesian relationship to being.⁶⁶ Claims such as the following abound: 'True understanding of the world is given indeed by the right metaphysics, which is just why it used to be called the kingly science.'⁶⁷ Meanwhile, philosophical systems such as Hegel's were dismissed as 'the absolute negation of all that is metaphysical'.⁶⁸ We saw earlier that Schelling approvingly noted the suspicion in which the Scholastics held the ontological argument, an argument which he himself dismissed in order to save the transcendence and the liberty of God.⁶⁹ He argued that it was precisely because reason was subsequent to God that it could not prove

---

59   Aquinas, *De Ente et Essentia*, Chapter 5.

60   Aquinas, *Summa Theologiae*, Part I, Question 3, Article 3, Response.

61   Aquinas, *Summa Theologiae*, Part I, Question 3, Article 4, Response.

62   Schelling, *Philosophie der Offenbarung* (1841–42) (Paulus-Nachschrift), p. 172.

63   Frank, *Der unendliche Mangel an Sein*, p. 147.

64   Adriano Bausola, *Metafisica e rivelazione nella filosofia positiva di Schelling* (Milan: Vita e Pensiero, 1965), p. 100.

65   Rüdiger Bubner, 'Dieu chez Aristote et Schelling', in Jean-François Courtine and Jean-François Marquet (eds), *Le dernier Schelling: raison et positivité* (Paris: Vrin, 1994); B. Majoli, 'La critica ad Hegel in Schelling e Kierkegaard', *Rivista di filosofia neo-scolatica*, XLVI (1954); Christian August Brandis, *Johann Gottlieb Fichtes hundertjähriger Geburtstag, gefeiert in der Aula der kgl. Pr. Friedrich-Wilhelms-Universität zu Bonn* (Bonn, 1862); see also Walter Kasper, *Das Absolute in der Geschichte, Philosophie und Theologie der Geschichte in der Spätphilosophie Schellings* (Mainz: Grünewald, 1965), p. 429.

66   For example *Philosophische Einleitung in die Philosophie der Mythologie, oder Darstellung der reinrationalen Philosophie* (1847–52), II/1, 281; *Einleitung in die Philosophie der Offenbarung oder Begründung der positiven Philosophie*, Berliner Vorlesung (1842–43), II/3, 82; Schelling, *Philosophie der Offenbarung* (1841–42) (Paulus-Nachschrift), p. 100.

67   *Einleitung in die Philosophie der Offenbarung* (1842–43), II/3, 28.

68   *Ibid.*, II/3, 31.

69   Xavier Tilliette, *L'absolu et la Philosophie: essais sur Schelling* (Paris: Presses Universitaires de France, 1987), p. 180.

His existence.[70] Reason reposed instead on an abyss which cannot be thought, *das Unvordenkliche* – a clearly anti-rationalist idea.

God does not *need* the world, as Schelling himself had suggested in the *Freedom* essay: he is its master. Schelling savaged the notion (which he himself once held) that the creation was the result of God's desire to achieve self-consciousness. 'This is really the lowest form of popularisation', he wrote.[71] '*God does not need to go through the world (*durch die Welt hindurch zu gehen) *in order to come to self-consciousness through man or through world history.* God is already master of the world *before* the world. He can posit it or not. It makes no difference to him to exist in this way or that; with respect to His being, it is all the same.'[72] By taking this position, Schelling was explicitly renouncing an earlier heretical thought. Creation was not the result of a logical process flowing out of God. Thus did Schelling reach Christian orthodoxy in his theory of the creation.

Because order was brought out of chaos and the void, Schelling insisted that understanding has the incomprehensible as its basis. Thus he returned to a scheme which was similar to that of the *Freedom* essay: all understanding and order depended on overcoming the incomprehensible and the orderless.[73] The very purpose of creation was that man should rest in God.[74] Schelling insisted on the freedom of revelation, as well as of creation.[75] His assessment of the powers of human reason strongly resembled that of the Scholastics:

> But even though the revelation cannot be a necessary process, the philosophy of revelation will not let it stand there as something incomprehensible. Even if it is admitted that the philosophy of revelation can only be a free act, a philosophy can still be conceived which holds it possible partly to grasp and partly to explain the will according to the way it revealed itself. That decision of revelation does indeed exceed human concepts, but it is conceivable as the greatness of the decision is the same as the greatness of God. All that man can do in this respect is extend the narrowness of his concepts to the greatness of the divine ones.[76]

As in the Munich Lectures, so in the late philosophy Schelling blamed Descartes for the fact that philosophy had broken off the dialogue between the positive content of religion, only in order to try to reproduce the same results by itself. Although God was greater than our thought, Schelling insisted that 'all the treasures of knowledge are hidden in Christ'.[77] Therefore, it was necessary that they be grasped through Him. 'Christum scire est omnia scire', he wrote.[78] Faith helped knowledge, but it was also the culmination of it. And, in a peroration which will warm the heart of anyone who finds modern philosophy cold, inhuman and devoid of any sense of the sacred,

---

70   *Einleitung in die Philosophie der Offenbarung* (1842–43), II/3, 158ff.
71   Schelling, *Philosophie der Offenbarung* (1841–42) (Paulus-Nachschrift), p. 133.
72   *Ibid.*, pp. 183–4, emphases original.
73   *Ibid.*, p. 186.
74   *Ibid.*, p. 199.
75   *Ibid.*, p. 253.
76   *Ibid.*, pp. 253–4; cf. Aquinas, *Summa Contra Gentiles*, Book 1, Chapter 7.
77   Schelling, *Philosophie der Offenbarung* (1841–42) (Paulus-Nachschrift), p. 254.
78   *Ibid.*, p. 255.

Schelling wrote, 'Nothing is more mournful than the business of all rationalists, who want to make that rational (*vernünftig*) which is above all reason.'[79] Attributing mind, love and even irony to God, Schelling insisted on his personality.[80] Positive philosophy, he reiterated, assumed a real relationship between man and God.

Revelation, Schelling argued, meant specifically Christianity, not mythology or any kind of paganism.[81] 'In a philosophy of revelation, it is a matter of explaining the person of Christ.'[82] He devoted many pages of extensive Biblical commentary to showing this. In particular, he used the opening verses of the Gospel of St John to defend his argument that the reasonable principle which brings light and understanding into an otherwise chaotic and formless void is also a person. The concept of revelation and the Incarnation was indeed so central that Schelling said that the Jewish God was 'not the true God'.[83] He argued that the culmination of revelation was when the word was made flesh,[84] and that this was the single crucial event in world history. He insisted that this event showed that Christianity is not a doctrine, but a thing (*eine Sache*).[85] This, it is clear, is quite congruent with the positive philosophy which, like Christianity itself, is not just a matter of concepts but rather of really existing things and historical events and people.

Schelling's insistence on the events of the Christian revelation as genuine historical events (an emphasis he makes with reference to Biblical texts as straightforward evidence of that history) was, of course, designed to show the revelation as the realisation of freedom in the world. Mythology was an example of a failed history of freedom but the Christian revelation was an example of one in which freedom is perfected.

Schelling and Aristotle

It is also significant for our appreciation of Schelling's development away from idealism that he admitted in the *Philosophy of Revelation* that he had known nothing of Aristotle while he wrote on Identity Philosophy. (It is true that the German idealists, Kant in particular, knew little about Plato and Aristotle, and still less about the great metaphysicians of the Middle Ages. When they dismissed 'metaphysics' they often associated it with the teachings of Wolff.[86])

The late Schelling's recourse to Aristotle was revealing, of course, because Aristotle was the first and definitive ontological realist. It is also interesting that Schelling should emphasise that the *Timaeus* was the summit of Plato's achievement,[87] for this is the most realist and least essentialist of Plato's works. Indeed, Tresmontant

---

79   *Ibid.*, p. 256.
80   *Ibid.*, p. 257.
81   *Ibid.*, p. 259.
82   *Ibid.*, p. 260; cf. *Philosophie der Offenbarung, Zweiter Theil*, II/4, 35.
83   Schelling, *Philosophie der Offenbarung* (1841–42) (Paulus-Nachschrift), p. 278.
84   *Ibid.*, p. 287.
85   *Ibid.*, p. 309.
86   Etienne Gilson, *L'être et l'essence* (Paris: Vrin, 1994), pp. 196–7.
87   Schelling, *Philosophie der Offenbarung* (1841–42) (Paulus-Nachschrift), p. 140.

argues that there are two tendencies in Plato: an Orphic one, according to which the created world is a degraded shadow of the Absolute, but also 'a more optimist tendency, which is expressed above all in his later works, the *Timaeus* and the *Laws*.'[88] Schelling's approval for the *Timaeus*, in other words, is more compatible with orthodox Christian metaphysics than attachment to other works of Plato would be.

Schelling used Aristotle's theology to attack Hegel's *Logic*. We have seen that Hegel's system pursued to the very end the 'revolutionary'[89] task of explaining reason totally from within. For Schelling, the error was precisely that Hegel, despite the Kantian critique, had tried to arrive at classical metaphysics exclusively by means of concepts. This was an error because beyond the concept there lay being itself, which was the foundation of the possibility of concepts. As Schelling said,

> Aristotle has this ultimate term (*to energeia on*) as the really existing, but only because his whole science is based on experience ... Even today, Aristotle's progression from the existent to the logical would be the only way for philosophy."[90]

For Aristotle, it was axiomatic that philosophy was attached to the cosmos, and that it did not operate with concepts which had nothing to do with reality. It was also obvious to him that it was not necessary to demonstrate the existence of the world before thinking about it. And the same time, the mystery of being is that it exists at all. As Schelling wrote in the *Philosophy of Revelation*, with reference to Aristotle,

> The contingent element in the unprethinkable existent had to be shown. It comes before that which exists, the existent itself (*dem Existierenden selbst*), so that the latter is not posited as an essence (*Wesen*), but is directly being (*das Seiende*) in a quite ecstatic (*ekstatisch*) manner, posited out of itself. The essence has not realised itself, but is realised before it thinks. In it is the antipode of all idea ...
>
> This *actus purus* has not become through another *actus* – then it would have to have been potentiality. Rather, it is inaccessible being (*das unzugängliche Sein*), to which thinking must renounce all priority (*Prius*), and thus itself. The being which cannot be thought in advance (*das Unvordenklichseiende*) has being in itself, in the sense that has been explained; it is therefore that which is in itself (*das Ansichseiende*). But what is it *itself*? It itself cannot be anything but *that which necessarily exists through its own nature*. But because it exists by itself (*vor sich*), so its necessity is not determined by its nature, it is just *actu*, that is, *only blindly, contingently existing*.[91]

Aristotle himself, according to Schelling, had fought a similar battle to his own. Existence, said Schelling, demanded an explanation,[92] and Schelling said that his positive philosophy was that which deduced the world from the 'really existing

---

88 Claude Tresmontant, *La métaphysique du christianisme et la naissance de la philosophie chrétienne: problème de la création et de l'anthropologie des origines à Saint Augustin* (Paris: Seuil, 1961), p. 276.
89 Bubner's adjective, in 'Dieu chez Aristote et Schelling', p. 123.
90 Schelling, *Philosophie der Offenbarung* (1841–42) (Paulus-Nachschrift), pp. 142–3.
91 *Ibid.*, p. 167.
92 *Ibid.*, p. 139.

God'.[93] By the same token, when philosophers like the relativist Heraclitus deduced everything from concepts, Aristotle dismissed them[94] – rightly so in Schelling's view. 'For mere movement in thought excludes all reality.'[95]

In some respects, therefore, Schelling did not vary between his early and his late philosophy. He had declared in 1797, 'Common sense has never separated the thing from the concept',[96] arguing that philosophy should not do so either. Again in 1799, he had insisted, 'We do not know only this or that, we know absolutely nothing except through experience, and to this extent the whole of our knowledge consists in the findings of experience (*Erfahrungssätzen*).'[97] In the later philosophy, he used Aristotelian realist arguments explicitly: 'When I know a plant and know what kind of a plant it is, I recognize the concept which I previously had of it in that which is present, that is, in that which exists here. In cognition there are always two things which come together, as the Latin word *cognitio* indicates.'[98] This compares to Aristotle's 'We acquire our knowledge of all things only in so far as they contain something universal ...'[99] The conceptual inheres in the real. Moreover, said Schelling, 'Reason can never affirm without experience that anything exists, and especially that this particular thing which has been seen *a priori* actually exists in the world.'[100]

Given that these apparently empiricist claims seemed to sit uneasily with Schelling's wild speculations about the history of the Absolute in the *Freedom* essay, we must remind ourselves that the point is this: the *fact* of being is something we know through experience, and something which philosophy must assume but cannot prove. To this extent, Schelling returns in some respects to a Kantian schema, albeit with the differences that he himself outlined. In Schulz's words, Schelling insisted that 'Experience does not give us distorted images in which essences (*das Wesen*) exist for a second time' – this would be a Platonist schema, or at least the one caricatured by Aristotle's 'third man' argument – 'it gives only that essence, which does not exist on its own, as really existing (*daseiendes*);[101] or, as Schelling himself puts it, 'this particular plant, at this point in space, in this moment in time'.[102] Essences, in other words, exist only in real things, not in some separate Platonic realm. According to him, reason grasps the real, and anyone who thinks that reason is a stranger to reality is mistaken:

---

93   *Ibid.*, p. 139.
94   'Philosophy has become mathematics for modern thinkers' (Aristotle, *Metaphysics*, I, ix, 27, 992b).
95   Schelling, *Philosophie der Offenbarung* (1841–42) (Paulus-Nachschrift), p. 139.
96   *Abhandlungen zur Erläuterung des Idealismus der Wissenschaftslehre* (1797), I/1, 362.
97   *Einleitung zu dem Entwurf eines Systems der Naturphilosophie* (1799), I/3, 278.
98   *Einleitung in die Philosophie der Offenbarung* (1842–43), II/3, 58.
99   Aristotle, *Metaphysics*, III, iii, 4, 1 (999a).
100 *Einleitung in die Philosophie der Offenbarung* (1842–43), II/3, 58–9.
101 Walter Schulz, *Die Vollendung des deutschen Idealismus in der Spätphilosophie Schellings* (Stuttgart and Köln: Kohlhammer, 1955), p. 23.
102 *Einleitung in die Philosophie der Offenbarung* (1842–43), II/3, 59.

The distinction (between reality and the real) has been interpreted to mean that philosophy or reason has absolutely nothing to do with existing being (*das Seyende*); it would, of course, be a poor version of reason which had nothing to do with existing being, but only with a chimera. But this is not the way in which the distinction was expressed: on the contrary, reason has to do with nothing other than existing being, and indeed with being according to its *matter* and *content* (this is existing being as it is in itself) *(das Seyende in seinem Ansich)* ... Of course, if I have grasped the essence *(das Wesen)* or the What *(das Was)* of a thing, a plant for instance, I have grasped something real, for a plant is not something non-existent, it is not a chimera, but something which does exist, and in this sense it is true that reality *(das Wirkliche)* is not something foreign, closed or inaccessible to our thought, and that existing being *(das Seyende)* does not have the concept outside it, but inside it.[103]

Chapter 2 tried to show that it has always been a cornerstone of traditional realist thinking that individual existing things have an intelligible essence within them, which it is the work of the intellect to discover, and that this view was undermined by idealism from Descartes onwards. This is what Schelling was saying here: being is the basis, source and root of all intelligibility. Philosophy since Descartes, by contrast, had presupposed the priority of the ideal over the real, and, as Schelling said of Hegel, encouraged the view that the whole of being could be comprehended within concepts. Schelling wanted to overcome the practice by which reason 'admires its own reflection in being'.[104] Indeed, in a strikingly realist vein, Schelling insisted that Hegel's fundamental idea was that reason should concern itself only with the essence of things,[105] and not with their existence.

Thus Schelling believed that reason could determine the real essences of things. He broke with idealism in his assessment of the knowledge which could be derived from the self-knowledge of the subject, for he repeated that actual knowledge of existing things came only from experience. He rejected self-consciousness as a source of knowledge of the outside world:

> Reason gives everything, according to content, which happens in experiences. It grasps the real, but not thereby reality. For this is a great difference. The science of reason does not give us (*gewähren*) the real existence of nature and of its individual forms; to this extent, experience, through which know the truly existent, is a source independent of reason."[106]

This was why, later, Schelling wrote in a very realist–Aristotelian vein:

> There is no wisdom for man, if in the objective run of things there is none either. The first assumption for philosophy, as a striving after wisdom, is that in the object, that is, in being, in the world itself, there must be wisdom. To demand wisdom means to demand being which is posited with wisdom, with foresight, and with freedom.[107]

---

103   *Ibid.*, II/3, 60.
104   Andrew Bowie, *Schelling and Modern European philosophy*, p. 128.
105   *Einleitung in die Philosophie der Offenbarung* (1842–43), II/3, 60.
106   *Ibid.*, II/3, 61.
107   *Ibid.*, II/3, 203.

The reasonableness of the world comes from the very fact that it was created by a wise and free God. All that experience does is to verify the constructions of being which reason builds *a priori*. It is only thus that reason can find out whether its constructions are mere chimeras or whether they have any basis in reality. 'This control is experience. For only experience, not reason, can tell that that which has been constructed exists.'[108] Later, Schelling wrote, 'Rational philosophy has its truth in the immanent necessity of its progress; it is so independent of existence that it would even be true if nothing existed.'[109] Schelling himself said he was starting not with mere thought but instead with true being itself. Only this approach could lead to a knowledge of God: 'It is not the Absolute *prius* which needs to be proved, but its consequence that must be factually proved, and thereby the divinity of the *prius*.'[110]

Schelling's view of God has also been compared to that of Aristotle.[111] Aristotle's starting point was change and movement in the world. Unlike Plato, Aristotle did not believe in the Forms, and did not believe that the principles that underlie change in the world existed only in eternity. On the contrary, those principles provided a true foundation for reality in its concrete being. Aristotle posited a sufficient ground for this eternal change and movement, which was itself immobile – the doctrine of the unmoved mover.[112] The unmoved mover operated as an efficient force as both substance and actuality for the good of the world, and was linked to it by love. Without this supreme being, there would be no being at all. It is important to emphasise that Aristotle's deduction of God moved in an opposite direction from that of the ontological proof: his argument deduced God's existence from the reality of being, not from the definitions attached to His name. Schelling attacked the ontological proof for this very reason.

Schelling said he considered Aristotle to be 'the summit of ancient philosophy',[113] praise he qualified only by saying that Aristotle's God was unsatisfactory for us, who have a Christian understanding of God that the ancient Greek obviously lacked. Writing about Scholasticism approvingly, Schelling insisted on the importance of the Church as a force for keeping intact the Aristotelian dual allegiance to experience and to reason.[114] This pleasant balance, he said, had been destroyed by Locke and Hume, who doubted the truth of general principles.

While Aristotle provided a cosmic principle for explaining the world, Schelling tried to explain why reality is given to us. The single most important difference between ancient and Christian metaphysics in this regard is that the latter insists on a personal God. It was emphasised in the opening chapters of this study that it is the particularity of the Christian God that He is personal, that He says 'I', and above all that He was incarnated as man. Christianity is indeed unique as a theology of incarnation. The Christian God is a God of love, of sacrifice and of suffering: these

---

108   *Ibid.*, II/3, 62.
109   *Ibid.*, II/3, 128.
110   *Ibid.*, II/3, 129.
111   Bubner, 'Dieu chez Aristote et Schelling', pp. 117–18.
112   Aristotle, *Metaphysics*, 1072a 20f.
113   Schelling, *Philosophie der Offenbarung* (1841–42) (Paulus-Nachschrift), p. 143.
114   *Ibid.*, pp. 143–4.

are personal attributes. God cannot be conceived of only as *actus purus*, the pre-Christian and Aristotelian view. Indeed, as has been seen, it is precisely the innovation of Christian metaphysics to have transformed the ancient metaphysical concept of being into a personal God who creates and speaks. The old abstract doctrine of the 'logos' turns into the word of God.

Schelling and Christian Metaphysics

This helps us to understand why Father Tilliette calls the *Philosophy of Revelation* of 1841/42 'a philosophy of the Christian *religion*'.[115] Realism is a key Catholic concept, whose influence is felt in the ethical, dogmatic and liturgical domains. Schelling even seems to endorse the liturgical consequences of realism when, at the end of the *Philosophy of Revelation*, he wrote that it was only through a religion based on the Incarnation, and kept alive by tradition and liturgy, that rationalism or individualist piety could be avoided. It is because of remarks like this that Schelling even said himself that those who interpreted his philosophy as tending towards Catholicism were right (even if he also expressed his differences with it).[116] And this is why, the influence of Schelling on twentieth-century left-wing and existentialist thinkers notwithstanding, Schelling's role as religious counterpart to Hegel is crucial.[117] Even though he was certainly not trying to be a theologian, Schelling explicitly called his own philosophy 'Christian' in 1827:

> Christianity in its purity is the archetype (*das Urbild*) towards which philosophy should direct itself. I am not saying this in order to defend myself against those who hold my philosophy to be irreligious or not upstanding – there is, in fact no irreligious philosophy, for philosophy without religion is a non-thing (*ein Unding*) – but instead because I would consider it to be unworthy cowardice not to declare that I have drawn my contentment (*Beruhigung*) from the New Testament and that I hope that others will find the same. The decisive name for my philosophy is *Christian philosophy*, and I have grasped this decisive element with seriousness. Christianity is thus the basis of philosophy.[118]

Later on, Schelling added tartly, 'Whoever is acquainted with rationalism knows that there is no transition from it to Christianity.'[119] It is for this reason that Klaus Hemmerle emphasises 'the explicit efforts Schelling devotes to thinking of God not only as the God of the concept but as the God who chooses freely his Other for himself, and relates to it, and who acts historically'.[120]

---

115   Tilliette, *Schelling, Une Philosophie en devenir*, Vol. 2, p. 467, emphasis original.
116   *Philosophie der Offenbarung, Zweiter Theil*, II/4, 324, note.
117   Thomas O'Meara, *Romantic Idealism and Roman Catholicism: Schelling and the Theologians* (Notre Dame and London: University of Notre Dame Press, 1982), p. 112.
118   Schelling, *System der Weltalter* (1827–28), 2. Vorlesung, p. 9, emphasis on 'Christian philosophy' original.
119   Schelling, *System der Weltalter* (1827–28), 3. Vorlesung, p. 13.
120   Klaus Hemmerle, *Gott und das Denken nach Schellings Spätphilosophie* (Freiburg im Breisgau: Herder, 1968), p. 11.

Emilio Brito comments on the thoroughly orthodox nature of Schelling's Christian anthropology in this later period. Schelling admitted the doctrines of original sin, of the Fall, the wrath of God, man's servitude to death, the enslavement of the devil, and the expulsion of Adam from Paradise: all these are in conformity with the teaching of the Council of Trent.[121] Schelling even corrected the thesis, typical of original Protestantism, that the Fall produced a radical corruption of human reason. The only real area of difficulty, from the point of view of Catholic orthodoxy, was the persistent Schellingian doctrine that God Himself was somehow dislocated by man's sin.

However, it is precisely when we see Schelling moving away from the Gnostic and idealist tradition into which he was born that we understand the close correlation between religion and philosophy. When Schelling attacked Hegel, he called him 'just as theosophical' as Böhme.[122] He attacked his own earlier idealist Identity Philosophy, and the neo-Platonism and Plotinism which had inspired it, for being hybrid and not fully Christian.[123] Again, in the 1842/43 Berlin *Introduction to Positive Philosophy*, Schelling demolished Hegelian theology, and especially the Orphic elements within it, according to which God undergoes an endless circular process of 'descent' into matter and return to Himself.[124]

In other words, it was precisely the differences between Schelling and Hegel over the meaning of God's revelation which drove them apart. For Hegel, God was simultaneously absolute ideality and reality: for Schelling, He was absolute reality and could not be reduced to ideality. Schelling understood the revelation as something that was based on 'an impenetrable basis of obscurity and of inaccessible majesty, the purely existing, the absolute transcendent, the *Vorbegriff* of God'.[125] It could not be grasped simply by reason, for revelation, like the existence which brings it about, was inaccessible to reason alone. 'The difference is profound between the philosopher who hypostatises and divinises the concept [that is, Hegel] so that the Revelation is entirely manifested in speculation, and the philosopher who determinedly preserves the inscrutability of the fact, and its irrevocable margin of unpredictability and mystery, in order later to make it impermeable to thought.'[126]

Schelling emphasised the derivative and feeble nature of human reason, and the logical pre-eminence of the creation and revelation. He spoke of the 'extra-logical character' of existence,[127] something which had been brought into being by God's free will alone, and it was his understanding of this which led him to abhor the divinisation of the capacities of human reason of which he accused Hegel. In the beginning was not the gradual unfolding of *Geist*, but rather the creation by an act of free will. This is why Schelling wrote, 'We live in this definite (*bestimmt*) world,

---

121 Emilio Brito, 'L'anthropologie chrétienne de Schelling', *Revue théologique de Louvain*, 18 (1987): 18–19.

122 *Einleitung in die Philosophie der Offenbarung* (1842–43), II/3, 122.

123 *Philosophische Einleitung in die Philosophie der Mythologie, oder Darstellung der reinrationalen Philosophie* (1847–52), II/1, 258.

124 *Einleitung in die Philosophie der Offenbarung* (1842–43), II/3, 106, note.

125 Tilliette, *L'absolu et la Philosophie*, p. 132.

126 *Ibid.*, p. 131.

127 *Ibid.*, p. 133.

The Religious Flowering in Schelling's Late Philosophy 141

and not in the abstract or universal world which we so enjoy imagining by hanging on only to most universal properties of things without penetrating into their real relationships.'[128] Or again,

> Nothing is easier than to displace oneself into the realm of pure thought, but it is not so easy to get out of it again. The world does not consist of mere categories or pure concepts, it does not consist of concrete categories, but of concrete and contingent things. What matters is the un-logical, everything else which is *not* the concept but its opposite, which simultaneously takes on the concept unwillingly ... The end of Hegel's 'Logic' is the perfected, closed-off idea. Nothing new can ever come to it. ... Hegelian philosophy is just Wolffianism raised to a higher power ... I, the one who philosophises (*der Philosophierende*) obviously demand more, because I have a real world in front of me, and I demand that I can make nature *conceivable*.[129]

He explained the fact that Hegel had overlooked the real by saying that it was inherent in the very notion of self-development. 'The whole opposition (that is, between real and ideal) only exists after an *extra-logical* world is *there*.'[130]

Schelling believed that Hegelian conceptualism was irreligious because it accorded divine capacities to human reason. This is the same attack made by traditional conservatives on rationalistic philosophy in general. His own God, unlike Hegel's, was absolutely real and revealed. It was only within a philosophy of reality, indeed, that real historical events – such as man's salvation by Christ – could occur. As Xavier Tilliette emphasises, 'This is why positive philosophy has the task of rejoining tradition, belief and common piety, the religious phenomenon – first mythological and then Christian; it must extend itself to the transrational and supra-real domain ... In these conditions, his philosophy is indeed an overcoming of idealism and a counter-offensive, and that it belongs to the anti-idealist reaction ... There is no need to contest Fuhrmans when he happily repeats that this philosophy is, in its initial intention, a philosophy of will and of liberty, or of history.'[131]

It was not, in other words, a philosophy of the idea or of reason. Precisely what Schelling denied to Hegel was the possibility that reason could complete itself. Tilliette writes, 'Hegel believes in absolute knowledge, in the circularity of reason installed in security and transparency. Schelling denies to thought this power of self-completion.'[132] Indeed, Schelling even got his own back against Hegel for the famous jibe in the *Phenomenology*, when he wrote, 'The perfect "maturity" of the Hegelian system is explained by the fact that it cannot be explained again (*wiedergegeben*) in anything other than its own words ... If (its ultimate thought) were clear, it (that is, Hegel's philosophy) would destroy itself.'[133] Hegelian philosophy was so devoid of content that its only merit was that it had shown the futility of negative philosophy.

---

128 *Philosophie der Offenbarung, Zweiter Theil*, II/4, 332.

129 Schelling, *Gründung der positiven Philosophie*, ed. Horst Fuhrmans, 29. Vorlesung, pp. 225 and 227, emphases original.

130 *Ibid.*, emphases original.

131 Tilliette, *L'absolu et la Philosophie*, p. 133.

132 *Ibid.*, p. 134.

133 *Grundlegung der positiven Philosophie* (Munich, 1832–33), 32. Vorlesung, ed. Horst Fuhrmans (Torino: Bottega d'Erasmo, 1972), p. 236.

It is also essential to grasp that Schelling believed that the Hegelian ontology destroyed both man's and God's freedom. As Alan White puts it, 'In stressing the importance of necessity, Hegel denies the reality of freedom; in stressing the eternal, he denies the temporal; in stressing unchanging essence, he denies historical existence.'[134] It is precisely because it was a mere science of concepts that Schelling said that Hegel's philosophy was not on the level of the Absolute. It was instead a mere movement in thought, much like Fichte's.[135]

Hegel on God

The difference between Hegel on God and Schelling on God, in other words, is best grasped using the template outlined in Chapter 1, when various Oriental cosmogonies were contrasted with the Christian one. There are excellent grounds for classing Hegel in the former category.

First, Hegel's theory of the creation is problematic from a Christian point of view. As Charles Taylor shows, '*Geist* or God cannot exist separately from the universe which he sustains and in which he manifests himself.'[136] This is incompatible with the fundamental Judeo-Christian notion that the universe and God are two different things, that creation is the result of the free choice of God, and that He could very well have continued to exist without creating the world. 'Absolute idealism (which Hegel embraces)', writes Taylor, 'means that nothing exists which is not a manifestation of the Idea, that is, of rational necessity ... Thus absolute idealism is related to the Platonic notion of the ontological priority of rational order, which underlies external existence.'[137] It certainly is. Hegel, as Taylor rightly says, is also, like Plotinus, and like the Greeks, committed to an eternal universe[138] and to the view that the creation is necessary for God to become aware of Himself.[139]

Hegel also believed that 'God eternally begets His son',[140] a remark that lent credence to Schelling's accusation that Hegel's God never rests: he never rests because Hegel has a straightforwardly Plotinian view of God, according to which God *must* reveal Himself in creation.[141] It is clear, once again, that such a cosmogony is not Christian: in Christianity, God begets His son once, and He creates the world once. By contrast, as Tresmontant says, there is no creation in Platonic or neo-Platonist

---

134 Alan White, *Schelling: An Introduction to the System of Freedom* (New Haven: Yale University Press, 1983), p. 152.
135 *Ibid.*, p. 155.
136 Charles Taylor, *Hegel* (Cambridge: Cambridge University Press, 1975), p. 87.
137 *Ibid.*, p. 110.
138 *Ibid.*, p. 102.
139 *Ibid.*, p. 490.
140 Hegel, *Vorlesungen über die Philosophie der Religion*, ed. W. Jaeschke (3 vols, Hamburg: Felix Meiner, 1983–85), Vol. III, p. 209.
141 Stephen Houlgate, *Freedom, Truth and History: An Introduction to Hegel's Philosophy* (London and New York: Routledge, 1991), p. 196.

systems, only necessary emanation.[142] And as Taylor rightly says, 'Hegel claimed to be orthodox Lutheran, but in fact he only accepted a Christianity which had been systematically altered to be a vehicle for his own philosophy':[143] Hegel's religious position was 'on a narrow crest between theism and some form of naturalism or pantheism'.[144] Taylor concludes, 'The Hegelian ontology itself, in which everything can be grasped by reason because everything is founded on rational necessity, is ultimately incompatible with Christian faith.'[145] And as Stephen Houlgate says (even though he tries to argue that there can be a Christian reading of Hegel), Hegel essentially equated God with rationality;[146] he had no real sense of the Incarnation[147] and indeed described it as a mere metaphor;[148] and he did not even really think Jesus was God, or rather only to the extent that all men are God.[149] It is all very well to say that Hegel thought that 'God is love', but what kind of a love is it that 'plays with itself'?[150] In truth, as Taylor says, 'There is no place for divine love in Hegel',[151] because Hegel's God has no personality: 'How does a Hegelian philosopher *pray*?' (Taylor again).[152] We can neither thank God nor petition Him, since everything is the result of necessity.

The fact is that many of Hegel's positions may be compatible with some strands of Protestantism but they are certainly not compatible with traditional Christian metaphysics in the way that many of Schelling's are. Hegel's views on the divine presence (or rather, lack of it) in the Holy Eucharist are certainly Lutheran, and he was very anti-Catholic in both political philosophy and metaphysics. Hegel's religion – which, in the words of Robert Solomon is 'a faith without icons, images, stories and myths, without miracles, without a resurrection, without a nativity, without Chartres and Fra Angelico, without wine and wafers, without heaven and hell, without God as judge and without judgement'[153] – cannot properly be called Christian at all.

Schelling on God

Hegel brought to a head the Protestant insistence, which Kant and Descartes also endorsed, that 'truth must be verified by my own insight'.[154] The fundamental Hegelian, Kantian and Lutheran value is autonomy: the freedom of individuals to

---

142 Claude Tresmontant, *La prescience de Dieu, la prédestination et la liberté humaine* (Paris: François-Xavier de Guibert, 1996), p. 42, quoted in Chapter 1.
143 Taylor, *Hegel*, p. 102.
144 *Ibid.*
145 *Ibid.*, p. 494.
146 Houlgate, *Freedom, Truth and History*, p. 183.
147 Taylor, *Hegel*, p. 209; Houlgate, *Freedom, Truth and History*, p. 186.
148 Hegel, *Vorlesungen über die Philosophie der Religion*, Vol. 1, p. 293.
149 Taylor, *Hegel*, pp. 209 and 495.
150 Hegel, *Phänomenologie des Geistes, Vorrede*, Reclam edition, p. 21.
151 Taylor, *Hegel*, p. 494.
152 *Ibid.*
153 Robert Solomon, *From Hegel to Existentialism*, p. 61, quoted in Houlgate, *Freedom, Truth and History*, p. 206.
154 Houlgate, *Freedom, Truth and History*, p. 225.

ascertain the truth for themselves. Schelling inverts this post-Reformation order of priorities.

To be sure, Christianity is itself specifically a religion of liberty: salvation depends on the free decision of each individual to obey or not the commands of God. But it begins with the incontrovertible that-ness of being – and of the revelation – and thus provides a *real* relationship between human liberty and the absolute liberty of God. This is incompatible with determinism, and certainly incompatible with Hegelian presuppositionless self-determination: there are presuppositions, and there is an absolute beginning. Schelling's purpose is precisely to restore that Christian liberty which has been threatened by the very attempt made in modern philosophy to make human liberty as absolute as God's.

On occasions, Schelling compared his philosophy of creation as a free act to a superior history of liberty, saying that revelation was 'an event in time ... revelation is an actual relationship'.[155] The resurrection of Christ re-established a relationship between the divine and the temporal. It was precisely by preserving the reality of revelation in all its aspects that the *Philosophy of Revelation* showed that Christ's death and incarnation were in no way nominal events, as a theology built on a metaphysics of immobilism or on a static monotheism would tend to suggest.[156] On the contrary:

> The resurrection of Christ is the decisive fact of the whole of this superior history, which is certainly incomprehensible from the ordinary point of view. Facts like the resurrection of Christ are like flashes of lightning in which the higher, that is, the truer, the inner history pierces through and steps into merely outer ... How mournful (*öd*) empty and dead, how robbed of all divine content, seems history when it is robbed of its connection with that inner, divine and transcendent history, which is alone the *true* history ...![157]

The Gospels did not present a doctrine that could be detached from historical events. Instead they were the definitive account of the actual facts by which redemption was purchased. In attacking the docetism which he believed to be inherent in all transcendentalist positions, Schelling was here adopting a deeply orthodox Christian position. In revelation (as in mythology), said Schelling, we observe 'a real relationship of human consciousness to God, while philosophy knows only of reason-religion (*Vernunftreligion*) and sees all religious development only as a development in the idea.'[158]

Schelling's emphasis on the revelation as an event in real history contrasts strikingly with Fichte (and to a certain extent with Kant) for whom religion was defined purely within the limits of subjective morality, and as a practical support for it.

---

155 *Historisch-Kritische Einleitung in die Philosophie der Mythologie* (1842), II/1, 141.
156 Maesschalk, *L'anthropologie politique et religieuse de Schelling*, p. 254.
157 *Philosophie der Offenbarung*, 32. Vorlesung, II/4, 219–20.
158 *Historisch-Kritische Einleitung in die Philosophie der Mythologie* (1842), II/1, 250–51.

The suffering of God is key. Schelling emphasised that God's decision to suffer for man, to redeem man's sins through death, surpasses in wonder even the miracle of the creation. The love revealed here, he said, was 'far greater than that love which moved the creator to create, it is a miracle of which we can only say: in truth, it is so'.[159] God showed by this that he was not prepared to let man or the world go. It is so impossible to grasp that man can only wonder as the 'that-ness' of this supremely loving act. The love of God the Father and God the Son – a love which is sometimes called the Holy Ghost – is the identity which unites two otherwise different persons.[160]

Schelling even emphasised that philosophy was precisely the way by which we approach the divine because 'philosophy' implies 'love' and 'wisdom': love is God's own good, wisdom is the activity of his purest thought. This is of course another reason to attack to abstractness of Kantian morality, for love is precisely that which is lacking from the rationalist approach to being:

> [The subject] demands God Himself. Him, Him it wants, the God which acts and in whom there is a providence, and who can therefore counteract the fact of the fall as Himself even more factual – in short, Him who is **Master** of Being ... In this alone it sees the highest good. Even the sense of contemplative life was none other than this: to penetrate to the personal via the universal. For person seeks person ... The demand for a real God and for redemption through him is, as you see, nothing but the explicit need for – religion. With this the path trod by the I comes to its end. To the happiness of being (*Freudigkeit des Daseyns*), which it could not attain on its own, it hopes to arrive when it has God in reality and when it is reconciled and united with Him ... *At the end of the negative philosophy I have only possible religion, not real religion, only 'religion within the bounds of pure reason'.* ... That one knows nothing of God is the result of all true rationalism which understands itself. But only by stepping over into positive philosophy do we arrive at the domain of religion and of religions, and we can only then expect philosophical religion to arise ... It has been shown how the need arises within the I to have God outside reason (God not just in thought or in its idea). This willing is not coincidental, it is a willing of the mind, which as a result of inner necessity, and in longing for its own emancipation, cannot remain locked in thought. As this demand cannot go out from thought, it is not a postulate of practical reason. Not this, as Kant wants, but the individual leads to God. For it is not the general (*das Allgemeine*) in man which leads to happiness, but the individual.[161]

Here, indeed, the true purpose of Schelling's life's work becomes clear. As Maesschalk is right to point out, Schelling's age was marked both by the realism of Catholicism and by the idealism which affirmed the rights of the subject, as a result of the political experience of the Reformation. Schelling's determination – maintained early on in his career, and reaffirmed at the end of it – was to achieve a 'real-idealism' which would show that God does not belong to some sphere of reality which is separate from reason, but rather that He stands behind it as its constantly

---

159 *Philosophie der Offenbarung*, 31. Vorlesung, II/4, 197.
160 Danz, *Die Philosophische Christologie Schellings*, pp. 124 and 126.
161 *Philosophie Einleitung in die Philosophie der Mythologie* (Zwischen 1847 and 1852), II/1, pp. 566, 568 and 569, emphases added except for 'Master' ('Herr') which is bold in the original.

operative ground. The cause of intelligibility in the world is God's manifestation of Himself, the revelation. Schelling says that God is the Master of Being (*Herr des Seins*): He is 'pure relation (*Beziehung*), for He is only Lord (*Herr*).'[162]

What matters, then, is His essence as Lord (*Herr*) and His attendant glory (*Herrlichkeit*). Where Spinoza made God into a substance, Schelling makes Him into a king. As such, Schelling's positive philosophy was not a sublime foundation of being but the opposite of a foundation: it was the experience of the phenomenology of the divine.[163] God, the supreme principle of Being, the author of being, cannot be experienced directly Himself: God is not a thing, and therefore not susceptible to experience. God is absolute activity, the absolute 'can', and it is obviously humiliating for reason to realise that it cannot accede to that which has made it possible. By definition, thought cannot think God, for thought can only think that which is conditional. Thus reason has to posit God out of itself.

At the same time, the meaningful and reasonable order of the world is always there. Reason must assume that God has put Himself into this world but it cannot know how or why. In this sense, God is immanent and not transcendent. God is the transcendent which has become the content of reason, and thus immanent.[164] The beginning of thought is therefore unthinkable, and in this sense Schelling's later philosophy was a critical reflection of reason on itself.

Dethroning Human Reason

Reason did not explain being: Schelling held that God's free creation explained even reason itself. The world was without form and void before it was fixed in creation: the creation was the creation of intelligibility in the world, the speaking out of the *word*. Schelling realised that thought was not self-creative, and that it could not found itself. In particular, it could not grasp the '"pure that" of existence': 'logical philosophy is unable to achieve its own self-justification ... Reason is not the ground of itself: its being is groundless and factual (*faktisch*).'[165]

This is why in his later work, Schelling used the notion of *Ekstasis* to describe the process by which reason steps out of itself and realises its own capacities. *Ekstasis*, indeed, is rather like *thaumazein*, the sense of wonder that is the true beginning of all philosophy, in that the apparent certainties of the self are shaken and questioned. (Schelling quoted the *Theaetetus* on *thaumazein* as being the main emotion the philosopher feels and creates, saying that it was illustrative of the moment he calls '*Ekstase*' in the later philosophy, the moment when the subject steps out of itself and realises, with astonishment, that it is not the Absolute.[166]) Indeed, he believed that philosophy should not stop until it had reached that which is absolutely astounding,

---

162 *Darstellung des philosophischen Empirismus* (1836), I/10, 260.
163 Jean-François Courtine, 'Schelling et l'achèvenement de la metaphysique de la subjecti(vi)té', *Les Etudes Philosophiques*, II (1974): 169.
164 *Einleitung in die Philosophie der Offenbarung* (1842–43), II/3, 170.
165 Frank, *Der unendliche Mangel an Sein*, pp. 148 and 149.
166 *Über die Nature der Philosophie als Wissenschaft (Erlanger Vorträge)* (1821–25), I/9, 229–30.

instead of contenting itself with the merely necessary. The necessary, after all, elicits no wonder at all! Hegel, after all, had declared that philosophy would extinguish astonishment completely.[167]

Finding itself to have unthinkable origins, and through the experience of its facticity, reason realises that it has being. Because it cannot ground itself, reason realises that it cannot produce being from within itself, and that being cannot be deduced from knowledge. Beyond its boundaries, there is transcendence: the eternity which remains transcendent, and thus unknowable to reason, is reason's that-ness. Man, therefore, does not need to reflect in on himself, but needs to turn outward, for that is the path which leads to truth.[168]

Christian tradition has always insisted that human reason is created, and that it is not the Absolute, nor even consubstantial with divine reason, but that it is created as capable of knowing God through His creation, and of knowing His Word as it has been addressed to man. Thus one can speak of a Christian rationalism, but it is a rationalism which, unlike modern rationalism, does not accord absolute status to the powers of human reason.[169]

Schelling's anti-rationalist stand had a very direct impact on his political philosophy. We have already observed him rejecting contractarianism (in the Stuttgart and Munich Lectures) a classic conservative anti-rationalist position. He returned to the theme in the later philosophy, writing of the 'given-ness of the community, which is independent of reason and thus also from law'.[170] In the *Philosophy of Mythology*, he attacked the 'total futility' of trying to create states from the first principles of individual reason.[171] He regarded such attempts as liable to lead to despotism and tyranny, because people would be dominated by the contingent majority of the moment. Citizens would have only rights and no duties.

> Reason – yes, but not the bad reason of the individual, but rather the reason which is nature itself, the lasting being (*bleibende Seyende*) which stands above the merely appearing and contingent being (*Seyn*), reason in this sense determines the state ...[172]

The community could not be understood as a conscious product of subjective reason. Instead, order and rules were presupposed in human togetherness, and were the necessary condition for the development of human freedom. The given-ness (and not the capacity to be rationally invented from scratch) of political constitutions is, of course, the bedrock of Burkean conservatism, as is the notion that there is a natural law inscribed into the very structure of being, which Schelling also embraced:

---

167 Karl Jaspers, *Schelling: Größe und Verhängnis* (Munich: Piper, 1986), p. 97.
168 *Über die Natur der Philosophie als Wissenschaft (Erlanger Vorträge)* (1821–25), I/9, 230.
169 Claude Tresmontant, *Les idées maîtresses de la métaphysique chrétienne* (Paris: Seuil, 1962), p. 103.
170 *Philosophische Einleitung in die Philosophie der Mythologie* (Zwischen 1847 and 1852), II/1, 536.
171 *Ibid.*, II/1, 537.
172 *Ibid.*, II/1, 538.

> It is in this sense that the moral law is also to be called the law of reason; because it is the law which comes from (*sich herschreibt*) the intelligible order, and through which the intelligible is also in the world ... it is the reason which dwells in being itself which makes itself the subject of will.[173]

Although he credited Kant with not making God the author of morality, the point is absolutely not to pretend that man is instead. Rather, it is to insist that God is to be praised for willing and creating that which is objectively good:[174] the laws of morality were not simply the result of God's arbitrary choice. Schelling insisted, in an appropriately conservative fashion, that Kant's choice of the word 'autonomy' in a moral context was unfortunate, precisely because he wanted to show that man cannot invent social or moral rules for himself and therefore is never really autonomous. 'An intelligible order thus precedes the ... community of men', he wrote.[175]

Because of the naturally authoritative principles inherent in being, to which the state is subject, any attempt to destroy the state was impious. Schelling considered the state a means, not an end in itself; but at the same time, it was not right constantly to question the state.

> The state has a root in eternity, and it is the lasting basis – which is not to be destroyed nor even to be examined – for the whole of human life and all its further development ... Being such a basis, the state is not a goal, but an eternal starting point for all the higher aims of spiritual life. It is neither to be dissolved, nor put into question.[176]

This is not far from Burke, who had written, 'It has been the misfortune (not as these gentlemen think, the glory) of this age, that every thing is to be discussed, as if the constitution of our country were to be always a subject of altercation than enjoyment.'[177]

It was in this vein that Schelling had attacked the incipient nihilism of Fichte, who had declared that the search for truth was the only valuable activity for a philosopher, even if it culminated in the conclusion that there was no truth. Against this, Schelling opposed his own conviction that there is objective truth and reasonableness in the outside world itself. Philosophy, he wrote, meant love or striving after wisdom.[178] In a strikingly teleological vein, he insisted that such wisdom could only be about ends.[179] This is the political significance of the passage quoted earlier: 'If man demands the knowledge that there is wisdom, he must assume that even in the object of this knowledge there is wisdom ... The first assumption of philosophy as striving

---

173 *Ibid.*, II/1, 532.

174 Cf. a similar remark with reference to Leibniz in *Über das Wesen der menschlichen Freiheit* (1809) I/7, 396; ref: Tentam. theod. Opp. T. I, pp. 365, 366.

175 *Philosophische Einleitung in die Philosophie der Mythologie* (Zwischen 1847 and 1852), II/1, 53.

176 *Ibid.*, II/1, 550.

177 Edmund Burke, *Reflections on the Revolution in France*, ed. Conor Cruise O'Brien (Harmondsworth: Penguin, 1968), p. 188.

178 *Philosophie der Offenbarung*, 10. Vorlesung, II/3, 201.

179 *Ibid.*, II/3, 202.

for wisdom is that there is wisdom in the object (*Gegenstand*), that is, in being (*in dem Seyn*), in the world itself.'[180]

This, indeed, was the most politically sensitive aspect to Schelling's metaphysics: there is a divinely ordained order of being, which man has the capacity to pervert by his capacity for good or evil. It is precisely because he conceived of liberty as definitive of the human condition, and because he saw that it must be located with relationship to being as a whole, that the very fact that man is in the world at all is of philosophical interest. To ask, as Schelling did, why the world is there at all is to try to comprehend its priority over human freedom. The result should be the modesty and the prudence that derive from finding a world already made, rather than inventing it. Just as reason and being are not self-legitimating, so the state, too, derives its legitimacy from outside itself, and indeed, partly from outside of mankind. Conversely, a modern revolution is ultimately a rebellion against being, comparable to the overturning of the divine order of which evil is capable when the ground rebels against existence. Seen in this light, evil is not merely immoral conduct, but the synonym for a profound ontological perversion of divine unity and harmony.

Schelling was above all concerned with the uncertainties which 'new' philosophy had introduced into modern life. His purpose was to counter the decline of the absolute and, as Xavier Tilliette writes, 'Schelling's best works have the value of appeals' against this decline.[181] He welcomed the fact that most people studied philosophy not to become philosophers, but rather in order 'to win those great unifying convictions without which there is no independence of mind and no dignity of life'.[182] 'Yes, in a time when everything has become unsteady, when everything positive is subject to disputes and attacks of different kinds, it appears doubly important and necessary that a virile philosophy, which comes from all the depths of the mind (*eine aller Tiefe des Geistes kundige Philosophie*) should replace and fasten the shaky foundations of all truly human convictions.'[183]

And this, he knew, could not come from the individualist exercise of human reason alone. Although he sometimes attacked Catholicism with such phrases as 'stony Papism',[184] Schelling had a profound understanding of the importance of embodied history in preserving religion intact. At the end of the *Philosophy of Revelation* he criticised the individualist religion of pietism that the Reformation had introduced (and which so heavily influenced Kant's philosophy) and he did so by implicitly approving the established Church with all its symbolic and communal aspects:

> What is common to all (different Churches) is the *historical way* that is characterised by doctrine, cult and the cycle of festivals. Only through this can the inner process be maintained alive, and only through the recognition of this historical origin can the church

---

180 *Ibid.*, II/3, 203.
181 Tilliette, *L'absolu et la Philosophie*, p. 25.
182 *Erste Vorlesung in München*, 26. November 1827, I/9, 359.
183 *Ibid.*
184 Schelling, *Philosophie der Offenbarung* (1841–42) (Paulus-Nachschrift), p. 321.

maintain its objectivity, and preserve itself from dissolution into pious subjectivity or *empty* rationalism.[185]

As Cardinal Newman wrote, 'To be deep in history is to cease to be Protestant.'[186] Although it cannot be denied that Schelling's idealist heritage continued to shine through his thought right until the very death – he retained elements of mystical and Messianic ecumenism which enabled him to write, at the end of his life, 'The true religion is the religion of the future'[187] – nonetheless, it was no doubt indeed 'a sign of fate'[188] that a Catholic priest read prayers over the Lutheran Schelling's open grave.

---

185 *Ibid.*, p. 325, emphasis original; cf. the same thought expressed in *Philosophie der Offenbarung, Zweiter Theil*, II/4, 333.
186 John Henry Cardinal Newman, *An Essay on the Development of Christian Doctrine* (London: Longmans, Green & Co., 1894), p. 8.
187 *Philosophie der Offenbarung*, 29. Vorlesung, II/4, 129.
188 Tilliette, *Schelling, Une Philosophie en devenir*, Vol. 2, p. 130.

Bibliography

Arendt, Hannah, *Der Liebesbegriff bei Augustin. Versuch einer philosophischen Interpretation* (Berlin: Springer, 1929).
——, 'What is Existenz Philosophy?', *Partisan Review*, 13/3 (winter 1946): 40.
Arquillière, H.-X., *L'augustinisme politique: essai sur la formation des théories politiques du moyen age* (Paris: Vrin, 1934).
Balthasar, Hans Urs von, *Prometheus, Studien zur Geschichte des deutschen Idealismus* (Heidelberg: Kerle, 1947).
Barth, Hans, 'Edmund Burke und die deutsche Staatsphilosophie im Zeitalter der Romantik', in *Schweizer Beiträge zur allgemeinen Geschichte*, Vol. 3 (1945).
Bausola, Adriano, *Metafisica e rivelazione nella filosofia positiva di Schelling* (Milan: Vita e Pensiero, 1965).
Béhar, Pierre, *Du 1er au IVe Reich, Permanence d'une Nation, Renaissance d'un état* (Paris: Desjonquères, 1990).
Beiner, Ronald (ed.), *Hannah Arendt: Lectures on Kant's Political Philosophy, Interpretative Essay* (Chicago: University of Chicago Press, 1982).
Bergson, Henri, *L'Evolution créatrice* (Paris, 1907).
——, *La pensée et le mouvant* (Paris: Presses Universitaires de France, 5th edn, 1996).
Bord, André, *Plotin et Jean de la Croix* (Paris: Beauchesne, 1996).
Bowie, Andrew, *Schelling and Modern European Philosophy* (London: Routledge, 1993).
Bracken, Joseph, *Freiheit und Kausalität bei Schelling* (Freiburg im Breisgau and München: Karl Alber, 1972).
Bréhier, Émile, *La philosophie de Plotin* (Paris: Vrin, 1998).
Brito, Emilio, 'La Création ex "nihilo" selon Schelling', *Ephemerides Theologicae Lovanienses*, 60 (1984).
——, 'Schelling et la bonté de la création', *Nouvelle Revue Théologique*, 108/4 (July–August 1986).
——, 'La création chez Hegel et Schelling', *Revue Thomiste*, 87 (1987).
——, 'L'anthropologie chrétienne de Schelling', *Revue théologique de Louvain*, 18 (1987).
——, *La Création selon Schelling* (Louvain: Louvain University Press, 1987).
——, *Philosophie et théologie dans l'oeuvre de Schelling* (Paris: Cerf, 2000).
Brown, Robert F., 'Resources in Schelling for New Directions in Theology', *Idealistic Studies*, XX/1 (January 1990).
Bruaire, Claude, *Schelling ou la quête du secret du l'être* (Paris: Seghers, 1970).
Brun, Jean, *Aristote et le Lycée* (Paris: Presses Universitaires de France, Collection 'Que sais-je?', 1961).

Brunneder, Gertrud, 'Das Wesen der menschlichen Freiheit bei Schelling und sein ideengeschichtlicher Zusammenhang mit Jakob Böhmes Lehre vom Ungrund', *Archiv für Philosophie*, 8 (1958).
Bubner, Rüdiger, 'Einleitung', in *Geschichte der Philosophie in Text und Darstellung*, Vol. 6, *Deutscher Idealismus* (Stuttgart: Reclam, 1978).
——, 'Dieu chez Aristote et Schelling', in Jean-François Courtine and Jean-Francois Marquet (eds), *Le dernier Schelling: raison et positivité* (Paris: Vrin, 1994).
Buchheim, Thomas, 'Das "objektive Denken" in Schellings Naturphilosophie', *Kant-Studien*, 81 (1990): 321–38.
Cesa, Claudio, *La filosofia politica di Schelling* (Bari: Laterz, 1969).
Challiol-Gillet, Marie-Christine, *Schelling* (Paris: Presses Universitaires de France, Collection 'Que sais-je?', 1996).
Coreth, E., SJ, 'Schellings Weg zu den Weltaltern', *Bijdragen Tijdschrift voor Filosofie en Theologie*, XX (1959).
Courtine, Jean-François, 'Schelling et l'achèvenement de la metaphysique de la subjecti(vi)té', *Les Etudes Philosophiques*, II (1974).
——, *Exstase de la raison* (Paris: Galilée, 1990).
—— and Jean-Francois Marquet (eds), *Le dernier Schelling: raison et positivité* (Paris: Vrin, 1994).
Couvert, Etienne, *La Gnose contre la Foi* (Chiré en Montreuil: Editions de Chiré, 1989).
Dallmayr, Fred. H., *Polis and Praxis: Exercises in Contemporary Political Thought* (Boston: MIT Press, 1990).
Danz, Christian, *Die philosophische Christologie F.W.J. Schellings* (*Schellingiana*, Vol. 9, ed. Walter E. Erhardt) (Stuttgart-Bad Cannstatt: Frommann-Holzboog, 1996).
Daujat, Jean, *Y a-t-il une vérité?* (Paris: Téqui, 1974).
Drago del Boca, Susanna, *La Filosofia di Schelling* (Florence: G.C. Sansoni, 1943).
Durner, Manfred, 'Zum Problem des "Christlichen" in Schellings "Weltalter" und Spätphilosophie', *Philosophisches Jahrbuch*, 89 (1982): 25–38.
Fackenheim, Emil L., 'Schellings Begriff der positiven Philosophie', *Zeitschrift für philosophische Forschung*, VIII (1954).
Frank, Manfred, *Der Unendliche Mangel an Sein, Schellings Hegelkrikitk und die Anfänge der Marxschen Dialektik* (Frankfurt am Main: Suhrkamp, 1975).
——, *Eine Einführung in Schellings Philosophie* (Frankfurt am Main: Suhrkamp, 1985).
—— and Gerhard Kurz, *Materialen zu Schellings philosophischen Anfängen* (Frankfurt am Main: Suhrkamp Taschenbuch Wissenschaft, 1975).
Franz, Albert, *Philosophische Religion, eine Auseinandersetzung mit den Grunlegungsproblemen der Spätphilosophie F.W.J. Schellings* (Amsterdam: Rodopi, 1992).
Fuhrmans, Horst, *Schellings letzte Philosophie* (Berlin: Junker und Dünnhaupt, 1940).
——, *Schellings Philosophie der Weltalter* (Düsseldorf: L. Schwann, 1954).
——, 'Dokumente zur Schellingforschung', *Kant-Studien*, 47 (1955/56).

——, 'Ausgangspunkt der Schellingschen Spätphilosophie', *Kant-Studien*, 48 (1956/57).
—— (ed.), *F.W.J. Schelling, Briefe und Dokumente* (Berlin: Bouvier, 1962).
——, Introduction to *Über das Wesen der menschlichen Freiheit* (Stuttgart: Reclam, 1964).
Genuyt, F.M., *Vérité de l'Etre et Affirmation de Dieu, Essai sur la philosophie de Saint Thomas* (Paris: Vrin, 1974).
Gilson, Etienne, *The Unity of Philosophical Experience* (London: Sheed & Ward, 1938).
——, *Le thomisme* (Paris: Vrin, 6th edn, 1989).
——, *L'être et l'essence* (Paris: Vrin, 1994).
Grosos, Philippe, *Philosophie et théologie de Kant à Schelling* (Paris: Ellipses, 1999).
Gulyga, Arseni, *Die klassische deutsche Philosophie, Ein Abriß* (Leipzig: Reclam, 1990).
Heidegger, Martin, *Schellings Abhandlung über das Wesen der menschlichen Freiheit (1809)* (Tübingen: Max Niemeyer, 1971).
——, *Die Grundbegriffe der Metaphysik* (Frankfurt am Main: Klostermann, 1983).
——, *Einführung in die Metaphysik* (Tübingen: Max Niemeyer, 1987).
——, *Die Metaphysik des deutschen Idealismus. Zur erneuten Auslegung von Schelling: Philosophische Untersuchungen über das Wesen der menschlichen Freiheit und die damit zusammenhängende Gegenstände* (*Gesamtausgabe*, Vol. 49) (Frankfurt am Main: Klostermann, 1991).
Hemmerle, Klaus, *Gott und das Denken nach Schellings Spätphilosophie* (Freiburg im Breisgau: Herder, 1968).
Hölderlin, Friedrich, 'Urtheil und Seyn', in Manfred Frank and Gerhard Kurz (eds), *Materialien zu Schellings philosophischen Anfängen* (Frankfurt am Main: Suhrkamp, 1975).
Holz, Harald, *Spekulation und Faktizität, Zum Freiheitsbegriff des mittleren und späten Schelling* (Bonn: Bouvier, 1970).
Houlgate, Stephen, *Freedom, Truth and History: An Introduction to Hegel's Philosophy* (London and New York: Routledge, 1991).
Hudson, Wayne, *The Marxist Philosophy of Ernst Bloch* (London: Macmillan, 1982).
Jacobs, Wilhelm G., 'Schellings Anfänge zwischen Orthodoxie und Revolution', in *Schellings Philosophie der Freiheit, Festschrift der Stadt Leonberg* (Stuttgart: Kohlhammer, 1977).
Jankélévitch, Vladimir, *L'odysée de la conscience dans la dernière philosophie de Schelling* (Paris: Félix Alcan, 1933).
Jaspers, Karl, *Schelling: Größe und Verhängnis* (München: Piper, 1955 [page references to Piper, 1986 edn]).
Jonas, Hans, *The Gnostic Religion* (Boston: Beacon, 2nd edn, 1963).
Kasper, Walter, *Das Absolute in der Geschichte, Philosophie und Theologie der Geschichte in der Spätphilosophie Schellings* (Mainz: Grünewald, 1965).
Kile, Frederick O., *Die theologischen Grundlagen von Schellings Philosophie der Freiheit* (Leiden: E.J. Brill, 1965).

Kojève, Alexandre, *Introduction à la lecture de Hegel* (Paris: Gallimard, 1947).
Kolakowski, Leszek, *Chrétiens sans église, La conscience religieuse et le lien confessionel au XVIIe siècle* (Paris: Gallimard, 1969).
——, *Metaphysical Horror* (Oxford: Blackwell, 1988).
——, *Religion, If There is No God* (London: Fontana, 2nd edn, 1993).
Kreiml, Josef, *Die Wirklichkeit Gottes, Eine Untersuchung über die Metaphysik und die Religionsphilosophie des späten Schelling* (Regensburg: S. Roderer, 1989).
Libera, Alain de, *La querelle des universaux de Platon à la fin du Moyen Age* (Paris: Seuil, 1996).
MacIntyre, Alasdair, *After Virtue: A Study in Moral Theory* (London: Duckworth, 1981).
Maesschalk, Marc, *Philosophie et Révélation dans l'itinéraire de Schelling* (Paris: Vrin and Leuven: Peeters, 1989).
——, *L'anthropologie politique et religieuse de Schelling*, Editions de l'Institut supérieur de Philosophie, Louvain-la-Neuve (Paris: Vrin and Leuven: Peeters, 1991).
Majoli, B., 'La critica ad Hegel in Schelling e Kierkegaard', *Rivista di filosofia neoscolatica*, XLVI (1954).
Mannheim, Karl, *Konservatismus, Ein Beitrag zur Soziologie des Wissens*, ed. David Kettler, Volker Meja and Nico Stehr (Frankfurt am Main: Suhrkamp, 1984).
Marquet, Jean-François, *Liberté et existence. Étude sur la formation de la philosophie de Schelling* (Paris: Gallimard, 1973).
Martensen, Hans L., *Studies in the Life and Teaching of Jacob Boehme*, trans. T. Thyr Evans (London: Rockliff, 1949).
Nichols, Aidan, *Looking at the Liturgy* (San Francisco: Ignatius, 1996).
O'Meara, Thomas, *Romantic Idealism and Roman Catholicism: Schelling and the Theologians* (Notre Dame and London: University of Notre Dame Press, 1982).
Ousset, Jean, *Pour qu'il règne* (Grez-en-Bouère: Dominique Martin Morin, 1986).
Pappin, Joseph L. III, *The Metaphysics of Edmund Burke* (New York: Fordham University Press, 1993).
Pegis, Anton C., *Introduction to Saint Thomas Aquinas* (New York: Randon House, 1948).
Philonenko, A., *Théorie et Praxis dans la pensée morale et politique de Kant et de Fichte en 1793* (Paris: Vrin, 1988).
Pinkard, Terry, *Hegel's 'Phenomenology': The Sociality of Reason* (Cambridge: Cambridge University Press, 1994).
Pippin, Robert B., *Hegel's Idealism: The Satisfactions of Self-Consciousness* (Cambridge: Cambridge University Press, 1989).
Richir, Marc, *Du sublime en politique* (Paris: Payot, 1991).
Rivelaygue, Jacques, *Leçons de métaphysique allemande*, Vol. I, *De Leibniz à Hegel* (Paris: Grasset, 1990).
Rothbard, Murray N., *Economic Thought before Adam Smith* (*An Austrian Perspective on the History of Economic Thought*, Volume I) (Aldershot: Edward Elgar, 1995).
Schulz, Walter, 'Das Verhältnis des späten Schellings zu Hegel: Schellings Speckulation über den Satz', *Zeitschrift für philosophische Forschung*, 14 (1954).

——, *Die Vollendung des deutschen Idealismus in der Spätphilosophie Schellings* (Stuttgart and Köln: Kohlhammer, 1955).
——, *Der Gott der neuzeitlichen Metaphysik* (Pfullingen: Neske, 1957).
——, 'Freiheit und Geschichte in Schellings Philosophie', in *Schellings Philosophie der Freiheit, Festschrift der Stadt Leonberg* (Stuttgart: Kohlhammer, 1975).
——, 'Die Wandlungen des Freiheitsbegriffs bei Schelling', in *Vernunft und Freiheit, Aufsätze und Vorträge* (Stuttgart: Reclam, 1981).
Scruton, Roger, *Spinoza* (Oxford: Oxford University Press, 1986).
——, 'Understanding Hegel' and 'Hegel as a Conservative Thinker', in *The Philosopher on Dover Beach* (Manchester: Carcanet, 1990).
Stüttler, Josef Anton, 'Das Gottesproblem im Spätwerk Schellings', *Scholastik*, 36 (1961).
Taylor, Charles, *Hegel* (Cambridge: Cambridge University Press, 1975).
——, 'Kant's Theory of Freedom', in Zbigniew Pelczynski and John Gray (eds), *Conceptions of Liberty in Political Philosophy* (London: Athlone, 1984).
Tillich, Paul, 'Schelling und die Anfänge des existentialischen Protests', *Zeitschrift für philosophische Forschung*, 9 (1955).
Tilliette, Xavier, *L'absolu et la Philosophie: essais sur Schelling* (Paris: Presses Universitaires de France, 1987).
——, *Schelling, Une Philosophie en devenir* (Paris: Vrin, 2nd edn, 1992).
Trapp, W., *Vorgeschichte und Ursprung der liturgischen Bewegung, vorwiegend in Hinsicht auf das deutsche Sprachgebiet* (Regensburg, 1940 and Münster, 1979).
Tresmontant, Claude, *La métaphysique du christianisme et la naissance de la philosophie chrétienne: problème de la création et de l'anthropologie des origines à Saint Augustin* (Paris: Seuil, 1961).
——, *Les idées maîtresses de la métaphysique chrétienne* (Paris: Seuil, 1962).
——, *La prescience de Dieu, la prédestination et la liberté humaine* (Paris: François-Xavier de Guibert, 1996).
——, *L'opposition métaphysique au monothéisme hébreu de Spinoza à Heidegger* (Paris: François-Xavier de Guibert, 1996).
Über Ernst Bloch, mit Beiträgen von Martin Walser, et al. (Frankfurt am Main: Suhrkamp, 1968).
Vaquié, Jean, *Abrégé de Démonologie* (Vailly-sur-Sauldre: Sainte Jeanne d'Arc, 2nd edn, 1988).
Villey, Michel, *Le droit et les droits de l'homme* (Paris: Presses Universitaires de France, 1983).
Walker, Graham, *Moral Foundations of Constitutional Thought: Current Problems, Augustinian Prospects* (Princeton: Princeton University Press, 1990).
Welte, Bernhard, *Über das Böse, Eine thomistische Untersuchung* (Freiburg im Breisgau: Herder, 2nd edn, 1986).
White, Alan, *Schelling: An Introduction to the System of Freedom* (New Haven: Yale University Press, 1983).
Zum Brunn, Emilie (ed.), *Voici Maître Eckhart* (Grenoble: Jérôme Millon, 1994).

Index

Especially important passages are highlighted in **bold**

Aquinas, St Thomas (and Thomism) **13-16**, 17, 18, 22, 23, 25, 28, 35, 37, 38, 39, 59, 72, **88-91**, 99, 100, 101, 102, 104, 106, 118, 121
   quoted by Schelling **131-132**
Aristotle **11-13**, 14-15, 22, 23, 32, 39, 125
   Schelling and Aristotle **134-139**
Augustine, St **8-10**, 15, 16, 23, 71, 73, 75, 79, 81, **88-91**, 118, 120, 130

Baader, Franz 38, 59, 60, 61, 78, 102, 119
being 8, 9, 10, **11-36**, 41-45, 47-50, 53-54, 56, 57, 58, 94, 95, 97-19
   in the *Freedom* essay, **63-91**
   in *The Ages of the World* 100-103
   in the *Munich* lectures 104-119
   in *Philosophy and Revelation* 123-150
Bergson, Henri 3, 23
Berkeley, George (Bishop Berkeley) 24, 25, 108,
Böhme, Jakob 27, 28, 61-62, 84, 96, 128, 140
Bruaire, Claude 4, 37, 82
Bruno, Giordano 6, 53, 62, 65
Burke, Edmund 34, 35, 147, 148

Calvin, Jean 10, 22, 80
cosmogony (see also 'creation') **1-10**, 84, 93-122, 142
   of Spinoza 18
   Schelling's evolving views on, 74,
creation, **1-10**, 65, 67
   Judeo-Christian theories of **2-6**
   & evil, 2, 4, 81, 98
   attacked by Fichte **30-31**
   & Hegel 114, 130, 142-143
   & Plotinus 6,
   & Spinoza 18, 132
   as a free and loving act of God 6, 9, 20, 82-83, 93-95, 101, 132
   as a locus of meaning 23
   no creation in neo-Platonism 7
   Schelling's evolving views on, 56-58, 68-69, 74-77, 82-83, 85-86, 93-95, 98, 101-103, 115, 119-121, 127, 129, 132-133, 140, 144, 146-147,

Descartes, René 14, 15, **16-18**, 21, 22, 24, 31, 49, 69, 78, 118, 137, 143
   Schelling on, **54**, **72**, 100, **104-106**, 108, 133
Devil, the 9, 71, 79, 81, 98, 107, 140

Eckhart (Meister Eckhart) 6, 7, 28, 59
Engels, Friedrich 21, 32, 39, 124, **125**
   attacks Schelling, 39
evil **1-10**, 23, 55-56, 60, 94, 96, 97, 107, 115, 121, 129-130, 149
   in Schelling's 1792 master's thesis 1
   in *Freedom* essay **61-91**
   in *Stuttgart Private Lectures* **98-99**
   in Manicheism 8
   & freedom 23
   in Gnosticism 46

Fall, the 9-10, 62, 74, 95, 110, 140, 145
   the notion of 'fall' in *Philosophy and Religion* 56-60
Feuerbach, Ludwig 39, 124
Fichte, Johann Gottlieb **28-31**, 36, 37
   and Schelling **40-45**, 50, 54, 58-59, 63-64, 69, 82-83, 86, 95-97, 99, **109**, 117, 126
freedom/ liberty (man and God's) **1-10**, 15, 17, 18, 19, 21-36, 37, 38, 49, 70, 75
   Hegel on **34-36, 142**
   Schelling on, 20, 37, 38, 39, 40-43, **55-60**, **61-91**, 94-99, 101, 102, 105, 107, 110-111, 115, 118, 120,

121, 128-131, 133-134, 137, 143, 147, 149

Gilson, Etienne 14, 27, 34, 100, 104, 106, 109, 112, 127, 128
Gnosticism 1, 67, 71, **76-78**, 83, 95-96, 100
  abandoned by Schelling 96, 100
  adopted by Schelling 38, 41, 44, 50, 52-54 (in the '*Identity philosophy*'), 56 (in '*Philosophy and religion*'), 61 (in the *Freedom* essay), 76 (*Freedom* essay), but attacked by Schelling 119, 140
  cosmogony of, 5
  & idealism 18
  incompatibility with freedom 95
  & Luther 71
  & Spinoza 19

Incarnation, the 3, 22, 102, 138
  Hegel on 143
  Schelling on **74**, 99, 130, 134, 139, 144

Hegel, Georg Wilhelm Friedrich 4, 9, 16, 20, 21, 23, 27, 28, 30, **31-36**, 37, 38, 40, 41, 42, 45, 46, 57, **59**, 60, 63, 69, 80, 83, 86, 93, 94, 95, 102, 119, 121,127-129, 130, 132, **135**, 137, 139, , 144, 147
  on Freedom **34-36**
  on God **142-143**
  Schelling attacks Hegel as 'Orphic' 127
  Schelling attacks Hegel's theology **140-143**
  Schelling called to Berlin to counteract Hegel **124-125**
  Schelling on Hegel in Munich Lectures **111-117**
  seems to attack Schelling in *Phenomenology* 59
  supported by Engels 125
Heidegger, Martin 21-22, 40, **62**, 72, 85, 129
Heine, Heinrich 29, 124
Hobbes, Thomas 23, 97, 99, 130
Hume, David 117, 138

Jacobi, Friedrich Heinrich 18, 43, 59, 68, 77, **117-119**, 128

Kant, Immanuel 4, 13, 16, 20, 21, 23, **24-31**, 37, 38, 41, 61, 62, 68, 69, 79, 112, 117, 134, 143, 149
  Hegel on, 34-35
  Schelling and, 44-50, 51, 54-55, 58, 64, 69, 78, 80, 81, 85, 86, **86-88**, 90, 97, 99, 106, 107, **108-111**, 120, 126, 128, 129, 130, 136, 144, **145**, 148,
Kolakowski, Leszek 5, 17, 51, 65, 67, 87, 98, 109
Leibniz, Gottfried 58, 72, 85, 93, 99, 107
Luther, Martin 10, 22, 27, 28, 71, 87, 143
love 3, 5, 6, 7, 9, **10**, 15, 17, 20, 35, 68, 75, 76-77, 80, 82-83, 84, 87, 88, 94, 95, 102, **130**, 134, 138, 143, **145**, 148

Manicheism 1, **8–10** , 16, 72, 99
Marx, Karl (and Marxism) 30, 32, 39, 124, 125

Neo-Platonism 1, 2, 6, 7, 8, 28, 38, 88, 142
  embraced and then rejected by Schelling 52-56, 61-62, 67, 72, 78, 82, 83, 93, 140

ontological argument 15, 104-106, 108, 113, 126, 128, 132,
Orphism 1, 5, 8, 56, 58, 135
  rejected by Schelling 94-95, 127, 140

Pantheism 17, 44, **55-56**, 63, 77, 89, 101, 103,
  discussed in *Freedom* essay **65-67**
  Hegel's 124, 143
  Pantheismusstreit 18
  Schelling brought to Berlin to combat Hegel's 124
pietism 28, 51, 52, 149
Plato 3, 11-3, 14, 30, 24, 75, 77-78, 95, 112,134-135, 136, 138, 142
Plotinus **6-8**, 18, 57, 72, 75, 80, 88, 130, 142
Pride 10, 17, 71, 81, 85
rebellion and revolt 2-3, 5, 8, 23, 27, 71, 78, 84, 87, 99, 149
Resurrection, the 3, 8, 143,
  Schelling on **144**

Schelling's main works discussed:

Index

Antiquissima de prima malorum humanorum origine etc (1792) 1
On the I as the principle of philosophy (1795) 41, 44
Philosophical Letters on Dogmatism and Criticism (1795) 41, 42, 44, 63
Ideas on a Philosophy of Nature (1797)/Nature Philosophy 43, 45, 47, 49
System of the whole of philosophy and of Nature Philosophy in particular (1804) 49, 53, 54, 55, 56, 81, 90, 129
Philosophy and Religion (1804) **56- 58,** 74, 80, 95
Freedom essay (1809) 23, 27, 38, 48, 55-56, **57-91,** 93-95, 98, 100, 110, 118, 119, 133, 136
Stuttgart Private Lectures (1810) **93-100**
The Ages of the World (1811-1827) 82, 86, 94, **100-103,** 120, 123
Munich Lectures (1827) **104-121**

Philosophy of Revelation and Introduction to the Philosophy of Revelation (1841-1843) **123-150**
Identity philosophy 40-46, 49, 50, **52-54**, 59, 62, 63, 126, 127, 134, 140
Nature philosophy **40-46**, 48-49, 51, 53, 57, 62, 63, 67, 73, 76,
Philosophy of Mythology (1847–1857) 113, 132, 140, 144, 145, 147, 148
Spinoza, Baruch
1, 4, 7, 9, **18-20**, 21, 30, 61, 72, 97, 99, 109, 112, 117
Schelling and, 40, 42-44, 49, 57, 65, 68, 72, 82, 95, **107-108,** 132, 146

Tresmontant, Claude 2, 6, 7, 75, 77, 134, 142

universals 11, 13, 14
Upanishads 4, 8, 75

Wolff, Christian 93, 134, 141